TARIFF PROCEDURES AND TRADE BARRIERS

No economic policy can be appraised without some knowledge of the actual processes used to enforce it and such knowledge is not always easy to come by. This book contains a non-technical and in part an historical description of the processes by which customs tariffs and certain other measures are applied to imported merchandise in Canada and the United States. Imported merchandise must be examined, classified, and valued before the amount of the duty can be known. The time, trouble, uncertainty, and expense involved in these processes are costs that must be borne by importers and exporters and ultimately by consumers and producers.

Customs procedures necessarily impose greater burdens when tariffs are complicated or include high rates of duty. Whether low or high these costs are a hidden part of the protection given by customs tariffs. Like other regulations intended primarily to preserve health, to prevent fraud or the infringements of patents, trademarks, and copyrights, or to enforce standards and uniform grading, they may be used to confer by stealth a greater measure of protection than would be approved by the electorate.

The book contains examples of difficulties and surprises encountered in importing merchandise into Canada or exporting to United States. It is intended for those who are interested in international economic relations and international commercial policy. It is not a customs house guide, nor a customs manual for importers and exporters. It may, however, help to convince those who propose to begin exporting and importing of the need to obtain technical information or advice.

This book is sponsored by the Canadian Institute of International Affairs.

G. A. ELLIOTT came to the University of Toronto in 1946 as Professor of Economics, having previously taught at the Universities of Manitoba, Chicago, and Alberta. In 1944-5 he was a Commissioner of the Royal Commission on Co-operatives, and since 1947 has served as Managing Editor of the *Canadian Journal of Economics and Political Science*. He is a member of the Board of Directors of the National Bureau of Economic Research and a Fellow of the Royal Society of Canada.

TARIFF PROCEDURES
AND TRADE BARRIERS

A STUDY OF INDIRECT PROTECTION IN
CANADA AND THE UNITED STATES

G. A. ELLIOTT

PUBLISHED UNDER THE AUSPICES OF THE CANADIAN
INSTITUTE OF INTERNATIONAL AFFAIRS, TORONTO, 1955

UNIVERSITY OF TORONTO PRESS

LONDON: GEOFFREY CUMBERLEGE
OXFORD UNIVERSITY PRESS

ANNOUNCEMENT

THE Canadian Institute of International Affairs is an unofficial and non-political organization founded in 1928. The Institute has as its objects to promote and encourage in Canada research and discussion in international affairs and to give attention to Canada's position both as a member of the international community of nations and as a member of the Commonwealth of Nations.

The Institute, as such, is precluded by its Constitution from expressing an opinion of any aspect of public affairs. The views expressed, therefore, are those of the writer.

PREFACE

THIS STUDY was begun several years ago at the suggestion of the Canadian Institute of International Affairs. Planned as a study of administrative protection it has come to cover a considerably broader field than was originally intended. Those procedural obstacles to trade that are adopted primarily in order to give protection to special groups of domestic producers are only examples of the much broader set of procedural costs and hurdles encountered by importers which arise in the enforcement of customs regulations and in the application to imports of a great many other sets of regulations. In a sense, then, this study illustrates the procedural costs of government regulation in general.

However, emphasis has been placed on the protective effects of the procedures described and to some extent, as one customs official has remarked, on the "horrible examples" rather than on the large proportion of trade which proceeds smoothly in well-worn, routine channels. That routine procedures favour old channels, methods, and content of trade is in itself, however, a necessary protective effect of the application of duties and regulations, no matter how carefully the procedures are planned, no matter how efficiently they are carried out.

Certain difficulties of phrasing have not been completely overcome. In the first place, certain sorts of problems and surprises have been described as characteristic of particular situations; this should not be interpreted to mean that, in the circumstances referred to, surprises are characteristic, but that the surprises and difficulties which are discussed exemplify or are characteristic of those surprises which do occur in these circumstances. In the second place, the term administration is used in a broad, rather than a narrow sense to include all administrative procedures whether they result from statutory prescription, judicial decision, executive or ministerial order, or the behaviour of customs officers. Except where specifically indicated, criticism of inept or intentionally protective procedures are not directed primarily against customs officials who, for the most part, do what they must do; and do it well.

Unfortunately this study cannot be regarded as a general comparison of the total protective effects of Canadian and United States procedures. For this purpose it is necessarily biassed in favour of the United States. It takes into account the procedural difficulties encountered in importing merchandise into Canada from every source; but it is concerned primarily only with that portion of imports to the United States which originates in Canada; and the potential imports of the United States from Canada are less varied than her imports in general, and consist more largely of raw materials. This circumstance affects especially the discussion of classification in chapter v. In addition certain procedures and practices have been excluded from the study which might reasonably have been discussed—shipping regulations, for example, and the purchasing policies and practices of governments.

Whatever its shortcoming, this study could not have been undertaken at all without help from a great many people. I am indebted to the Canadian Institute of International Affairs for patient encouragement and for financial assistance which enabled me to stay, for brief periods, in different parts of Canada and the United States that I visited for other reasons; and which obtained for me the help of two assistants to whom I am grateful for companionable and effective help: Gordon Blake, who during the important initial period of the investigation collected much of the historical, and some of the current, Canadian material; and Stephen Kaliski, who gave able assistance for two months during 1953.

I am indebted, too, to the University of Toronto and to my colleagues in the Department of Political Economy who suggested sources of information and gave me time to pursue this study; especially to Professor S. D. Clark who during several summers assumed my duties as managing editor of the *Canadian Journal of Economics and Political Science*. Some parts of the manuscript, too, were completed or revised while I was on leave from the University on a fellowship from the John Simon Guggenheim Foundation engaged, for the most part, on another project; I am grateful for this assistance.

I am also indebted to a multitude of busy specialists, both in the United States and in Canada, who must for reasons of space remain anonymous, but who gave time and energy to instructing me in their practices and problems; importers and exporters, wholesalers, retailers, manufacturers, and the officers and officials of their associations and of chambers of commerce; customs brokers, customs attorneys, as well as customs officers and other government officials concerned with tariff matters. I am grateful to members of the staffs of the Ontario Provincial Library and the Library of the University of Toronto for prompt and sympathetic assistance.

I am particularly indebted to Andrew W. Brown of the Department of National Revenue, William R. Johnson of the United States Bureau of Customs, Ben S. Shapiro of the Department of Trade and Commerce, and others who read all, or substantial parts, of the first draft of the manuscript and made many corrections and valuable suggestions. They cannot be held responsible, however, for any of the errors and defects that remain, nor for any of the interpretations, arguments, or suggested remedies, nor for the viewpoints adopted in this study; for these I must take sole responsibility.

The manuscript was completed in mid-November 1953, but has been revised to include comments on the amendment to the Canadian Customs Act in December 1953, and a few references to events in the first quarter of 1954.

Publication of this volume was made possible by funds from the Rockefeller Foundation and the Canadian Tax Foundation.

G. A. E.

Toronto, June 30, 1954

CONTENTS

TARIFF PROCEDURES AND TRADE BARRIERS

I

INTRODUCTION

Let me write the Administrative Act and I care not who
writes the rates of duty.

BENJAMIN A. LEVETT[1]

A MANUFACTURER of motor tires found that his products could
not be admitted to the United States as "automobile tires of rubber,"
dutiable at 10 per cent *ad valorem*, because they contained synthetic
as well as natural rubber. He was given an "opinion," however, that
truck tires were probably dutiable at 45 cents a pound plus 65 per cent
ad valorem as "manufactures of rayon not specially provided for,"
while the passenger car tires were probably dutiable as "articles composed wholly or in part of carbon" at 30 per cent *ad valorem*. Some
years ago a Canadian importer purchased several small shipments of
cotton net in the United States and cleared it through customs at
27½ per cent *ad valorem* plus 3½ cents per pound, less 20 per cent.
A large shipment of 20,000 pounds, however, was classed as knitted
goods and entered at 35 per cent plus 25 cents per pound: though
indistinguishable from ordinary cotton net in use or general appearance, it had been manufactured on a knitting machine. Nearly half the
maple sugar offered for entry at customs ports in the United States in
the fiscal year 1937–8 was rejected by food and drug officers, as were
more than half the dried figs presented for entry into Canada in 1950.
The declared value of shipments of firebrick products to the United
States was appealed by the collector of customs; after nearly fifteen
years of dispute and litigation the dutiable value of the shipments
was fixed at approximately the value originally declared by the importer; but the case was reopened, and another and higher basis of
valuation was selected. If the foreign publisher of a book in the English
language obtains provisional copyright in the United States, no more
than 1,500 copies of the book will be admitted into that country.
Though these were unusual incidents, they resulted from the logical

[1]*Through the Customs Maze*, p. 11.

3

application of usual and legal procedures; and they serve to illustrate
the surprises, costs, and losses which interpose indirect, and sometimes even unintentional, barriers to international trade. This study
explores some of the laws, regulations, and procedures that occasion
such costs and surprises. It describes and illustrates the obstacles to
international trade incidental to the administration of customs tariffs
and of certain other measures that relate ostensibly to sanitation and
the preservation of health, to the maintenance of standards, to the
prevention of misleading or fraudulent labelling, packaging, and advertising, and to the protection of copyright, patents, and trade marks.
Primarily it is concerned with these barriers as they are encountered
by Canadians when importing into Canada or exporting to the United
States. It is illustrative and descriptive rather than exhaustive or
statistical. Of necessity, it is not a customs house guide; customs laws
and regulations are detailed, technical, and complicated; they are
subject, continually, to change and reinterpretation. Only a few
specialists are competent to advise concerning their current practical
application: customs officers, customs brokers, customs lawyers, for
example, and some importers and their agents; and the author is none
of these.

The barriers mentioned have sometimes been called "the invisible
tariff,"[2] sometimes "administrative protection."[3] Accordingly, use of
the phrase "indirect protection" requires some explanation and defence.
The term "protection" is here interpreted very broadly. It is used in
the sub-title as a short method of referring to all the expenses, uncertainties, and delays in international trade that are incidental to the
payment of customs duties or to conforming with the other regulations
mentioned above; whether they are part of the necessary costs of
collection and enforcement, the unintended result of inept regulations
or administrative inefficiency, or intended burdens designed to discriminate unobtrusively against imported merchandise: results are
independent of purpose, and proof of intention is often difficult.

As used here the term includes such special burdens even though
identical commodities are not produced in the importing country.
Many regulations apply to all imports; and, in any case, over wide
ranges, many different commodities are partial substitutes for one
another. Imported figs, for example, are substitutes for domestic dried,
and even preserved, fruit; fringed rugs are substitutes for rugs without
fringes even though they may be classified for tariff purposes as different articles. In a very general sense most commodities are substitutes

2Bidwell, *Invisible Tariff*.   3Winslow, "Administrative Protectionism."

for most others: if one sort of thing is not available or is exorbitantly high in price, other things will often be used instead. General hindrances to trade, accordingly, affect the ways in which domestic resources are used and they diminish, as well, the variety of commodities from which the consumer may choose; if neither the foreign nor an identical domestic article is available he will have to do without, or be content with something that is less satisfactory and may require a greater use of resources than the thing he really wants. In addition, obstacles to the importation of an article may affect the domestic and international distribution of income even though no close substitute is produced domestically. The measures here discussed need not affect all importers, or even all customs ports in the same way. Indeed, importers not only fear lest their imports may attract higher duties than expected; they often fear even more that their competitors may be treated less badly.

The term "indirect" is used to exclude those charges and quantitative restrictions which are explicitly and publicly imposed on imports. It excludes, for example, the rates of duty explicitly stated in the customs tariff, and direct restrictions imposed by quotas and by the rationing of foreign exchange. The United States has used quotas more sparingly than many countries, though recently other countries have been reducing while the United States has been increasing quantitative restrictions. In peacetime Canada has scarcely used quotas at all, except temporarily from November 1947 to December 1950. Even then, some attempt at least was made to counteract their protective effects; and as soon as the balance of international payments permitted, they were discontinued. The United States has not adopted foreign exchange control. Except, perhaps, for ten days or two weeks in 1947, Canada has always permitted the acquisition of foreign exchange to pay for goods that could be lawfully imported, and in 1950 abandoned foreign exchange control altogether. Generally speaking, then, the special measures in force during the war years and the years immediately following are not treated at all in this study, or are mentioned only incidentally. In Canada, at any rate, trade was then controlled by more direct methods; and many of the earlier, more burdensome procedures here to be considered were removed, suspended, relaxed, or simplified.

The term "indirect protection" is chosen in preference to "administrative protection" because the latter phrase has sometimes been restricted to the protective effects of actions left to the discretion of administrative agencies in contrast with those prescribed by statute, and for the purposes of this study this distinction is not fundamental. Indeed, one of the interesting contrasts in the procedures of Canada and the United States is that in the United States many of the protective procedures are made mandatory by the Tariff Act; whereas in Canada the statutes have often conferred on the government broad powers which might be used to restrict or to relax restrictions. These broader powers have been used flexibly to implement government policies; policies not determined primarily by the Department of National Revenue, which performed the narrower function of applying the laws and regulations to particular imports.

"Indirect protection" is used in preference also to "invisible protection." The latter term has been used to suggest, quite correctly, that the protective effect of the procedures here considered is not clear and obvious and knowingly ratified by the electors or even by a majority of their representatives. However, the phrase also suggests that the legislators and the public do clearly understand the degree and kind of protection afforded by the rates of duty themselves, and this suggestion is probably misleading. The tariff rate structures of the two countries are so complex that their implications can be understood, if at all, only by the expert. Indeed, when a tariff is as complex as these, it is often very difficult, even for the expert, to determine the protective effects of specified changes. Under certain circumstances, aggregate protection can be increased by decreasing a particular rate.[4]

In this study it is assumed that indirect obstacles are worse, or less good, than direct obstacles. In the first place they require importers, if they choose to trade, not merely to make payments but to use up labour, materials, and initiative in conforming with customs and other requirements, in providing against the risk of incurring unforeseen costs or penalties, and in costly litigation which often absorbs the energies of unusually capable persons. In the second place they may confer protection on certain domestic producers (often at the expense of others) in addition to the amount indicated by the duty; they may be used to confer this additional protection intentionally by stealth, or they may confer it unintentionally through inadvertence. Finally, even when the uncertainties, delays, and costs are reduced as low as is possible by appropriate laws and administrative procedures, they cannot be eliminated completely. They then form a necessary cost of the measures in question which should be taken into account in assessing their effects and in deciding whether to retain, extend, or complicate them.

[4]Viner, *The Customs Union Issue*, p. 48.

Customs duties, like other taxes and regulations, should be designed to secure their objectives with as little cost as possible. In fact, with certain necessary qualifications and interpretations, they may be judged by the same standards as other taxes. Statements of the requisites of a good tax system usually include, in some form or other, the four canons of taxation enunciated by Adam Smith, which prescribe equity or equality, certainty, convenience, and economy. In 1924 the International Conference on Customs and Other Similar Formalities listed five characteristics which customs procedures must possess if they are to impose no unavoidable costs or hindrances to international trade: publicity, simplicity, expedition in releasing goods, opportunity of appeal to an independent tribunal, and equality.[5] "Equality" appears in both these lists; "expedition" is partly analogous to Smith's "economy" and "convenience"; and "publicity," "simplicity," and "redress" are presumably means of providing what Smith called "certainty."

More explicitly, the importer wants to know the duty he will ultimately be required to pay: before purchase if possible; if not, at least before sale. He wants the goods released promptly and at as little cost as possible. Also he wants to know that other importers will not be given more favourable treatment. Even if he has no direct competitors he still wants to know at least the upper limit of the costs he may have to incur; a high upper limit may reduce sales or prevent trade altogether.

A foreign manufacturer considering developing the protected market, or a domestic producer considering developing foreign sources of supply, will be interested in these considerations, and others too; especially, in the prospective treatment of his imports over a reasonably long period in the future. In a democracy, this assurance of reasonable customs treatment can be given most adequately by a consistent refusal of the electorate to support protectionist policies, and especially concealed protection; on the other hand, a tendency to condone indirect protection, even in prosperous times, is likely to prevent foreign producers from committing their resources to provide capacity to produce goods for the uncertain protected market; or to the establishment of merchandising and servicing channels in that market.

Accordingly it would appear that uncertainty concerning foreign duties is a greater deterrent to the opening up of new channels of

[5]League of Nations, International Conference on Customs and Other Similar Formalities, *Proceedings*, vol. I, p. 135. Quoted by Bidwell, *Invisible Tariff*, p. 24.

trade than it is to established ones. Procedural protection (as well as quotas and duties) is more likely to preserve obsolete channels of trade and methods of production than to stimulate innovation in these matters.

Indirect protection has been repeatedly condemned and many proposals for reform have been approved. Recommendations designed, if put into practice, to minimize indirect protection have been drawn up and approved by a number of international conferences under the auspices of the League of Nations, by the International Chamber of Commerce, and by importers' and exporters' associations. Between the wars several commercial agreements contained articles relating to customs regulations and procedures. Currently, the General Agreement on Tariffs and Trade contains important restrictions with respect to anti-dumping and countervailing duties; valuation for customs purposes; and formalities relating among other things to consular certification and documentation, to analyses and inspection, to quarantine, sanitation and fumigation, and to marks of origin. It forbids the imposition of internal taxes or regulations that discriminate against imports; and it requires prompt publication of general administrative rulings and the provision of facilities for appeal from administrative decisions to tribunals independent of the agency charged with enforcement.[6] The Havana Charter for the proposed International Trade Organization included substantially similar provisions.[7]

With respect to indirect obstacles to imports, the United States and Canada have not, perhaps, been the worst offenders. In neither of these countries is it true, for example, as it has at times been true in certain others, that bribes or gifts to customs officials form a necessary and important part of the cost of importing merchandise; nor do importers sustain massive losses from pilfering or spoilage occasioned by the gross inefficiency, dishonesty, carelessness, or ill-will of government officials. On the other hand, neither country has completely eschewed procedures that afford indirect protection; and each has perfected some of them. Canada, for example, in the early thirties, instead of imposing the obstacles then fashionable, such as quotas and exchange controls, perfected a combination of anti-dumping duties and official valuation of imports that was much less visible though perhaps equally effective in excluding imports. In the United States, on the other hand,

[6]United Nations, *General Agreement on Tariffs and Trade* (G.A.T.T.), arts. III, VI–X.

[7]United Nations, *Charter for an International Trade Organization* (Havana Charter), arts. 18, 34–8.

there has gradually evolved a method of valuation for customs purposes which is probably unrivalled in its precision, in its intricacy, and in its effectiveness in producing uncertainty and delay. In the United States, too, domestic interests have been allowed, at times, to convert an admirable system of judicial appeal into an unusually effective method of harassing the importers it was originally intended to protect.

In both countries, the level of indirect protection has changed over the years. In both, it reached a peak between 1930 and 1934; in the United States the peak had been reached gradually, in Canada more suddenly. In Canada, too, the descent from the peak was the more rapid. The use of discretionary powers, for example, was limited by agreement with the United States, the United Kingdom, and other British and foreign countries, in return for commercial concessions; the Customs Act and the Customs Tariff Act were amended as required by these agreements. In the United States, the Trade Agreements Act of 1934 removed from domestic competitors the power to protest the classification of articles mentioned in any trade agreement, and the Customs Administrative Act of 1938 liberalized the provisions of the Tariff Act of 1930 in certain other respects. Meanwhile, a series of decisions of the customs courts had the general effect of determining a foreign value for imports that ranked higher and higher in the hierarchy of prices in the foreign market. These decisions had the effect at the same time, however, of narrowing the meaning of foreign value, one of the preferred bases of customs valuation, so drastically that in more and more cases it was found that a foreign value did not exist. In these cases the value determined on an alternative basis was often lower than the price proposed as the foreign value.

Though by 1940 procedural protection had diminished in intensity in both countries, it was still an important obstacle. Even in Canada between 1938 and 1940 the combined operation of valuation, dumping duties, and sales tax occasionally increased the landed costs of certain textile items by as much as 25 per cent of the invoice price. And in one post-war survey of Canadian firms nearly half of those who had discontinued exporting to the United States mentioned United States customs procedures as one of the factors forcing them to discontinue export; of those who gave reasons for not exporting, more mentioned customs procedures than rates of duty.

In recent decades the United States has sponsored a world movement toward less restrictive trade policies; and Canada has given strong support. In multilateral negotiations both countries have made considerable reductions in rates of duty, though the reductions made by the United States were necessarily restricted within the limits prescribed by the Trade Agreements Act and the various extending Acts. Certain changes too have occurred in customs procedures in each country. In 1947 each undertook to apply provisionally the General Agreement on Tariffs and Trade; that is to say, they agreed to adopt the negotiated changes in rates of duty and to conform with those procedural provisions which did not require amendment of statute. It was understood that as soon as practicable each would propose the legislation necessary to permit its government to conform completely with the provisions of the Agreement. Each of the governments adopted the tariff rates agreed upon and began to make the procedural changes within its power; and each introduced appropriate legislation; but the two legislatures have behaved quite differently.

In Canada, the powers of the Government were already so broad that most of the procedural provisions could be implemented at once; indeed, with a few exceptions, discussed later, Canadian practice already conformed with them. Nevertheless, the Canadian Customs Act and Customs Tariff were amended in 1948; amendments of less importance were adopted in subsequent years. The principal effects of the Canadian amendments were to make more adequate provision for appeals; to narrow certain discretionary powers of the Government, especially concerning valuation; to remove the provision that value for duty must not be less than cost of production; to permit the Governor in Council to declare any goods or classes of goods exempt from dumping duty, and to bring the wording of the Acts in certain other respects more closely into correspondence with the actual phrases of the General Agreement. The Government has retained certain discretionary powers, concerning valuation for example, which could not be used against imports from a signatory of the General Agreement, or if so only under its escape provisions.[8] These changes were not made without opposition; but they were defended, as were later the statutory amendments proposed in the United States, on the grounds that they were desirable in themselves, as well as in relation to the General Agreement. Their adoption was assured by the substantial and well-disciplined parliamentary majority of the Government and the post-war prosperity of the country, as well as by the direct advantages accruing to many sectors of the economy from the lowering of barriers to international trade. For a time, too, domestic producers were shielded from the full effects of the tariff concessions and the changes in customs practices by the Emergency Foreign Exchange

[8]G.A.T.T., art. xix.

Conservation Regulations, imposed immediately after the conclusion of the General Agreement to check the loss of external reserves that had begun in 1946, but removed as rapidly as practicable. Recently, protectionists in Canada have begun to advocate more forcibly a return to restrictive customs practices, on the grounds, in part, that the United States has failed to adopt correspondingly liberal procedures.[9]

Legislative events in the United States have followed a different course. After the completion of the General Agreement at Geneva, the United Nations Conference on Trade and Employment met at Havana and by March 24, 1948, had prepared a Charter for the International Trade Organization which included many of the provisions of the General Agreement with respect to customs procedures. The United States Administration chose to introduce a bill based on this Charter but the bill met with such determined opposition, partly at least concerning non-tariff matters, that it was not reported out of committee.

During 1949 and 1950 (and, it may be assumed, at other times as well), the United States Government was receiving representations from Canada and other countries urging it to make further reforms in customs procedures.[10] In 1950 a Customs Simplification Bill to amend the Tariff Act[11] was introduced but was not advanced very far. In 1951 an identical bill was considered by the House Committee on Ways and Means. These bills were based on "a survey conducted in 1938 by a private firm of management consultants[12] and some of the provisions contained in the bill paralleled certain of the customs administrative

[9]H. Crombie, President, Canadian Manufacturers' Association, "Canadian Industry Needs Protection—Report of an Address to the Rotary Club of Toronto, Mar. 28," *Industrial Canada*, May 1952, p. 53; J. T. Stirrett. "General Manager's Report," *Industrial Canada*, July 1952, pp. 56 *sq.*; and extract from speech of G. K. Sheilds, President, Canadian Manufacturers' Association: ". . . our government should realize, now, that it is elected primarily to protect the interests of Canada, the nation—not to attempt, starry eyed, to lead the world into Elysian fields of International Free Trade." *Industrial Canada*, Feb. 1953, p. 43.

[10]Rt. Hon. C. D. Howe, "The Return of Competitive Market," *Industrial Canada*, July 1950, p. 87; and R. C. Isbister, as reported in *Industrial Canada*, July 1951, p. 197.

[11]U.S., House of Representatives, 81st Congress, H.R. 8304 (1950).

[12]"Management Survey of the Bureau of Customs" by McKinsey & Co. of New York (nine volumes unpublished). Of the 178 recommendations, 87 had been put into effect by administrative action by 1951; 36 required legislative action; 20 of the latter were involved in H.R. 1535: U. S. House, Committee on Ways and Means, *Hearings on 1535*, 1951, pp. 37–38. One copy of the report was made available to the appropriations committee of each of the Houses; it was not available to the author.

provisions of the General Agreement on Tariffs and Trade." The Treasury expressed the view that even had there been no General Agreement the amendments were "needed to improve the administration and procedural aspects of the customs service and thereby expedite the movement of merchandise in regular channels of trade."[13] At the committee hearings many opposed the bill, partly on the grounds that the State Department was making use of the Treasury to implement the provisions of the General Agreement.[14] The House passed the bill after deleting two provisions; one would have removed American selling price as a basis for dutiable value, and the other was intended to remove discrimination against foreign spirits. In the spring of 1952 the Senate Finance Committee held hearings on the bill but made no report on it, and the bill lapsed with the end of the 82nd Congress. In 1953 another bill was introduced, similar to that passed by the House in 1951. In the hearings, many witnesses represented themselves as favourable to *real* simplification of customs administration, but opposed several of the proposals which lessened the burden on the importer. The bill was amended and enacted as the Customs Simplification Act of 1953.

Of the seven provisions of the bill mentioned separately by the Treasury in 1951[15] as being of great importance, three were retained in the Act: those relating to marking, undervaluation duties, and the correction of admitted errors. Three were deleted, relating to valuation, conversion of foreign currency, and proof of injury in applying countervailing duties.[16] The seventh important item, relating to administrative exemption of small shipments, was enacted; though the amount of one of the proposed exemptions was reduced. Of the provisions deleted, the Treasury even in 1953 had classed that relating to valuation as the most important of its proposal; the currency pro-

---

[13]U. S. House, *On H.R. 1535*, p. 15. The U.S. Tariff Commission described the position as follows: "The pertinent provisions of G.A.T.T. are not definitely effective, and cannot be made so until after appropriate legislation; the enactment of the amendments proposed in H.R. 8304 (H.R. 1530) would make it possible for the United States to accept G.A.T.T. . . . These changes would also meet the requirements of corresponding provisions in the Charter for an international Trade Organization." From "Memorandum of United States Tariff Commission" in U.S. House, *On H.R. 1535*, p. 222.

[14]See e.g. testimony of O. R. Strackbein, U.S. House, *On H.R. 1535*, p. 408.

[15]U.S. House, *On H.R. 5106* (1953), p. 15.

[16]The provision requiring proof of injury before applying countervailing duties was not included in the original bill in 1953, although favoured by the Treasury. It was inserted by the Committee and deleted on the floor of the House.

visions were also held to be of substantial, though not comparable importance. The currency and valuation proposals (as well as one other provision inserted in the House) were removed from the bill because they were regarded as controversial and there was not enough time to hold hearings. A new bill containing these deleted provisions was introduced in the House and passed next day. It is now pending in the Senate Finance Committee.[17] The other proposals of the bill were regarded by the Treasury as "less important individually but cumulatively of considerable importance." Many of these clauses were enacted, including a few that granted limited increases in the discretionary powers of the administration.

Meanwhile, Congress was demonstrating by other legislative acts (and pranks) that, on particular issues, it was inclined to increase rather than remove protection.[18] "Section 104 of the Defense Production Act of 1950 . . . directed the President to impose import controls including quotas and embargoes on a number of commodities whenever the Secretary of Agriculture determines that such imports would reduce domestic production below present levels or such higher levels as might be considered necessary, interfere with orderly domestic storing and marketing, or result in any unnecessary burden or expenditure under any Government support program."[19] An amendment in 1952 softened the effects of this measure by permitting the Secretary of Agriculture to exercise import controls by type and variety of a commodity; in 1953 these provisions were removed to a more permanent, and less anomalous position in the Agricultural Adjustment Act.

Similarly the provisions of the successive Reciprocal Trade Agreements Extension Acts, and the committee hearings with respect to them, suggest the very considerable congressional influence of those opposed to a reduction in trade barriers. In particular, the Extension Act of 1951 included several restrictive provisions. In the first place, it required that an escape clause be included in all future trade agreements and inserted in all existing agreements as soon as practicable.

[17]H.R. 6584, 1953.

[18]On the protectionist bias of Congress, John Day Larkin remarks: "For tariff-making purposes practically all congressmen may be divided into two groups: those who are frankly on the protectionist side at all times and are willing to give any interested group whatever it seeks in the way of protective rates; and those who are in principle opposed to this sort of protection, but who feel that while a tariff bill is in the making, they must not let their constituents down." *Trade Agreements: A Study in Democratic Methods*, p. 3.

[19]U.S., Public Advisory Board for Mutual Security, *A Trade and Tariff Policy in the National Interest* (*Bell Report*), p. 25.

This provision made mandatory by statute a practice which had formerly been established by an Executive Order of the President of 1947. Under the escape procedures, the Tariff Commission is required upon request of the President or on a motion of either House, or upon application of any interested party, to report whether, as a result of a trade-agreement concession or tariff concession, imports of a specified kind have increased so as to cause or threaten to cause serious injury to a domestic industry "producing like or directly competitive products." If it finds that imports have so increased, it is required to recommend to the President the withdrawal of the concession wholly or in part, its suspension, or the imposition of a quota. If the President does not accept the recommendation, he is required to submit a report to the appropriate committee of each House giving his reasons for not acting on the recommendation of the Commission.

In the second place, the Trade Agreements Extension Act of 1951 included a "peril point" provision requiring the President to submit to the Tariff Commission a list of the commodities on which it is proposed to negotiate concessions. The Commission is then required to determine for each a peril point beyond which a concession might threaten serious injury to domestic producers of like or directly competitive articles. The President is required to report to Congress within thirty days after making a concession that reduces duties below the peril point.

The Act of 1951 also had the effect of restoring to domestic producers of competing products the privilege of carrying to the customs court a protest against the classification of an imported article even though mentioned in a trade agreement, and it amended the Agricultural Adjustment Act to provide that "no trade agreement . . . heretofore or hereafter entered into by the United States shall be applied in a manner inconsistent with the requirement" of section 22, that the administration restrict imports under certain conditions. Finally, lest there be any danger of conveying the opposite impression, the Act provided in its penultimate section that the passing of the Act "shall not be construed to determine or indicate the approval or disapproval by the Congress of the Executive Agreement known as The General Agreement on Tariffs and Trade." These unsatisfactory legislative results have occurred in spite of the appearance of several able and well-authenticated reports from governmental and from responsible private sources.[20]

[20]For example: U.S., Dept. of Commerce, U.S. Economic Co-operation Joint Mission, *Report of the . . . Joint Mission to Investigate Possibilities of Increasing*

Much of what has been written concerning customs procedures has quite properly emphasized the extent and the precise details of the revisions required immediately to facilitate trade. The difference in the history of customs legislation in Canada and the United States since 1948, however, suggests that broader studies of long-run tendencies may be needed as well. What are the underlying factors which have made for the differences and similarities, and how are they likely to affect future behaviour with respect to customs procedures? These are large and difficult problems and this study can do little more than raise a few such issues incidentally to its more specific tasks, and suggest a few of the more obvious hypotheses.

Western European Dollar Earnings; U.S., *Report to the President on Foreign Economic Policies (Gray Report);* Bell Report*;* Fletcher School of Law and Diplomacy, *International Trade Policy Issues;* Council on Foreign Relations, *Foreign Trade and U.S. Tariff Policy.* See also U.S., Commission on Foreign Economic Policy, *Report to the President and Congress (Randall Report); Staff Papers* of the *Randall Report;* and Klaus Knorr and Gardner Paterson, *A Critique of the Randall Commission Report,* published after this manuscript had been written.

II

TARIFF STRUCTURE

*In the Arithmetic of the Customs House two plus two seldom
makes four.*

NO ATTEMPT is made in this study to apportion praise or blame
among different departments or agencies of government concerned
with the formulation and administration of customs procedures in
Canada and the United States. However, a brief statement of their
functions and relationships is necessary. In Canada, the Department
of Finance is primarily responsible for formulating government policy
and proposing legislation on customs matters, in consultation, of
course, with other departments: with the Department of Trade and
Commerce, for example, concerning trade negotiations, and with the
Department of National Revenue (Customs Division) concerning administrative feasibility. The Department of National Revenue, on the
other hand, is responsible for applying the legislation and the orders that
reflect the policy of the Government. The Tariff Board of Canada
performs two distinct functions. In one capacity it is a court of record
and acts as a tribunal to decide appeals from decisions of the Deputy
Minister of National Revenue (Customs Division) on matters relating
to customs duties and excise taxes; in its other capacity it conducts
enquiries and makes reports on matters relating to the Customs Tariff
referred to it by the Minister of Finance. Since, in Canada, the Government is responsible to the House, it has often been given rather larger
discretionary power under statutes which are less detailed than those
of the United States; and its majority in the Commons, together with
the stronger party discipline incident to maintaining that majority, has
made it possible to open up for revision the Acts relating to Customs
with less danger than exists in the United States, that the legislature
may subordinate the general public interest to the pressures of special
interests.

In the United States the Treasury is charged with the administration
of the Tariff Act and makes recommendations concerning its amend-

ment; the Department of State and the Treasury, in consultation with other departments (e.g. the Department of Agriculture), are directly concerned in negotiating commercial agreements. The United States Customs Court is an administrative court which hears appeals from decisions of customs officials subject to appeal on matters of law to the United States Court of Customs and Patent Appeals. The Tariff Commission is a fact finding and advisory body which reports to the President and to Congress. In the United States, legislative and administrative powers are constitutionally distinct and Congress has shown itself to be particularly jealous of its authority in customs matters. The legislation under which customs duties are collected, accordingly, often prescribes procedures in great detail, the Tariff Act is revised infrequently, and appeals to the Customs Court are numerous and important.

In each country, the governmental organization is only part of a complexly interacting set of circumstances which condition the formation and application of tariff laws and regulations. National resources, population, production techniques; constitutional law and procedures, legislatures, courts; governmental officials, central and local government departments; brokers, domestic importers, foreign exporters, domestic producers, and their attitudes and organizations all have effects. In addition, a network of communication—telephone and telegraph and word of mouth; letters, bulletins, court decisions, government memoranda; privately prepared guides, journals, magazines, and newspapers—determines the extent and distribution of knowledge of cutsoms precedure. The cost and complexity of this network of communication and its success in diminishing the uncertainties of importing and exporting depend, among other things, on the complexity of the tariff structure: on the number of rates prescribed for each article or item; on the number of special taxes or imposts not prescribed by the tariff itself; on the methods of distinguishing between articles subjected to different rates of duty (that is to say on the wording of the tariff items), and on the number of items for which the tariff prescribes different rates. Both Canada and the United States have developed extremely complex tariffs.

1. NORMAL RATES OF DUTY

With respect to the number of rates prescribed for a single article the Canadian Tariff is the more complicated. In 1897 Canada reverted to the colonial practice of admitting goods from British countries at reduced rates of duty, and since 1907 the Canadian Tariff has contained three columns specifying the rates of duty payable under the British Preferential Tariff, the Most-Favoured-Nation Tariff (formerly the Intermediate Tariff) and the General Tariff. For some items the rates under the different tariffs are identical but for many they are different. The rate applicable to a particular importation may depend then on the country of origin and also, since to enjoy the lower rates the goods must be imported directly, on the way in which it was transported to Canada. Indeed, the articles included in a single tariff item may be dutiable at more than three alternative rates. The Chairman of the Tariff Board of Canada described this complexity to the Senate Committee on Canadian Trade Relations: ". . . the Canadian tariff, as it stands today, is easily one of the most complicated in the world. I am . . . referring to its structure. . . . Where the United States will have one rate on a given commodity applicable to all the world, we may have in our tariff at the one time as many as five different rates on one and the same commodity"; and later "I was trying to talk about a given tariff item, senator."[1]

To enter under the British Preferential Tariff an article must be, to the extent of a substantial proportion of its value (often 50 per cent),[2] the product of one or more of the specified British countries entitled to the preferential rates and it must be shipped directly to Canada; that is "conveyed into a sea, lake or river port of Canada, on a bill of lading from the country of origin showing the ultimate destination as Canada, without contingency of diversion, and without transhipment except at a port of any British Country."[3] If the British product is shipped on a through bill of lading to a sea, lake, or river

[1]Hector B. McKinnon, in Can., Senate, Standing Committee on Canadian Trade Relations, *Proceedings [on]* . . . *G.A.T.T.*, no. 5, March 6, 1948, pp. 105–6. On the other hand Mr. McKinnon states elsewhere: "Our Canadian formalities were not involved or vexatious and this comes closer to our law, as it now stands than it probably does to the law of most of the countries who signed at Geneva." *Ibid.*, no. 9, May 18, 1948, p. 388.

[2]Earlier provisions had required successively that one-fourth of the *value* of the article be added in countries entitled to the preference (P.C. 1871, July 14, 1898); that it be finished in a country entitled to the preference and not less than one-fourth of the *cost* of production be incurred in one or more British countries (P.C. 2527, Dec. 17, 1909); "one-fourth" was changed to one-half in 1928 (P.C. 2138, Nov. 28, 1928). For a consolidation of orders reducing the required British content on certain goods to 25 per cent see P.C. 822, Feb. 26, 1948. As an example of amendments to content requirements see P.C. 1646, changing British content requirement for manila rope from one-quarter to one-sixth; *Can. Gaz.*, April 9, 1952, p. 245.

[3]P.C. 3659, Dec. 2, 1935.

port in Canada without transhipment, the importer is entitled to a discount of 10 per cent of the duty otherwise payable, provided the preferential rate of duty exceeds 15 per cent *ad valorem*. This discount, however, is not allowed on tobacco products, wines, or spirits; or on imports which attract the same rates under the British Preferential and the Most-Favoured-Nation Tariffs;[4] or on goods admitted under the special rates provided for in the Canada–West Indies Trade Agreement of 1926. From the Canadian (as distinct from British) point of view the discount and the provisions for direct shipment are intended to give protection to Canadian ports and transportation facilities. Similarly, to enter under the Most-Favoured-Nation Tariff, a substantial proportion of the value must be added in a country whose exports are entitled to enter at the Most-Favoured-Nation rate and it must have been imported directly from such a country.

In contrast with the Canadian Tariff, the Customs Tariff of the United States until recently has been unilinear; by exception, preferential treatment has been extended to Cuban imports under a trade agreement of long standing, and more recently to imports from the Philippines under the Philippine Trade Act of 1946. Otherwise, except for retaliatory measures, uniform rates of duty have been charged without respect to country of origin. In the Trade Agreements Extension Act of 1951, however, the President was required to withdraw from products of Communist areas "concessions made in any trade agreement."[5] At the moment, then, the tariff of the United States, too, is formally multilinear. It is true, of course, that little would be imported into the United States from Communist countries in any event; but it is also true that the Canadian General Tariff is applied to only a few countries.

The regulations of the United States require, primarily, a statement of the country of export, not of origin. Formerly they did not require evidence concerning the amount of value added to an imported article

[4]This provision results from a compromise reached at Geneva where many countries claimed that the 10 per cent discount was a "hidden extension of our British preferential system." (See letters of L. D. Wilgress, Oct. 30, 1947, to acting chairman of U.S. delegation and to acting chairman of the U.K. delegation. Can., Dept. of External Affairs, *Treaty Series*, 1948, no. 31.) The change affected only some $3,120,000 worth of a total of $504,000,000 of British imports in 1948. The only items of importance affected were manufactured brass (1948 value $330,000), cotton clothing ($2,298,000), and mixed clothing ($422,000). Can., Commons, *Debates*, 1950, p. 2175.

[5]For an example of multiple rates in the tariff of the United States see the *Bell Report*, p. 42.

in particular countries, in order that it might qualify for admission under the rates of duty to which it was entitled. At present, however, invoices of products of Cuba, the Philippines, and certain insular possessions of the United States must contain or be accompanied by certain statements concerning origin.[6] Even when the tariff of the United States was unilinear, knowledge of the country of origin was, in fact, required for many imports. Most imports, moreover, must be marked with the name of the country of origin—not necessarily the country whence exported. The value for duty may depend on the cost of production in the country whence the imported article was sold to the United States, but the question is not well settled,[7] and the classification of some articles depends on the component of chief value. Accordingly, it would be easy to exaggerate the difference in procedures occasioned by Canada's multilinear tariff.

2. Additional Duties

In addition to normal rates, other special duties may be collected. In the United States countervailing duties must be collected, equal to any bounty on any dutiable article. If it is shown that a domestic industry is being seriously damaged or that a prospective one is being prevented from developing, a dumping duty may be imposed, equal to the difference between fair market value of the imported article in the country of origin and the actual selling price. A marking duty of 10 per cent is collected if goods are not marked to show the country of origin before the entry is finally liquidated, unless the goods are of a kind exempted from the marking requirement. Until 1953 an undervaluation duty was imposed if the appraised value exceeded the value stated on the entry form; this duty, however, might be remitted on a finding of the United States Customs Court that the undervaluation was not intended to defraud. Under certain specified conditions, discussed later, Canada imposes dumping duties on goods of a class or kind made in Canada. In each country the administration is empowered to impose punitive duties on imports from countries which discriminate against its exports. These other duties serve not only from time to time to increase the amounts of duty payable, but also, by making the procedures more complex, to increase the time, expense, and uncertainty of international commerce.

[6]U.S. Customs Regulations, 16.23 and 16.26.

[7]Two judicial decisions have indicated that a product made in country A, exported to B, and thence sold to the United States was subject to appraisement on the basis of cost of production in B rather than its cost in the country of origin.

3. ADDITIONAL CHARGES ON IMPORTS

Internal taxes that discriminate against imports may be used to give concealed protection to domestic producers. Most commercial agreements contain provisions intended to ensure that the advantages gained through reduction of duties will not be offset by discriminatory increases in other taxes. The General Agreement provides for national treatment of imports with respect to internal taxes, prohibits the imposition of new taxes designed to protect untaxed substitute products of domestic origin, and provides that existing taxes of this latter kind be subject to negotiation.[8] The Havana Charter contained a similar but less detailed provision.[9]

In the United States import fees are collected on certain agricultural imports under section 22 of the Agricultural Adjustment Act; taxes which are not levied against similar domestic goods apply to certain lumber products, petroleum products, copper ores, fish oil,[10] and certain related products and to certain oil-bearing seeds; and processing taxes are imposed on coconut, palm, and palm-kernel oil. Of these the processing taxes on certain oils afford concealed protection. The others, though imposed by the Internal Revenue Act, are described in the customs regulations and elsewhere as ordinary customs duties and are listed in the official schedules of import duties. They serve not only to increase the tariff rates explicitly but to increase their complexity.[11]

Some Internal Revenue taxes give protection in more complicated ways as well. The Internal Revenue Code of the United States imposes a tax of $10.50 (formerly $6.00) on each proof gallon of distilled spirits, or on each wine gallon. In effect, domestic spirits are taxed on the proof content while imported spirits testing under proof (about

[8]G.A.T.T., art. III.

[9]Havana Charter, arts. 17 and 18, and Annex P, Interpretative Notes Relating to art. 17 and art. 18, par. 2.

[10]U.S. Tariff Commission, *The [First] Trade Agreement With Canada* (*Report 111*): "The provision of the United States Revenue Act of 1934 levying taxes on certain animal and vegetable oils affected Canada substantially only with respect to fish oils or relatively minor items on the trade with the U.S."

[11]The complex distinctions involved in the taxes on ordinary oils and fats under ss. 2490–2493 of the Internal Revenue Code (U.S. Code, 1946 ed., title 26) which are negotiable in trade agreements, and the processing taxes on coconut oil and palm oil, which are not negotiable, as well as the taxation of imported oleomargarine, adulterated butter, and filled cheese, are recounted in U.S. House, *On the Customs Simplification Bill of 1951*, pp. 28 *sq.*, also pp. 531–2. For the complicating effects concerning the measurement of lumber see *infra* chap. IV.

86 proof is usual) are taxed as if they were 100 proof. This treatment is said by United States distillers to increase the excise payable on imported Canadian whisky by more than $1.00 per gallon.[12] The sections in the original Customs Simplification Bill designed to apply these taxes more equitably were rejected by the House in 1951.

In Canada, a special excise tax of 1 per cent was imposed in 1931 on the duty-paid value of nearly all imports. The rate was increased to 3 per cent in 1932. On goods entitled to preferential treatment, it was reduced to 1½ per cent in 1934 and removed entirely in 1935. In the second trade agreement with the United States, Canada agreed to end this concealed discrimination in favour of British goods, and in 1939 the tax was dropped entirely.[13]

During the last war Canada collected a 10 per cent Exchange Conservation Tax (repealed in 1945) on imports from non-British countries. The customs officials also collect excise and sales tax on imported goods but these taxes are collected also on similar domestic products. It is to be noted, however, that the Canadian sales tax is collected on the duty-paid value of the goods, so that any overvaluation or increase in duties tends to raise the value base to which this tax is applied. Also, in September 1939, additional duties were placed on tea, coffee, cigars, tobaccos, cigarettes, distilled spirits, and wines, for revenue purposes. They were increased in 1940 and 1941, but were taken off tea and coffee in the war years. The additional duties on liquor were raised in 1949.[14]

4. STATEMENT OF TARIFF ITEMS

Of more importance, perhaps, than the number of columns in the tariff are the number of items and way in which they are described. Unless a country is prepared to prescribe a uniform rate of duty (or free entry) for every imported article some method must be developed of deciding which rate is to be applied to each imported article. The legal basis of this process is the customs tariff, which defines certain classes or items into one of which each imported article must be fitted, and which prescribes either free entry or a definite rate of duty for each such item. A customs tariff may include either few or many items attracting distinct rates. The tariffs both of Canada and of the

[12]U.S. House, *On H.R. 1535*, p. 384.

[13]For a more detailed examination of the tax see Parkinson, *Memorandum on the Basis of Canadian Commercial Policy 1926–38*, pp. 130–1.

[14]Can., Commons, Standing Committee on Banking and Commerce, *Torquay Negotiations, 1951*, no. 3, pp. 118–19.

United States are highly specialized; each contains a multitude of items and for each of them a rate of duty is prescribed (or a set of rates). These items vary in type and extent and in the basis of classification.

Schedule A to the Customs Tariff of Canada states the rates of duty (or free entry) prescribed for each item. Schedule B lists the goods, eligible for drawback, used to produce goods for the domestic market; and Schedule C lists the prohibited items. The administration of the Canadian Customs is regulated by the Customs Act, the Customs Tariff, the Tariff Board Act, and other statutes. In the United States the basic tariff law is the Tariff Act of 1930 as amended. Title I sets forth the dutiable items and the corresponding rates; Title II specifically exempts those imports that are admitted free; Title III contains special provisions including certain of the import prohibitions;[15] and Title IV contains the administrative provisions.

The number of items in each tariff changes from time to time. As of May 30, 1951, following the changes agreed to at Torquay, the Canadian Tariff contained about 2,038 items.[16] But a mere statement of the number of rates and items gives little indication of the complexity of the classification for the items vary greatly in scope. For example, in the Canadian Tariff, a commodity may be specifically designated by name (eo nomine); or by the nature of its components (manufactures of rubber, etc.); by the status of the importer; by the specific end use to which it is to be put, as one of a number of related commodities under a general term (entering into the cost of production of . . .); by its suitability for a general end use; or it may be left to fall in "the ambit of the 'basket' item of the Tariff Schedule 711."[17]

The United States Tariff Act of 1930 as amended contains 734 numbered paragraphs in its dutiable and free lists; recently the number of groups and subgroups individually mentioned in the tariff was

[15]There is no definite collection of all import prohibitions in Title III or anywhere else. Some are in the tariff schedules, some in Title III; others are in agricultural, copyright, trade-mark, food and drugs, cosmetics, and other legislation.

[16]Of these, 446 were free under all three columns; another 141 were free under the British Preferential and Most-Favoured-Nation Tariff and another 576 were free under the British Preferential Tariff, leaving 875 items that were dutiable under all three tariffs. On 1450 items, rates on British goods were lower than those on imports from most favoured nations. See evidence of W. J. Callaghan, Can. Banking & Commerce, Torquay, May 9, 1951, pp. 41-2.

[17]Statement of F. J. Leduc in A-260, Tariff Board of Canada, Appeal no. 272.

estimated at 8,000.[18] Not all of these items, however, have separate rates. Even the thousands of dutiable items separated out for special treatment are only a small fraction of the total number of dutiable imports; by far the greater number fall within basket items which usually prescribe relatively high rates of duty and there are more than 250 of these basket items.[19] As a result

the task of classification is extremely complex and involves not only an examination of the merchandise, but a thorough knowledge and understanding of the schedules of the Tariff Act, of the decision of the courts, and of rulings of the Bureau of Customs. The determination of the proper classification may necessitate the submission of samples of the products for analysis in the chemical laboratory maintained in the appraiser's stores. Occasionally it is necessary to undertake a foreign investigation of the process of manufacture in order to ascertain what is the component material of chief value in the articles as ready to be assembled, a factor which frequently determines the appropriate tariff classification.[20]

The complexity of the tariffs is increased by use of a number of different bases of classification. It might be supposed, superficially, that a satisfactory classification could be secured by placing in the same paragraph and subjecting to the same rate those articles that resembled one another closely in significant physical (or chemical) qualities. However, the relevant test of the significance of the physical resemblance is the ease with which the articles can be substituted for one another in use or in production. Even the proposal that close substitutes be classed together fails to take account of fundamental complexities. There is no simple correspondence between "articles" and "uses." Most articles have several uses, and some a great many. For certain uses, in certain quantities or for certain people, two articles may be almost perfect substitutes; for others, not. Even if substitutability were used as the sole basis of classification, then, no simple pattern would emerge. In fact, however, each of the tariffs is arranged primarily on the superficial basis of material content; and each is further complicated by the use of a number of other bases, reflecting partly the complexity of the commodities to be classified, and partly the unresolved conflict between the purposes for which customs duties are imposed.

In addition to the increase over time in the number and complexity of the commodities entering international trade, several factors have

[18]Estimate attributed to "an informed authority" in the Bell Report.

[19]Bell Report, p. 45.

[20]U.S. Senate, Committee on Administrative Procedure, (Attorney General's Committee), Administration of Custom Laws, Monograph 27 (A.G. Com., Mon. 27), pp. 108–9.

favoured the growth of specialization. In each country the principal (and not wholly compatible) objectives of the customs duties have been to provide a revenue to the government and to give to domestic producers a type and degree of protection consistent with the attitude of the electorate and the developmental objectives of the government. The rates of duty appropriate to the raising of revenue differ from commodity to commodity and even as between different grades of the same commodity. Higher rates of duty can be collected on some articles than on others without preventing importation. Heavy duties, like high taxes, give rise to more widespread resentment when imposed on some commodities than when imposed on others. Moreover, a specific duty collected uniformly over a wide range of qualities and values of an article tends to be regressive; so far as it is passed on to the consumer it tends to collect a larger proportion of the expenditures on the cheaper grades of the article, usually purchased by consumers with lower incomes. Even an *ad valorem* rate, uniform over a wide range of qualities, is at best only proportional and, relatively to the total incomes of the consumers, it may well be regressive. Accordingly, in periods and in countries which have come increasingly to favour progressive taxation there has been some tendency to remedy the regressive features of the tariff as a form of taxation by increasing the number of classes and imposing higher rates on luxuries and on the more costly qualities of dutiable commodities.

The objective of giving protection to domestic producers has produced even more complications than that of raising a revenue. In the first place, if protection is to be given to each of the consecutive processes required to produce the finished article it is necessary to distinguish not only between the raw materials and the finished product but also between these and the semi-finished products resulting from each process. Accordingly, to divide the total protection appropriately, different rates and items are provided corresponding to the degree of finish. A drastic increase in rates backed by a firm determination to give adequate protection may, of course, be accompanied by a reduction in the number of items, such as that which occurred in the revision of the textile items in the Canadian Tariff in 1930. However, the reaction to general and drastic increases has led to piecemeal reduction of duties on goods that were formerly only a part of some item.[21] Similarly a more discriminating policy of increasing protection

[21]See, for example, the following Tariff Board recommendations, taken almost at random from references in the 1930's: T.B.C., Ref. 47, caps and cones of paper, free entry recommended, new item; Ref. 49, wooden doors not less than 6 feet

is associated with the separation of narrower items from larger classes in order to subject them to higher rates.[22] The attempt to set rates that will equalize domestic and foreign costs of production increased the number of items in the United States Tariff very considerably. It has had some, though rather less, effect in Canada.

Efforts to give and promise general and flexible protection to Canadian producers without raising the costs of other producers or consumers more than is necessary have increased the number of items in the Canadian Tariff in still another way; and at the same time have introduced still other bases of classification. Many items allow entry free or at a low rate of duty if the articles described are of "a class or kind not made in Canada": other articles similarly described but considered to be of a class or kind made in Canada do not qualify for entry at the lower rate. Sometimes these items occur in parallel pairs, for example the important basket items relating to machinery.[23]

The Canadian Tariff also contains a large number of special classes (holes in the tariff wall) to permit entry free or at a reduced rate to materials for use in a particular industry or for a particular purpose. This procedure involves specialization of the tariff through the introduction of items that are based not on the observable characteristics or on the origin of the imported commodity but on the status of the importer and the use that is to be made of the imported merchandise; sometimes a lower duty or a drawback is conditional even on the use made of the commodity produced from the imported material.[24]

---

by 2 feet, free under Preferential Tariff, new item; no recommendation, however, was made for a reduction of duty on "meat grinders" for use in the fox-breeding industry because the volume was too small and the interest in the reduction too little.

[22]For example, T.B.C., Ref. 59, rabbit skins, wholly or partially dressed, specific duty recommended and a new item.

[23]"427 All machinery composed wholly or in part of iron or steel, n.o.p., and complete parts thereof . . . 10 p.c., 22½ p.c., 35 p.c.
"427a All machinery composed wholly or in part of iron or steel, n.o.p., of a class or kind not made in Canada; complete parts thereof . . . Free, 7½ p.c., 35 p.c."

[24]Item 1019, for example, provides for a drawback of 99 per cent on bituminous coal "when imported by proprietors of coke ovens and converted at their coke ovens into coke for use in the smelting of metals from ores and in the melting of metals." Formerly, another item (1070) made the payment of a similar drawback, if the coke was sold, provisional among other things on an appropriate amount of domestic coal being used in producing it. Again, at one time, provision was made under item 506f for the temporary free admission of "staves and headings of wood, finished or unfinished, for use in the manufacture of barrels to be used exclusively in the packing of apples, in their natural state." Currently,

In the United States the desire for protection has had important effects on the tariff structure in rather different ways. Specific duties imposed on raw materials are often carried through to the finished product which is protected by an *ad valorem* duty as well. But specific rates of duty have been used also to conceal the height of some protective duties. Congress has been unwilling to adopt openly rates in excess of 100 per cent but with respect to specific duties it has proved to be either astute or complacent. During the thirties rates equivalent to several hundred per cent were thus concealed. Benjamin Levett has made famous the case of the specific duty on low-valued pocket knives.[25] If valued at more than 50 cents and not more than $1.25 per dozen, they were dutiable at 55 per cent plus 11 cents *each*; making a total rate of nearly 320 per cent on the lower-priced knives. Even though prices have risen and trade agreements have reduced the duty on certain grades of imports the compound rate on pocket knives valued at $3.00 a dozen (25 per cent *ad valorem* plus $12\frac{1}{2}$ cents each) amounts to 75 per cent *ad valorem*. Canadian tariff makers have not been guiltless of using regressive specific rates to conceal the extent of protection but the Tariff Board has, recently at least, condemned the practice and refused to adopt it; for example, in revising the tariff on plastics.[26]

On the whole the tariff makers of the United States appear to have been more successful than those of Canada in introducing and retaining trick classes (or "sleepers") designed to conceal the degree of protection from Congress or the general public. A high rate has sometimes been attached to an item which, though appearing unimportant, was so worded as to draw within its compass an important volume of imports. The fewness of trick classes in the Canadian Tariff may be attributable in part to the more frequent piecemeal changes in the Canadian Tariff, associated perhaps with the fact that in Canada the administration is responsible to the legislature, and with the correspondingly greater significance of the judiciary in the United States.

Customs duties are used not only to raise revenue and to protect domestic producers but also as bargaining instruments in international negotiations to secure access to foreign markets. Different countries are often interested in different types, grades, or sizes of a commodity,

---

staves and headings of wood are admitted free of duty under item 506c "for use in the manufacture of light barrels or kegs."

[25]See Levett, *Reduction of Trade Barriers*; also *Bell Report*, pp. 21–2.

[26]See T.B.C., Ref. 109, *Inquiry Respecting So-called Plastics Including Synthetic Resins* (mimeo.), p. 36.

and specialization has been used by both Canada and the United States to narrow the concessions made in international commercial agreements. Even in her earlier commercial agreements Canada specialized her tariff to give France, for example, concessions on such narrow items as mineral water from the springs of Vichy and certain other French resorts,[27] and recently the Torquay negotiations resulted in the addition of ninety-seven items to the Canadian Tariff. On the whole, however, until recently, Canada's multilinear tariff and her willingness to discriminate openly relieved her from some of the pressures to specialize for purposes of negotiation.

The United States, on the other hand, has adhered formally, with only minor exceptions, to the principle of non-discrimination; that is of quoting one rate for each commodity or item without reference to country of origin; correspondingly she has tried to negotiate concerning each item with its principal supplier. Even before the second world war the United States Tariff Commission recognized that bilateral bargaining with the main supplier was assisted by multiplication of classes and that specialization might be used to limit the responsibilities arising from trade agreements; but it argued that the multiplication of items after treaty negotiations should not be assumed to indicate any general attempt to escape most-favoured-nation obligations. "Often differences exist in the conditions of competition of imported with domestic goods even between different types and grades of a single commodity. The careful consideration of competitive conditions which accompanies the negotiation of a trade treaty often brings to light these differences and results in greater specialization."[28] William Diebold reports succinctly: "Reclassification proved such a useful tool that the United States negotiators made frequent use of it; of the 1,014 reductions in tariff rates in the trade agreements, 436 involved reclassification."[29] It appears then that, while the United States eschews formal international discrimination, she achieves many of the same results by specialization of her tariff.

Under an older dispensation, when the bilateral most-favoured-nation treaty was the instrument commonly used for reducing tariffs and extending the area of non-discrimination, extreme specialization was regarded with suspicion as an underhand method of lessening the common benefits from bilateral negotiations or of avoiding most-

[27]Exception to Canadian Tariff, item 711; June 10, 1933, *Customs Memo.*, no. 658.
[28]U.S. Tariff Commission, *Extent of Equal Tariff Treatment in Foreign Countries.*
[29]Diebold, *New Directions in Our Trade Policy*, p. 18.

favoured-nation obligations.[30] Now that the objectives have been changed to removing discrimination and reducing tariffs, "reasonable specialization" apparently has come to be regarded as a necessary condition to lowering tariffs at all.[31]

5. KINDS OF DUTY RATES

The tariff of each country is further complicated by the variety of ways in which the rate of duty is stated. Some rates are specific; some, *ad valorem*; some include both a specific and an *ad valorem* rate. In some items a specific, or *ad valorem*, or compound rate varies with the value of the article or with one or more of its physical characteristics. Some items impose a specific rate of duty with an *ad valorem* floor or ceiling; others are *ad valorem* rate with a specific floor or ceiling. Some instances of these latter methods of stating the rate have resulted from a change in the method of quoting a rate previously bound in a trade agreement.[32]

[30]See, e.g., Culbertson, *International Economic Policies*, pp. 88–9.

[31]For a survey of the uses and abuses of specialization see Hawkins, *Commercial Treaties and Agreements*, pp. 88–96.

[32]For the United States see *Bell Report*, p. 41.

III

ENTRY AND DOCUMENTATION

It should not be inferred that conditions, similar to those mentioned by Hawthorne, now prevail in the "Customs Service" department. . . . Vast improvements have been made since his time.

WILLIAM H. FUTRELL[1]

1. ENTRY

PREPARATIONS for clearing shipments through customs must begin long before the shipment arrives—often even before the goods are produced; and uncertainties and disputes concerning rates of duty and other customs matters may continue long after the shipment is sold. Nevertheless, customs formalities are focussed on the processes of entering merchandise and securing its release from custody. Clearing procedures in the two countries are very similar.

When imports arrive at a Canadian customs port they must be reported inward to the local customs officials, who check the list of shipments, the manifest, against the goods imported; shipments not reported are liable to seizure. Shipments that are not to be cleared at the border may be forwarded in bond to a sufferance warehouse maintained by the transportation agency in an interior port to be held in customs custody until released after payment of duty or, if entry is delayed, until sent to the Queen's Warehouse. When the shipment arrives by land for clearance at any port it must be accompanied by a

[1]*The History of Customs Jurisprudence*, p. 5. Many prominent persons besides Hawthorne have been customs officials, including Chaucer, Burns, and Adam Smith. In the Introduction to *The Scarlet Letter* Hawthorne wrote: "More frequently, however, on ascending the steps you would discern . . . a row of venerable figures, sitting in old-fashioned chairs, which were tipped on their hind legs back against the wall. Oftentimes they were asleep. . . . These old gentlemen . . . were Custom House officers. . . .

"It is a pious consolation to me, that, through my interference, a sufficient space was allowed them for repentance of the evil and corrupt practices into which, as a matter of course, every Custom House officer must be supposed to fall."

way-bill if shipped by freight or express; and it appears on the ship's manifest if it arrives by sea. The importer receives a notice of arrival from the transportation company, or from customs officials if it arrives by parcel post. Meanwhile he should have received from the shipper a commercial invoice, in the form prescribed by customs regulations, made out and certified by the exporter.

From the information contained in the invoice and notice of arrival the importer or his broker prepares the entry form. On this form the shipment is identified; the articles included are described and classified under the appropriate items of the customs tariff; the amount, the value, and the rate of duty are stated; the total amount of duty and excise and sales taxes if applicable are computed. Entries relating to food, drugs, and certain other kinds of merchandise subject to sanitary or other special regulations must also be stamped by officials of the appropriate departments of the government. The entry, the invoice, the notice of arrival, and certain other documents are filed at the customs house for detailed checking. If incomplete or incorrect the entry is blocked and after correction it must be refiled. When complete it is sworn to and the duty is paid; one copy of the entry is sent to Ottawa for central checking while the original and the other documents including a release warrant go to the appraisers' department for distribution to the place where the merchandise is being held. If the shipment apparently conforms with the entry and with the manifest or way-bill, the goods are released, except such designated packages, normally one in ten, as are sent to the warehouse or otherwise held for examination. When sample packages are retained for examination the merchandise must be held by the importer for three days unless the samples are sooner released.

In the interest of speed or convenience departures from this usual process of entry are permitted in certain cases. Goods may be entered for consumption as described above; or they may be entered for storage in a bonded warehouse without payment of duty until they are entered for consumption and withdrawn from the warehouse.[2] On withdrawal they need not be appraised a second time but the rate of duty applied is that prescribed on the date of withdrawal. Special provisions are made to speed the release of perishable goods; travellers' baggage is also dealt with quickly and informally; for gifts and small shipments of goods that are not for resale a simple form is used entitled "appraisal note for small collections." If an adequate invoice has not been received, goods may be admitted on a sight entry, after

2In this case a different entry form is used.

being examined at the expense of the importer in the presence of a customs officer, on deposit of a sum judged to be sufficient to pay duties on them and a declaration that information available is not sufficient to make a perfect entry. Unless a complete entry is made within the time specified by the collector, however, the money deposited is taken as the duty; and unless a satisfactory invoice, certified by the foreign seller or exporter is presented, an additional penalty may be exacted equal to the amount so deposited.[3] Highway shipments by truck may be spot-checked and entered at border ports or, since 1952,[4] they may be carried in bond over approved routes, to sufferance warehouses at interior ports. Similarly, in conformity with the provisions of the General Agreement on Tariffs and Trade goods may now be transported by truck across Canada in bond in a continuous journey from one point in the United States to another. This latter concession had been strongly resisted by certain Canadian interests.[5]

In many respects the United States procedures in entering imports resemble the Canadian though there are certain differences. Articles imported to the United States in a shipment valued at more than $250 (formerly $100) and subject to a duty in any way dependent on value must be accompanied by an invoice certified by a consular official of the United States in the country whence exported; though entry may be made on the basis of a suitable commercial invoice, on giving bond to produce a proper invoice within six months. The importer, or his agent, is required to state the tariff classification, the value, and the total duty payable on the importation. This estimated amount is deposited in making entry. Though the final decision of the customs as to the amount of duty payable may not be known for some time the merchandise is usually released on a re-delivery bond.[6] One package

[3]For a clear and concise description of entry procedures in Canada see Nuttall, *Functions of a Licensed Customs Broker* (an address given on Nov. 25, 1947, sponsored by the International Trade Section of the Montreal Board of Trade in co-operation with Sir George Williams College).

[4]Shipment by trucks in bond from border ports to larger customs ports had been permitted prior to Jan. 30, 1936; *Importer and Trader* (Toronto), Nov. 1936, p. 4.

[5]See discussion, Can., Banking & Commerce, *G.A.T.T.*, no. 3, April 15, 1948, pp. 191–3.

[6]Prior to 1938, section 499 of the Tariff Act of 1930 provided that goods might be held, except as otherwise provided in the Act, until reported by the appraiser to have been correctly invoiced and found to comply with other requirements of the law. Section 15 of the 1938 Amending Act allowed release of the goods "under

from each lot of uniform goods and not less than one of each ten packages of other goods must be held for inspection by the appraiser; and, unless the packaging permits appropriate selection, the whole shipment may be held.[7] As in Canada, goods arriving in the United States may be entered at the port of arrival or they may be entered for transport in bond to be entered for warehouse or consumption at an interior port. Clearance at a border port of imports to be forwarded for entry at another port may be made by the consignee, by the carrier, by a customs broker, or by any other person having a sufficient interest in the goods. If the arrangements for clearance from the border port are made by a broker a fee, of course, is charged. If arrangements are not made the goods are held at the border port. United States officials state that commercial shipments are seldom held at a Canadian border port; several Canadian exporters, however, have complained of delay supposedly because shipments were not cleared at the port of arrival.

In the United States, as in Canada, goods may be entered for warehouse and later withdrawn for consumption. On withdrawal from warehouse for consumption they are subject to the rate of duty in effect on the date of withdrawal.[8] Sometimes, however, in the United States two different rates of duty have been in effect at the time of withdrawal, one on withdrawals from warehouse for consumption and another for entries for consumption; and slight, though definitely adjudicated, differences in the terminology of particular paragraphs of the Customs Tariff Act determine which is to apply. A dispute concerning one of these items illustrates the uncertainties which the administrative customs provisions may occasionally introduce into international trade. In the General Agreement the United States granted a concession on certain types of red beans "when *entered for consumption* during the period from May 1 to August 31" and also on green peas and certain other fresh vegetables "when *entered* during the period. . . ."[9] Certain other paragraphs of the Agreement provide for

such bond or other security as the Secretary of the Treasury might prescribe." Levett, *Customs Administrative Act of 1938*, p. 16. I am informed that section 15 provided specifically for a practice that had long been considered to be "otherwise provided in The Act" and did not change any procedure actually followed at that time. A clear and brief description of entry procedure in the United States is included in statement of John S. Graham, Assistant Secretary, Treasury Dept., in U.S. Senate, Committee on Finance, *Hearings on H.R. 5505* (1952), p. 26.   [7]A.G. Com., Mon. 27, p. 96.   [8]U.S. Tariff Act, s. 315.
     [9]G.A.T.T., Schedule XX, pars. 765, 769; see also pars. 772, 774.

tariff quotas which restrict the amount that may be entered at a lower rate of duty during any one year. Note 3 appended to the schedule of concessions granted by the United States provides: "Wherever in this Schedule the word 'entered' is used it shall mean 'entered, or withdrawn from warehouse, for consumption.' " The United States Customs Court has recently decided that "entered for consumption" in the paragraph concerning beans is to be interpreted as entered directly for consumption. Beans entered for warehouse and later withdrawn from warehouse for consumption during the low-duty season are not entitled to the lower rate.[10] It is not suggested that this decision is contrary to the intention of the Agreement or to the general principle stated above. It is clear, however, that the interpretation of such slight differences in wording requires highly specialized knowledge of customs law: indeed, documents were produced in this case to show that the appraiser's original report advised the collector that the lower rate was applicable.

The great bulk of highway shipments from Canada (though not from Mexico) are spot-checked and released on immediate delivery bonds within a few hours but the absence of or inadequacy of the commercial invoices or the statement of products, quantities, and values has at times occasioned a shipment with its truck and driver to be delayed.[11]

2. Speed of Release and Customs Staffs

Generally speaking, routine clearance of shipments at Canadian customs ports is reasonably prompt. In one large port, for example, if no special circumstances intervene, entries sworn to at three o'clock on one day are released by three o'clock the following day. It is estimated that at least three-quarters of shipments are so released. However, vacations make for occasional delays; sometimes the documents go to one warehouse when the goods are in another and several days may elapse before the goods are located; a few shipments are never found. Sometimes an unusually large number of ships dock on the same day. Generally speaking again, samples taken to a warehouse for inspection are delayed longer; also, the parcels designated for

[10]28 U.S. Customs Court 112, C.D. 1396, March 11, 1952.

[11]See e.g. *Industrial Canada*, July 1952, p. 376. No invoice is required for entry for immediate transportation without appraisement but the merchandise must be described on the combined entry invoice and manifest form (customs form 7512) in such detail as to allow the collector to make an estimate of the duties. The collector may require evidence to satisfy him of the approximate correctness of the value or quantities stated in the entry.

inspection because, contrary to the regulations, they are small rather than because they are representative, may, for example, contain all the nuts and bolts for a shipment of machinery, so that none of it can be assembled until the sample packages are released.

Between 1928 and 1950 the staff in the ports (as distinct from headquarters) has increased by 35 per cent from 3,578 in 1928 to 4,923 in 1950 while the number of import entries has increased 50 per cent. However, the number of ports has been cut in half from 729 in 1928 to 361 in 1951 with a corresponding increase in effectiveness of personnel, as well as, one may suppose, a considerable increase in uniformity of appraisement. Complaints that delay has been occasioned by understaffing have not been numerous in Canada, although from time to time it appears that at certain ports staff and facilities (and also the number of brokers) has not kept pace with rapidly increasing imports. In these rare cases there has been for a time congestion and delay[12] but they have not been numerous.[13] In a number of cities importers have complained that facilities for clearing postal shipments were inadequate and congested. Facilities for clearing such shipments by mail seem to be unequally provided or, perhaps, unequally publicized.

Clearance at United States ports, too, in most periods has been reasonably prompt and efficient, though from time to time there have been delays. Some Canadian exporters of seasonal goods have complained that shipments intended to be cleared at large interior ports are sometimes delayed at border ports; and that, in any event, brokers' fees are incurred in getting them forwarded to the port where they are to be entered and cleared. Some of the delay at border ports may have arisen because of lack of a statement of the value of the shipments or through misunderstanding as to who would make the arrangements for forwarding the goods in bond to the interior port at which they were to be entered. The Detroit Board of Commerce complained in 1951 that the customs staff at that port had not been increased since 1937

[12]Unusually rapid growth of imports and other special factors occasioned delay at the port of Edmonton, for instance. For an earlier example see reference to delay in expanding the staff at Regina in the early twenties. Can., Royal Commission on Customs and Excise, *Interim Report*, no. 10, p. 22.

[13]In 1947 there were some complaints that customs facilities in Toronto had not expanded to correspond with the increase in imports; *Canadian Importers and Traders Association Bulletin*, April 19, 1947, p. 1. In 1951 a proposal was made to the Tariff Committee of the Canadian Manufacturers' Association which was intended to speed up entry. No action was taken because the association had not been receiving complaints of delay. *Industrial Canada*, Oct. 1951, p. 63.

while traffic had increased considerably.[14] Serious and more general complaints were published, especially in 1951, to the effect that in the period from 1946 to 1951 customs staff, owing to budgetary retrenchment, had been reduced while the volume of unfinished business continued to increase.[15] In one editorial it was charged that the average time for removing a case from the pier to the examining shed had increased from three to eight days.[16]

The speed and effectiveness of entry and liquidation of entry as well as the impartiality of treatment may be affected by the quality of the customs staff as well as their numbers. On the whole the quality, training, and conditions of tenure in both countries is reasonably good. The rank and file of local officials in the United States are now appointed and hold office under civil service regulations and conditions. Those who have had experience with the United States customs officials may be quoted; many changes have evidently occurred since Hawthorne wrote *The Scarlet Letter.*

The rank and file of employees of the Customs Service to-day, totalling over 10,000, are appointed subject to the rules of the Civil Service Commission. As a result, we have far more efficient men in the Government service than we formerly had.[17]

One finds occasionally men who want to help domestic producers, or who want to help importers. But they are exceptions. As a rule, the motive which animates the customs officers and the officers of the Department of Agriculture, in dealing with imports, is to move the goods as rapidly as is consistent with the spirit and letter of the law, keeping in mind always that their decisions are subject to review and, it may be, reversal by the courts.[18]

Customs brokers do not complain of stupidity or inattention to duty

[14]Statement of John C. Ray, Chairman, Import and Customs Committee of the Detroit Board of Trade, U.S. House, *On H.R. 5106*, p. 195.

[15]Supplementary statement of Mr. David B. Strubinger, Acting Commissioner of Customs, concerning administrative simplifications. U.S. House, *On H.R. 1535*, p. 211.

[16]See also editorial from the *New York Journal of Commerce*, reported in *Industrial Canada*, Jan. 1951, p. 132; and *Industrial Canada*, April 1951, p. 108.

[17]Futrell, the *History of Customs Jurisprudence*, p. 5. Futrell notes that most collectors and certain other customs officials are "political appointees." His comments do not suggest, however, that the political appointment of special attorneys is detrimental to importers, at least in the long run: "Under the circumstances, realizing that their heads may 'fall' by political changes, their heart is not in their work. It is not surprising that these lawyers [special attorneys in the Customs Division of the Department of Justice] after familiarizing themselves with the work of the Customs Division, resign and 'take the other side'—that is, represent the importers of merchandise in their claims against the government."

[18]Bidwell, *Invisible Tariff*, p. 18.

of local officials in the United States.[19] Members of customs staff have been helpful, on invitation from Canadian organizations, in explaining United States customs procedure.[20] Customs officials sometimes tutor groups who gather on their own motion or at the suggestion of a supervisory officer. There have been some complaints that reductions of financial provisions have at times interfered with the training programmes.[21]

In Canada too, political favouritism is no longer important in the actual administration of customs duties, though the division between tariff policy and tariff administration is not always easy to define. Appeal from administrative decisions of the Department of National Revenue is now made to the Tariff Board, not to the Cabinet. Customs officials are now appointed and promoted under civil service regulations; patronage no longer dominates personnel administration. Occasionally, however, there are awkward delays in making appointments or promotions.[22] Published comments have recognized the improvement in the Canadian Civil Service over the years.

Canadian political mores together with a healthy concern with this problem [personnel administration] have kept patronage in the civil service below the level prevailing in either the federal or state governments in the United States. At the same time the Canadian standards of performance in such technical matters as classification and in-service training fall considerably below acceptable American standards.[23]

Impartiality of the civil servants in their relations with the public and with changing governments has been maintained . . . within a framework of democratic principles.[24]

The Customs and Excise . . . (division of D.N.R.) . . . is under the jurisdiction of the Civil Service Commission and has a sound personnel organization.[25]

---

[19]*Ibid.*, p. 33. But this judgment is based on statements by brokers at a public hearing; and brokers value good relations with customs officials.

[20]See speech and correspondence of E. J. Cannon in Canadian Manufacturers' Association, *Customs Aspects of Exporting to the United States.*

[21]"For instance, at the Port of New York our National Vice-President Doyle conducted a class for liquidations in 1946. . . . He had another class in 1950. . . . Time and again the Bureau has tried to get Congress to provide funds to re-establish the activities of the Division of Training but the request has been denied." Statement of Alfred F. Beiter, President, National Customs Service Association before U.S. House, *On H.R. 1535*, p. 413.

[22]The congestion in the port of Edmonton was attributed in part to delay in appointment and promotion; in part doubtless it was attributable also to failure of customs and brokerage facilities to keep pace with accelerated growth in the number of entries. With respect to the effects of divided authority on promotions and certain other matters see Dawson, *The Government of Canada*, 308–9; and Brady, *Democracy in the Dominions*, p. 90.

[23]Cole, *The Canadian Bureaucracy*, p. 275.   [24]*Ibid.*, p. 278.   [25]*Ibid.*, p. 21.

Canadian brokers and importers usually speak well of their local officials, and report that, on the whole, they are diligent, fair, and co-operative.[26] On the other hand, it is not unusual to hear an importer or broker remark that the success of his business depends on maintaining good relations with local customs officials. (In central Canada especially, some appear to be almost equally concerned with being on good terms with the officials in Ottawa.) Some sorts of criticism are frequently made. An almost universal complaint is that the local officials are not given, or will not take, responsibility for classifying or valuing unusual shipments except after consultation with Ottawa. This complaint is coupled in the far eastern and the far western provinces with the criticism that centralization favours those who clear their entries at centres close to Ottawa. Some importers, though not all, believe that the older port officials who were appointed and acquired their early experience in the protectionist atmosphere of the early thirties are inclined to give less favourable (and less rapid) decisions than more recent appointees or Ottawa officials. It is commonly reported that shipments to importers with an established reputation for fair dealing are cleared with little delay and difficulty. Some who report that they have now acquired this happy status, however, recall their own early experiences and remark that the newcomer to importing is likely to experience delays and disputes. In both countries, it appears, local officials sometimes use discretionary powers to penalize (or train) importers (and brokers) who have not yet established a reputation for probity and co-operativeness.

3. BROKERS

Accuracy of entry and speed of settlement depends in part on the persons who enter the merchandise. Any importer may make entry for his own importations but no person may act as a customs house broker unless licensed to do so. In Canada the prospective customs broker is required to be a British subject, a resident of Canada, at least twenty-one years of age, and of good character; recently the requirement was introduced that before being licensed he must pass an examination. A customs broker's licence may be revoked at any time by the Minister of National Revenue for what he considers sufficient reasons. Accordingly, the broker is dependent upon the goodwill of the customs officials. However, the Canadian Customs Brokers Association, a voluntary organization which includes 85 or

[26]In the past, however, customs personnel at certain ports have not always been proof against the corruption associated with prohibition. See Royal Commission on Customs and Excise, *Interim Report*, no. 10.

90 per cent of the licensed brokers in Canada, have from time to time made representations to Ottawa proposing, for example, certain simplifications in customs procedures and documents and more complete notification of brokers and customs officials of certain types of decisions and rulings.

Brokers receive the published customs memoranda and bulletins which include all the general customs regulations and decisions of the Department of National Revenue; but they do not receive confidential appraisers' bulletins. When the confidential bulletins affect valuation, an amended entry is required in the first instance, but the local appraiser then gives the broker the information applicable to subsequent entries. Both brokers and importers complain that failure to receive routine notification of all orders and decisions may prevent entry of an importation at a low rate to which it is entitled or which might be obtained for it on application to Ottawa. The principles that govern the granting of certain special reductions or remissions of duty are not readily discoverable.[27]

In the United States, as in Canada, brokers are investigated, licensed,[28] and subjected to rules of conduct. While in Canada many importing companies employ members of their own staff to make entry for their imports, in the United States it is uncommon for an entry to be made except through a broker. Casual importers who are unfamiliar with the procedures may obtain advice from the information bureau in the customs house. The enquirer is usually advised to employ a broker, but the customs officer may assist him in the preparation of his entry though not permitted to act as an agent or to prepare entries for importers.[29]

4. DOCUMENTATION

Before a complete or perfect formal entry can be made certain documents must be received from abroad and presented along with the entry form. The more elaborate, detailed, and difficult the requirements imposed on the foreign exporter in invoicing his shipment the more frequent are likely to be the misunderstandings and the inadvertent omissions which may not legally be remedied by the importer when entry is being made and which involve delay in clearing the

[27]Notice of certain decisions as to goods not made in Canada is sent only to the collector through which the shipment was made. Orders in council relating to special temporary reductions of tariff rates are published in the *Canada Gazette* and circulated to the ports; see R.S.C., 1952, c. 58, s. 273 (j), (k), (l), (m), and s. 277. Remissions and refunds of duties paid on entry are reported only as an aggregate; see Table I, chap. IV, *infra*.

[28]U.S. Tariff Act, s. 641.   [29]A.G. Com., Mon. 27, pp. 84–6.

imports, or the additional trouble and expense of securing release on a *pro forma* or imperfect entry and perfecting it later. Neither country normally requires unusually elaborate documentation. However, Canadian importers and brokers are almost unanimously of the opinion that a missing, inaccurate, or incomplete invoice is the most frequent cause of delay in entering and securing the release of imports. And the many suggestions contained in *Customs Information for Exporters to the United States*[30] indicate that importers and customs officers in that country encounter similar difficulties. The documentary information and evidence required for entry should, ideally, be sufficient to allow customs officials to classify and value the imported merchandise, and to determine whether it conforms with the marking, sanitary, and other regulations of the importing country. The details of the information that must be included in the documents depend then on the tariff structure and on the number and terms of the non-tariff regulations. The strictness of the requirements and the insistence with which their minute details are enforced tend to depend too on the traditional height of the duties and generally on the strength of the incentives to smuggle that exist or have existed. Both countries have complex customs tariffs and that of the United States has included many high rates.

In Canada the Customs Act requires that a sufficient invoice be presented with the customs entry; the exceptions are few and narrow. Six forms of invoices, each for a different kind of commercial shipment, are prescribed by order in council. The form required depends on whether the goods were sold prior to shipment, or shipped on consignment; and on whether they enter under the British Preferential, the Most-Favoured-Nation or the General Tariff. Accordingly goods certified for entry under different Tariffs must be entered on separate forms. In addition to the name and address of the exporter and the importer, the marks and number of packages, the content of each package, and a full description of the goods, the invoice must state the date and place and method of shipment, the country of origin, the fair market value at the time and place of shipment, the selling price to the purchaser in Canada, the amount of freight prepaid, if any, and any discounts that have been allowed.[31] The invoice must

[30]U.S., Treasury Dept., Bureau of Customs, *Customs Information for Exporters to the U.S.*, pp. 4–5. For complaints of U.S. customs officials see, e.g., *Industrial Canada*, June 7, 1952, p. 734.

[31]There are, of course, many other detailed requirements: for instance invoices of certain kinds of glassware imported in sets must specify the separate value of each component article. *Industrial Canada*, Nov. 1952, p. 48.

bear a certificate of origin signed by the shipper in the country of shipment and a certificate of value signed by an officer of the exporting company. However, in certain special cases, a separate certificate of origin is acceptable; coal or coke, for example, imported direct by rail from the point of production or by water from Great Lakes ports may be accepted for entry under the Most-Favoured-Nation Tariff without the certificate of origin.[32]

The behaviour of exporters abroad affects the speed of entry and the number of delays and errors. One of the most frequent defects of invoices received from abroad arises from failure to state on the invoice the *country* of origin. In domestic invoicing it is usually sufficient to state the *place* from which the goods have been shipped; but the customs invoice must state the *country* and not simply the *place* of origin. Not infrequently, too, the shipper fails to sign the declaration of country of origin. The shipping clerk who processes the invoices for presentation to customs is often sorely tempted to remedy both these defects illegally.

Most importers take great pains to instruct their foreign shippers as to the information that must be contained in the invoices and the form in which it must be made out. Those who maintain a buying agency in a foreign country usually have their foreign branch inspect all invoices to see that they are accurate and complete before forwarding them to Canada. In spite of such precautions many imperfect invoices are received.

The proportion of inadequate invoices varies also from one exporting country to another. It is reported, for example, that exporters from the United Kingdom are usually more familiar with the information required with respect to the intricate textiles items than are exporters from other European countries. Information concerning certain special regulations, also, is not uniformly well known or observed by foreign exporters; Mexican exporters of jewelry, for example, are said not to be well informed concerning the Canadian regulations for the marking of precious metals.

In commenting on faulty invoicing, more than one Canadian merchant engaged in importing and exporting remarked on the valuable reports of foreign tariff changes provided by the Department of Trade and Commerce in *Foreign Trade* and wished that all foreign countries would provide equally effective information concerning changes in Canadian regulations. In fact, the governments of both

[32]Can., Dept. of National Revenue, *Information for Exporters Concerning Shipments to Canada*, Series D, no. 43; *Supplement*, no. 1.

Canada and the United States attempt to give effective information concerning changes in their own and in foreign regulations. In addition to the official notification of changes in their own regulations, both prepare instruction booklets for foreign exporters, explaining their regulations.[33] The United States Commerce Department and the Canadian Department of Trade and Commerce each give advice to their own exporters.[34] In addition a network of private journals and associations assists in supplying customs information. In Canada, for example, such bodies as the Canadian Manufacturers' Association, the Canadian Exporters' Association, and the Canadian Importers and Traders Association as well as certain chambers of commerce furnish customs information to their members.

5. DOCUMENTATION—UNITED STATES

The principal document with respect to most imports into the United States is the consular invoice. If the value of a shipment exceeds $250,[35] it must, unless exempted, be accompanied by a "consular invoice"; an invoice, that is to say, made out on the appropriate prescribed form and certified by a United States consular official. Each shipment requires a separate invoice.[36] The information required to complete the United States consular invoice is very similar to that required for the Canadian invoice. However, there are certain differences; instead of the fair market value the United States invoice requires, in addition to the purchase price, the current price for home consumption *or* the price for export to the United States, whichever is the higher; it requires also information concerning taxes applicable to the merchandise when sold for home consumption, and a detailed statement of all costs, charges, and commissions (buying and selling to be distinguished) incidental to the shipment of the merchandise. Space is provided for the manufacturer's catalogue numbers or symbols and those of the importer. Additional information, in some cases supported by special consular declarations, is required with respect to merchandise subject to regulations under special acts designed to protect health and property. Additional information is required also

[33]Can., D.N.R., Series D, no. 43; U.S. Treasury Dept., Bureau of Customs, *Customs Information for Exporters to the United States.*

[34]U.S., Dept. of Commerce, *Preparing Shipments to Canada.* See *International Reference Service*, vol. VII, no. 130. Can., Dept. of Trade and Commerce, *Foreign Trade.*

[35]Changed from $100 under authority of the Customs Simplification Act of 1953, 67 U.S. Statutes at Large 507, P.L. 243, s. 16.

[36]A carefully delimited exception is made for instalment shipment.

with respect to some thirty-seven classes of goods including copper ores, concentrates, and copper articles, oils, lumber (including sawed timber), fish or fish livers in air-tight containers, screenings, grain, or grain and screenings.[37]

Though no certificate of country of origin is required, except on goods entered as from Cuba, the Philippines, and certain insular possessions, the consular invoice must ordinarily be certified by an official of the consular district in which the goods were manufactured, purchased, or delivered; and if a shipment contains goods assembled from different districts and repacked, the consular invoice must have attached to it the original invoices or excerpts from them. A certified invoice may be required as well from the consular office in the district in which any part of shipment was manufactured or purchased. Invoices covering shipments from places remote from consular office of the United States may be certified by a consular officer of a friendly nation; or by a notary public provided that the place in question has been placed on the no-consul list by decision of the United States Treasury.

Typically, certification at the United States consulate is reasonably prompt, and consular clerks in the Canadian centres are quite helpful in interpreting the voluminous instructions. "It is the duty of the consul to examine the invoice to see whether the required information has been supplied" but defects in invoicing are by no means completely prevented. According to the Attorney General's Committee, "it is said that many consular invoices are particularly deficient in respect of the description of the merchandise. . . . The inadequacy of invoices is probably the result of the failure of many consular officials to scrutinise them with sufficient care."[38] It is a duty of the consul, too, to advise the appraiser at the point of entry of such additional facts as may be of importance in determining the value or the amount of duty and to communicate to him any suspicions he may have as to fraud or as to the accuracy of the information supplied.

The United States Treasury has used its authority to permit the entry without a consular invoice of specific classes of articles including articles unconditionally free of duty or subject only to a specific rate of duty not depending on value. A substantial list of articles has been thus exempted including, among others, standard newsprint paper, pulpwood, planks and boards, most agricultural products, crude

[37]As of 1950; see Treasury Dept., *Customs Information for Exporters to the United States*.

[38]A.G. Com., Mon. 27, p. 82.

minerals, fish, fertilizer and fertilizer materials, and shingles (except red cedar shingles).[39]

Under the 1938 Trade Agreement red cedar shingles were admitted free of duty under a tariff quota equal to 30 per cent of the average consumption in the United States over the previous three years. The excess-quota duty of 25 cents per 100 square feet was imposed by Congress only for as long as they remained the subject of a trade agreement. Accordingly Canada agreed at Geneva to drop red cedar shingles from the agreement.[40] Canadian exporters have contended that no special reasons remain for requiring consular certificates for red cedar shingles.

Many countries besides the United States require consular invoices. In some cases, it may be that the requirement lessens the delay in clearing a shipment or in liquidating an entry, or assists in detecting evasion or fraud; though for the United States the evidence in support of this conclusion is not strong.[41] Against this possible advantage must be set the expense of preparing another set of documents, the fee of $2.50 charged for certification, and the time and trouble of securing consular certification and of conforming with one more set of meticulously detailed regulations. The fee is not large but when shipments are relatively small and frequent the additional expense is not negligible. Also, at times, Canadian exporters have been misinformed or have misunderstood instructions concerning the number of certified invoices required, for example, when different parts of a shipment are consigned to several importers; and the consular invoice sometimes gets sent to one port of entry while the shipment has been diverted to another. Representatives of air companies in particular complain that consular certification, requiring even a day, delays the arrival of the consular invoice and defeats attempts at speedy delivery and release.[42]

[39]In 1938 some 260 commodities were listed (Treasury Decision 49742). The exemptions were broadened in 1950 (T.D. 52430).

[40]Can., Banking & Commerce, G.A.T.T., no. 2, April 13, 1948, pp. 71–2.

[41]See, however, e.g., U.S. Senate, On H.R. 5505, p. 216, evidence of Benjamin M. Altschuler, Counsel for Customs Brokers and Forwarders Association of America Inc. Also F. McDonald, President of the United States Customs Warehouse Officers Association of New York, U.S. House, On H.R. 1535, pp. 430–3. This testimony might suggest to the reader that customs officials may develop vested interests.

[42]See evidence of Stuart G. Tipton, General Counsel, Air Transport Association, in U.S. Senate, On H.R. 5505, p. 94. Also letter to Secretary of the Treasury from Joseph A. Sinclair, Secretary, Import Division of the Commerce and Industry Association of New York, in U.S. House, On H.R. 5106, p. 141.

Objection has been taken, too, to the number of copies of the transportation entry form required to enter merchandise which is to be shipped across the United States in bond and re-exported. Nine copies of this form are required; and if precautions are taken in case the port of re-export may have to be changed, another two copies are needed.[43]

It is interesting to note that there were complaints from Canadian exporters even before Confederation concerning the consular certificate required by the United States Treasury for which a fee of $2.00 was then charged.[44]

6. ATTEMPTS TO SIMPLIFY DOCUMENTATION

Reduction or abolition of consular requirements and fees have been advocated in many reports, official, semi-official, and private. Article VIII of the General Agreement on Tariffs and Trade notes among other things that documentation requirements should be kept as simple as possible; and that fees, for consular certification, should be limited to the approximate amount of the cost of the service. In 1952 a resolution was adopted at the seventh session of the Contracting Parties calling for the abolition of all consular formalities as soon as possible, and at least by 1956. The International Chamber of Commerce has supported their abolition.[45] In a report approved by the Joint Canada–United States Committee maintained by the Canadian Chamber of Commerce and the Chamber of Commerce of the United States it was recommended that the statutory requirement of a consular invoice be eventually abolished and that meanwhile, by administrative action, all commodities from contiguous countries not subject to duties depending on value be admitted to the United States without consular invoice.[46] In 1949 the Import Advisory Committee of the United States Department of Commerce recommended that consular invoices should not be required if the wholesale purchase price of the shipment is less that $250 (or even $500); that the list of commodities for which consular invoices are not required be examined and extended; that chambers of commerce or other responsible trade bodies be recognized

[43]U.S. Senate, On H.R. 5505, p. 96.

[44]In a petition in 1860 to Sir William Fenwick Williams, Administrator of the Government of Canada, Public Archives of Ontario, The Merritt Papers; quoted in Gordon Blake, "Customs Administration in Canada," p. 164.

[45]Evidence of D. P. Cruikshank, President of the Canadian Council of the International Chamber of Commerce, Can., Trade Relations, N.A.T.O., April 22, 1953, p. 69.

[46]Chamber of Commerce, Joint Canada–United States Committee, Customs Administration and Procedure between Canada and the United States.

as an alternative to notary publics in no-consul areas; and that the content of customs invoices be simplified by omitting the statement of commissions paid by the foreign seller or shipper to an agent in the United States.[47] The *Bell Report* concluded that the consular invoice executed in the country of export is unnecessary. It also recommended that the formal entry should be eliminated for imports that are clearly non-dutiable; the much simpler informal entry is handled at a cost to the government of $1.60 as compared with $9.00 for a formal entry of Free-List goods.[48]

The Customs Simplification Act of 1953 gave the Secretary of the Treasury discretionary powers, unusually broad for the United States, to prescribe by regulation "for the production of a certified invoice with respect to such merchandise as he deems advisable and for the terms and conditions under which such merchandise may be permitted entry under the provisions of this section without the production of a certified invoice." In addition it empowered him to prescribe rules for the entry of shipments not greater than $250 instead of $100 as at present.[49] Although the statutory discretion might conceivably be used to change the requirements in either direction,[50] the administration, in fact, issued a customs regulation in September 1953 which permitted a shipment to be entered without a consular invoice when valued at $250 or less.

[47]U.S. Dept. of Commerce, Office of International Trade, Import Advisory Committee, *First Interim Report on Customs Administrative Laws.*

[48]*Bell Report,* p. 53.

[49]H.R. 5877, s. 17 (a), (c), and (d), and P.L. 243, 83rd Congress, s. 16.

[50]Not all opinion in the United States was favourable to such liberalization. See e.g. statement of Benjamin M. Altschuler, U.S. House, *On H.R. 1535,* p. 451; also, *On H.R. 5106,* p. 164.

IV

LIQUIDATION AND LITIGATION

"When *I* use a word," Humpty Dumpty said in rather a scornful tone, "it means just what I choose it to mean—neither more nor less."

"The question is," said Alice, "whether you *can* make words mean different things."

"The question is," said Humpty Dumpty, "which is to be master—that's all."

*Through the Looking Glass**

1. REFUNDS OF DUTIES OVERPAID

THE AMOUNT of duty estimated and paid on entering a shipment is not necessarily the final amount; for example, under certain conditions, the importer may secure refunds of duty overpaid in error; or he may be required to pay an additional amount.

In Canada refunds of excess duty paid on imported goods may be secured, but application must be made within a specified time after entry. To obtain refund of duty, goods found to be defective, or not according to order, or ordered by mistake, must be returned to customs for re-export within six months (formerly ninety days) of entry.[1] No refund is allowed for overpayment occasioned by misdescription of the goods in the invoice or entry unless the error is reported within fourteen days after entry. When goods have been delivered to the importer no refund may be made because of errors in values or quantities, except clerical errors, unless reported within thirty days (fourteen days prior to 1947). Refunds of duties overpaid on erroneous construction of the law as decided by the courts, the Tariff Board, or the Deputy Minister, will not be refunded unless application in writing has been made within twelve months of payment of duty (three years prior to 1948). In other cases of overpayment in error, application for refund must be made within two years (three years prior to 1948). It is to be noted that most of these refunds may be made without court pro-

---

*With apologies to Sir Dennis Robertson.

[1]S.O.R., 1952, 422, *Can. Gaz.*, II (Oct. 8, 1952), p. 903.

ceedings. No separate statement of the administrative refunds is available; Table 1 shows total import refunds of duties and taxes including administrative refunds, refunds based on decisions of the Tariff Board, and remissions outside the law made by order of the Governor in Council.

TABLE 1

CANADA, IMPORT REFUND CLAIMS[a]
(including duties and taxes)

Fiscal year ending March 31	Total amount paid
1947–48	$6,405,972
1948–49	9,718,623
1949–50	8,171,362
1950–51	8,640,581
1951–52	9,349,328

[a]Information furnished by Dept. of National Revenue.

In the United States if imported goods are found to be not in accordance with the order or shipped without the consent of the consignee[2] a refund of 99 per cent of the duty may be obtained by returning the goods to customs custody within ninety days (thirty until 1953) after they were released or longer in some cases and exporting them under customs supervision. When a deficiency in amount of the import is found by the appraising officer in examining a package, allowance of duty is made for the deficiency; and also for deficiencies in packages not held for examination if the importer files a claim within ten days of the discovery of the shortage and satisfies the collector of customs that the missing goods were not landed in the United States.

2. INFORMAL APPEAL AND AMENDING ENTRIES—CANADA

If a Canadian importer disagrees with the decision of the local collector he usually "pays first and talks later." To avoid delay he pays the amount of duty demanded, secures release of his merchandise, and then appeals to customs officials at Ottawa. Quick and informal administrative appeal may be made to the chief appraiser, and if necessary to the Deputy Minister; from his decision to the Tariff Board, and thence on matters of law to the Exchequer Court. Most disputes are settled without recourse to the Tariff Board—often by

[2]The provision was extended to goods "shipped without consent" in 1953.

telephone or air mail. This informal Canadian procedure is consistent with a greater degree of centralization than exists in the United States. Local customs officers frequently refer to officials at Ottawa difficult cases of classification and valuation. Importers and brokers in central Canada find this arrangement convenient since a firm decision can frequently be obtained from Ottawa immediately by an inexpensive telephone call. In more distant parts of the country it is a cause of complaint that local officials are not encouraged and permitted to make their own decisions, at least on small matters, since communication with Ottawa involves either delay or considerable expense, and the resulting uncertainty handicaps the Canadian importer as well as the salesman of the foreign product.

Even when the importer and local port officials agree as to the duty, an amending entry may be required. The Customs Act empowers any Dominion Customs Appraiser to review the treatment accorded any importation.[3] A copy of every customs entry at every port is sent to Ottawa to be checked by the checking branch. When an error is discovered, the collector at the port of entry is instructed to secure an amended entry and duties are refunded or additional duties collected as required. Doubtful cases are referred to the chief appraiser for decision. In 1951 Ottawa required 120,405 amending entries to be made at the ports, a number amounting to 4.4 per cent of the import entries in that year. Of these, however, 21,040 (about 17 per cent of the amending entries) involved refunds to importers.[4] Officials report that the need for many of these amending entries was discovered by local port officials on checking at the end of the day but by that time a copy has already gone forward to Ottawa. Although most entries are checked within thirty days, no limit is set by law to the time within which an amending entry and payment of additional duties may be required. However, the Department has not been permitted to make refunds on applications made more than three years (two years since 1951) after payment of duty;[5] and, in practice, it has seldom required an amended entry after the lapse of more than thirty days unless it appeared that the irregularity was so serious that it might have required seizure of the goods had it been discovered at the time of

[3]Can., Customs Act, s. 43.

[4]Statistics courtesy Customs Division: see Gordon Blake, "Customs Administration," p. 407.

[5]Can., Customs Act, s. 112 (1). The amendment of 1951 reduced the period to one year for application made on the basis of a decision of the Deputy Minister, or an order or finding of the Tariff Board, or a judgment of a court.

entry. Even in these cases of serious irregularity, prosecutions or suits for recovery of penalties or forfeiture cannot be commenced after the lapse of more than three years from the time the offence was committed.[6] Importers are required to preserve the relevant records for six years.

Canadian importers of goods which are difficult to classify or value complain of the uncertainty occasioned by the prospect of being required unexpectedly to amend entries and pay additional duties even after the imported goods have been sold. The evidence does not suggest, however, that Canadian importers are now required to pay unexpectedly greater duties as frequently as are importers into the United States; nor that, on the average, even in difficult cases as much time elapses between the arrival of the shipment and the final determination of the duty. It does appear, however, that, in periods when protectionist feeling was strong, amending entries were required very frequently with respect to imports such as textiles which compete with the products of especially sensitive sectors of the Canadian economy. This result is not surprising since many such imports were subjected to compound *ad valorem* and specific duties, and since the classification of such goods requires much detailed information and is difficult even when all relevant information is available. It would appear reasonable, however, to prohibit the Department, except on appeal by the importer or on proof before the courts of serious irregularity, from requiring entries to be amended after the lapse of some specified time, long enough to allow for checking if done with a reasonable promptness.

3. Uniformity of Treatment—Canada

Checking not only serves the purpose of correcting gross discrepancies in relation to past entries but, what is or should be more important, it may help to reveal and correct discrimination as between ports of entry with respect to subsequent imports. Any lack of uniformity between ports of entry tends, of course, to discourage importation. It introduces the risk that a competitor may be able to import the same article at a lower cost by clearing it through a different port; accordingly, if the article is to be stocked with reasonable safety, time and energy must sometimes be expended in finding (and keeping track of) the "soft" ports of entry.

The belief is expressed by some Canadian importers that certain

---

[6]Can., Customs Act, s. 265.

kinds of goods are treated differently at different ports;[7] and Canadian exporters have repeatedly expressed similar beliefs with respect to United States ports. Typically, neither exporters nor importers are anxious to make public current "soft spots" nor to have them enquired into too closely. Some, but not all, of the instances cited of lack of uniformity between Canadian ports have coincided approximately with changes in the regulations. Canadian procedures, on the whole, are well designed to allow the importer to secure without unreasonable delay information as to how his importations will be treated. To the extent that local officials, importers, or brokers consult with Ottawa, a relatively short delay at the time of entry may avoid subsequent demands for amended entries and additional duties; to the extent that the central checking is done thoroughly and rapidly, gross discrepancies as between ports may be remedied and, except for relatively short periods, avoided. It is to be noted, however, that for the importer a discrepancy may be quite important even if it is not continued over long periods.

4. LIQUIDATION OF ENTRY—UNITED STATES

In the United States the amount of duty stated and deposited at the time of entry is regarded as an estimate. The amount of duty finally fixed by the collector will not be known until the entry has been liquidated; that is to say, until the appraiser has reported the value to the collector who in turn has determined the rate and the amount of duty, and, after having the entry checked by the office of one of the seven regional comptrollers of customs, has deducted the duty from the amount deposited (or has collected additional duty). Until the appraiser reports the value to the collector the importer is encouraged to give him all relevant information at his disposal. Before 1953, if the importer at the time of entry had filed a written request for information concerning the value of the import, the appraiser was empowered to disclose the value he proposed to report and permit the importer to amend the entered value to correspond. Valuation once reported to the collector was final, subject only to judicial appeal. With respect to other matters concerning the amount of duty the col-

[7]There is a widespread impression among importers and domestic producers that truck entries at small border ports have been treated more leniently than entries at the larger customs ports. To confirm or refute this would require a very detailed investigation. For early complaints based in part on the effects of lack of uniformity between ports see Public Archives of Canada, Incoming Letters to the Inspector General, 1840; cited by Gordon Blake, "Customs Administration." p. 240.

lector, on receipt of a protest within sixty days of liquidation, may review his decision and alter it within ninety days after the protest has been filed. In recent practice the period of the collector's review within which administrative relief may be given has not infrequently been extended beyond ninety days. Until 1953, the administration had no power to refund duties overpaid by reason of an error in valuation, nor to refund overpayments attributable to errors in other customs procedures except to correct a clerical error in an entry or liquidation discovered within a year of entry (or sixty days after liquidation if that were longer). "Reliquidation almost invariably occurs only on request of the importer; on a few occasions, however, the discovery of new facts (in connection with the liquidation of a later entry) has led to a different decision on classification and the reliquidation of entries recently liquidated."[8]

These restrictions on the power of the administration to refund duties admittedly overpaid occasioned grievance and complaint. The Customs Simplification Act of 1953 widened the possibilities of securing refund through administrative action. It empowered the Secretary of the Treasury to correct an overpayment arising from a clerical error in appraisal (as well as in other procedures) or from a mistake of fact or other inadvertence, not amounting to an error in the construction of the law, adverse to the importer and manifest from the record or established by documentary evidence.[9]

Subject to these narrow administrative powers the duty determined on liquidation becomes final unless fraud is proven or an appeal is filed within thirty days after appraisement or a protest is made within sixty days after liquidation. At this time, then, the importer knows the maximum duty he will be required to pay. There can be no valid liquidation until appraisement has become final; that is until thirty days have elapsed after appraisement; or until a timely appeal has been finally adjudicated. No limit is set to the time that may elapse between entry and liquidation; and it has often been very long, not by reason of inefficiency of staff, but because of the intricacy of the customs laws, especially concerning value. Recently the number of invoices held for more than ninety days in the offices of appraisers has come to form a substantial fraction of the annual number of dutiable entries[10] as appears from Table 2 and Table 3.

[8]A.G. Com., Mon. 27, p. 135.
[9]Customs Simplification Act of 1953, s. 20, which amends s. 520 of the Tariff Act of 1930.
[10]*Bell Report*, p. 50.

5. UNIFORMITY OF TREATMENT—UNITED STATES

Some of the delays in liquidation, too, are associated with the methods adopted of securing uniformity of treatment as between different ports of entry. The United States customs administration is more decentralized than the Canadian and the methods used to secure uniformity are more elaborate and more highly formalized. *Treasury Decisions*, published weekly by the Treasury Department,

TABLE 2

IMPORT ENTRIES, CANADA AND U.S.

Annual average	Total Canada[a] (thousands)	Total United States[b] (thousands)	United States[c] warehouse and dutiable consumption entries (thousands)
1949	2,318	4,035	411
1950	2,516	4,234	483
1951	2,723	4,563	664
1952	2,941		

[a]Can., D.N.R., *Annual Reports*.
[b]U.S., Treasury Dept., *Annual Reports on the State of Finances*.
[c]U.S. House, *On H.R. 1535* (1951), p. 60.

TABLE 3

INVOICES ON HAND OVER 90 DAYS IN OFFICES OF APPRAISERS, 1950 AND 1952[a]

Reason for delay	June 30, 1950	June 30, 1952
Foreign enquiry report	9,876	34,831
Action by examiner	1,576	22,016
Court action on related cases	12,999	10,805
Reply from Customs Information Exchange	435	10,466
Amendment by importer	3,236	6,276
Information from importer	1,582	5,752
Consular invoices	1,065	1,960
All other causes	11,705	7,642
Total	42,474	99,748

[a]By the end of 1952 the backlog had increased to 124,000: U.S. Treasury Dept., Bureau of Customs, quoted in *Bell Report*, p. 49. It is reported to have decreased under the operation of the Customs Simplification Act of June 30, 1954.

contains notices of changes in rates of duty, changes in tariff classifications, and changes in the regulations governing import procedures, in addition to the text of relevant presidential proclamations, principal court decisions affecting customs, the proclaimed values of foreign currencies and other matters relevant to customs administration, and such decisions of the Treasury as are circulated generally. *Treasury Decisions* is readily available to the public in the United States and, in the form of bound volumes, is supplied to depository libraries at home and abroad. In addition, port officials are presumably furnished with much unpublished material concerning appraisement, including confidential comments on consular invoices, the results of investigations abroad, and information made available at other ports.

Local collectors and appraisers are required, at least tentatively, to classify and appraise each importation. But the Customs Information Exchange in New York plays an important part in securing uniformity. To it, when any article is first imported, the port of importation is required to forward a report from the local appraiser giving the price at which the merchandise is invoiced, the price at which it is proposed to appraise it, and the classification and rate of duty believed to be applicable, as well as all other pertinent information available. A similar report must be made by each port at least every three months with respect to each type of merchandise entered at that port. Examination of these reports serves to disclose discrepancies which are removed by correspondence; or, in case of continued disagreement, referred to the Commissioner of Customs in Washington for an opinion. Pending such decision final appraisement or classification is withheld. Local customs officials may also request information from the Customs Information Exchange.[11] If a decision cannot be secured on the basis of information available at the ports, the Customs Bureau may make an investigation through its officers abroad.

In addition the accuracy of the collector's determination of duty is checked by the comptroller of customs in one of the seven regional offices. This process serves as a check on collections "and to a considerable extent, ensures that rates of duty will be uniformly applied over the country."[12] The Customs Simplification Act of 1953 allows the administration somewhat more discretion than formerly in the matter of requiring checking.[13]

[11]See Canadian Manufacturers' Association, *Customs Aspects of Exporting to the United States.*

[12]Testimony of Alfred F. Beiter, National President, National Customs Service Association, U.S. House, *On H.R. 5106*, pp. 75–6.

[13]See Customs Simplification Act, 1953, s. 2.

The United States procedures thus involve a multilateral exchange of information and eventually secure a decision (subject to appeal to the courts) which will be applied uniformly at all ports. The process, however, is not rapid. In some cases liquidation has been delayed for ten or twelve years.[14] Release may be and usually is secured prior to final appraisement, of course, usually by deposit of the duty based on the customs estimate of the value; or, in cases of doubtful classification, by deposit of the estimated duties under an enforced agreement that liquidation be suspended pending determination of proper classification. In such cases, however, the importer may be forced to choose between quoting a non-competitive price on the merchandise, based on the estimated duty, and bearing the risk of loss if the price is based on what he thinks the duty will be. Hand woven women's garments, for example, shipped from Canada in time to arrive in New York for the Easter trade were delayed more than six weeks while a decision was being reached as to their value. They were released too late. Similarly, sale of a shipment of garden tractors entered in the spring as duty-free agricultural implements was delayed while information was sought through the usual channels. After six weeks an opinion was received from Washington that they should be admitted free of duty. Such delays tend to discourage the importation of any commodity; they are likely to exclude completely small shipments of seasonal goods.

This process of exchange of information makes it impossible to rely on the initial treatment accorded sample shipments. Even though the classification and value proposed by the importer be accepted as the initial estimate the final duties as determined at liquidation may be different; and liquidation may be delayed again. If the shipment is very small it may be passed under informal entry procedure without the expert attention accorded larger shipments entered formally. Finally, any United States producer, manufacturer, or dealer in a competing domestic product may file a complaint with the Secretary of the Treasury concerning the classification or appraisement of imports of a class or kind he produces.[15] If not satisfied with the action taken, he may, with certain exceptions, file an appeal or protest which must be decided by the Customs Court. However, since 1938 a domestic producer's protest has no effect on the customs treatment of the product against which it is directed until thirty days after publication of a notice that the protest has been allowed administra-

[14]See testimony of Harry S. Radcliffe, U.S. House, *On H.R. 5106*, pp. 178, 197.
[15]U.S. Tariff Act, s. 516.

tively, or until after publication of a judicial opinion contrary to an adverse administrative ruling on the protest. No formal or compulsory provision is made in the Act for appeal by an importer directly to the Commissioner of Customs, but this avenue of informal appeal is available and frequently used.

In January 1954 procedures were changed to provide the importer with a prompt notice of proposed disagreement with the entered rate of duty: as soon as possible after the release of the packages held for examination, and even before final appraisement. It is possible that this provision may further assist in the informal settlement of disputes concerning classification.[16]

6. Administrative Discretion and Appeal—Canada

In each country a system of appeals has been established. The two systems, however, differ considerably in degree of formality, extent of use, and speed of operation. The scope and procedures of appeal have changed from time to time but typically in Canada administrative discretion has been relatively great and administrative channels of appeal have been more important than judicial.

The Canadian Government has been granted wide powers of changing (especially of reducing) rates of duty or of allowing free entry; and the procedures which govern such decisions are not as narrowly prescribed by statute as in the United States. It may by order extend the British Preferential Tariff, or lower rates, to any British country, or the Most-Favoured-Nation Tariff to any country; it may withdraw these concessions and the decision of the Minister is final as to the tariff applicable to imported goods by reason of their origin;[17] it may also reduce duties by way of compensation for concessions granted by another country.[18] These provisions facilitate the negotiation of trade agreements since they ensure that the Government will be able to introduce the rates promised in the agreement. It may provide by order in council for the entry of articles used by Canadian manufacturers free, or at a reduced rate, or subject to drawback. The Government makes a multitude of decisions as to whether, and under what conditions, particular importations are thus to be admitted free or at a low rate under special classes designed to encourage certain kinds of manufacturing.[19] Of similar significance are

[16]U.S., *Federal Register*, Jan. 12, 1954.   [17]Can., Customs Tariff, s. 4.
[18]*Ibid.*, s. 10.

[19]Can., Customs Act, s. 273 (j), (k), (l), (m), and s. 277. The extent of this discretionary power is illustrated by provisions of section 277 of the Customs

the powers of the administration with respect to drawbacks of duty. These flexible powers can be used to adjust the amount of protection given at various stages of manufacture; but, obviously, they might easily be abused, their existence may raise suspicions that they are being abused, and their administration can be allowed to occupy much of the attention of important officials without achieving the results intended.[20] The Government's powers to remove or reduce a duty, if domestic producers raise prices unduly,[21] has seldom been actually used; nor its more limited powers with respect to a combine of domestic producers.[22] Its power to impose a retaliatory surtax on some or all of the products of a country which discriminates against Canadian products was used in a brief trade-war with Japan.[23] Goods or classes of goods may be declared exempt from dumping duty by order in council.[24] The powers granted to the administration of determining value for duty, and of including or excluding foreign taxes or duties, have varied from time to time, as has the scope of appeal from decisions concerning value.[25]

In earlier periods the administration of the tariff appears to have been considered to be primarily a political matter. Redress of grievances was sought by appeal to higher officials within the Department of National Revenue or to members of Parliament or to the Governor in

Act: "The Governor in Council may interpret, limit or extend the meaning of the conditions upon which it is provided in any Act imposing duties of Customs that any article may be imported free of duty for special purposes, or for particular objects or interests; and may make regulations for declaring or defining what cases shall come within the conditions of such Act, and to what objects or interests of an analogous nature the same shall apply and extend, and may direct payment or non-payment of duty in any such case, or the remission thereof by way of drawback, if such duty has been paid."

[20]See K. W. Taylor, "Tariff Administration and Non-Tariff Methods of Trade Control," p. 38: "There is a great need for reducing the present chaos of regulations to a coordinated body of administrative law. The conduct of government so far as details are concerned tends almost universally to be more and more by administrative regulation within the framework of general policies laid down by statute. This, I believe, is a necessary and quite satisfactory trend, provided that a harmonious system of rules is built up and there are adequate avenues of appeal from anonymous and what are often in fact 'secret' rulings."

[21]Customs Tariff, s. 16.

[22]Ibid., s. 14.

[23]Ibid., s. 7. A surtax was imposed on Japanese goods during part of the 1930's.

[24]See Customs Tariff, s. 6, subs. 2 (ii).

[25]For a summary of administrative discretionary powers in tariff matters in Canada see O. J. McDiarmid, *Commercial Policy in the Canadian Economy*, chap. XII.

Council. Provision was made at an early date, however, for the setting up of an *ad hoc* tribunal to hear and finally decide a formal written complaint by an importer concerning the appraisal of a particular shipment. Such a board was composed of one member selected by the importer, one by the collector, and, as chairman, a Dominion appraiser selected by the Minister. This procedure was seldom used.[26]

Other procedures were suggested from time to time. In 1926 the Royal Commission on Customs and Excise recommended that a staff of Dominion appraisers be appointed, instead of only one, then known as the textile appraiser; that, acting as a Board of Appraisers, they should hear appeals and make final decisions with respect to values; and that, to hear appeals on matters other than values, a Board of National Revenue be established to consist of a superior court judge and two other members.[27] Though certain changes were made in 1927[28] following the *Report,* no provision was made for judicial appeal. Appeal was provided from decisions of the port officials, chiefly on matters of classification, to the Board of Customs composed of senior officials of the Department of National Revenue and thence to the Governor in Council.

Finally in 1931 the Government was given power to appoint a Tariff Board with the powers of a court of record to assume the quasi-judicial duties of the Board of Customs and to exercise as well the broad fact-finding and advisory powers including those formerly possessed by the Advisory Board on Tariff and Taxation. The United Kingdom–Canada Trade Agreement of 1932 stipulated that the Tariff Board should be required to rule on protests by the United Kingdom that the duties applied by Canada were too high to allow United Kingdom producers a "full opportunity of reasonable competition."[29] It consists of three members appointed for a term of ten years and eligible for reappointment. In its advisory capacity it reports to the Minister of Finance or to the Governor in Council.

Not long after it was constituted, its powers were challenged in the courts. The power had been granted to the Government in 1930[30] of fixing officially the value of "imported goods of any kind"; and many values were fixed accordingly. In 1932, as required by the Ottawa

---

[26]R.S.C., 1927, c. 42, s. 52 and s. 53; repealed, S.C., 1948, c. 41, s. 5.

[27]Can., Royal Commission on Customs and Excise, *Final Report*, pp. 8, 14.

[28]17 Geo. V, c. 50.

[29]Arts. 11–15.

[30]Customs Act, R.S.C., 1927, c. 42, s. 43 (12), (2), as amended; continued in part in R.S.C., 1952, c. 58, s. 38.

Agreements,[31] this power was restricted to valuing goods "of any kind not entitled to entry under the British Preferential Tariff or any lower tariff."[32] No additional kinds of British goods were officially valued but customs officials continued to apply those values which had already been fixed by order in council. An importer applied to the Tariff Board for a ruling against this procedure. The Board heard the application and decided that the orders in council were annulled by the amendment, whereupon a Canadian manufacturer appealed to the Governor in Council on the grounds that the Tariff Board had exceeded its jurisdiction. On a reference from the Governor in Council, the Supreme Court of Canada ruled that the Tariff Board had no authority to determine that the orders in council in question were annulled by the 1932 amendment. The Court noted that the Board had inherited from the Board of Customs the power to review customs decisions "as to the principal markets or as to the fair market value" but that it did not have the power to review values fixed by the Minister since in these cases the provision respecting the fair market value did not apply; that value fixed by the Minister was not fixed by appraisement; further, that the matter at issue was not governed by the Customs Act but was purely a question of law, and the power to determine such questions of law lay with the Exchequer Court and not with the Board.[33] On November 9, 1935, the Exchequer Court ruled that the repeal of the section annulled the orders in council, and that the importer was entitled to refund of excess customs duties paid, as well as excess excise and sales taxes which are computed on the duty-paid value.[34]

A subsection added to the Customs Act in 1936[35] gave the Tariff Board power to hear appeals from any decision of the Minister fixing the value of an import that he considered was endangering domestic producers.[36] At the same time the door was closed to appeals for

[31]In the United Kingdom–Canada Trade Agreement of 1932, Canada undertook that customs administration in Canada should be "governed by such general principles as will ensure (a) the avoidance, so far as reasonably possible, of uncertainty as to the amount of customs duties and other fiscal imports payable on the arrival of goods in Canada; (b) the reduction of delay and friction to a minimum; and (c) the provision of machinery for prompt and impartial settlement of disputes in matters appertaining to the application of tariffs" (art. 16). The United Kingdom made no similar undertaking.

[32]23–24 Geo. V, c. 7.   [33][1934] S.C.R. 538.

[34]*Blakey and Co. Ltd.* v. *The King*, [1935] Ex. C.R. 223.

[35]R.S.C., 1927, c. 42, s. 43 (3), as amended by S.C., 1936, c. 19, s. 6.

[36]Repealed 1950.

refunds of duty previously exacted by inserting a new section (43A) which validated all official valuations that had been made and confirmed the duties collected under them.[37] In 1937 the powers of the Board were further extended and confirmed. It was given power, in case of doubt, to determine whether a particular import is of a class or kind produced in Canada "if there has been no previous decision concerning it binding throughout Canada." It was empowered also to review the value for duty applied by customs officials when based on cost of production.[38] However, the Board was, and continues to be, bound by the Supreme Court opinion that it may not hear appeals that relate purely to questions of law.[39] It was never empowered to review values fixed administratively by the Minister in certain difficult cases.[40]

In the period 1936–43 inclusive, the Tariff Board ruled on some 40 appeals from decisions of the Department of National Revenue. Of these, 38 related to classification, 2 to "Made-in-Canada" status, and 2 to valuation. Twelve of the appeals were allowed, including one with respect to valuation. With few exceptions, the appeals that were allowed granted more lenient treatment than had the rulings of the Department of National Revenue; the remainder confirmed the decisions of the Department in charging more duty than the importer thought should be paid. During the later war years and the early post-war years there were few appeals and no references from the Minister, partly because the Customs Tariff, though still an important producer of revenue, had largely been superseded as a method of regulating trade. The terms of two of the members expired in 1943 and the Board no longer had a quorum of two members.[41] Accordingly, until the Board was reconstituted, the system of informal appeal within the Department of National Revenue became even more important and was more fully developed. Departmental officials express pride in this informal, cheap, and speedy method of appeal.[42]

[37]1 Geo. VI, c. 24, s. 3. Section 43A was repealed in 1950.

[38]Under s. 36; repealed 1948, c. 41, s. 2.

[39]See A–155, T.B.C. 200, March 16, 1950.

[40]R.S.C., 1927, c. 48, s. 46, which became s. 41 in the revision of 1936; repealed in 1948, c. 41, s. 4. In *The King* v. *Noxzema Chemical Co.*, [1942] S.C.R. 178, it had been held that the price determined by the Minister for the application of taxes under the Special War Revenue Act was a purely administrative act and not open to review by the Exchequer Court. The latter Court applied the same reasoning to the Minister's determination of value under section 41 of the Customs Act (repealed 1948, c. 41, s. 4): *The King* v. *Weddell Limited*, [1945] Ex. C.R. 97.

[41]Mr. Abbott, Can., Commons, *Debates*, 1948, vol. V, p. 5156.

[42]In spite of the informality of the methods and the absence of an independent

In 1948 and 1950 the appeal provisions of the Customs Act were revised and amended. The obsolete provision for appeal to an *ad hoc* board of three evaluators was deleted; the method of informal intra-departmental appeal to the Deputy Minister was specifically prescribed in the Act; and his power to review appraisal as well as classification was confirmed. As revised, the Act provided for an appeal to the Board (if made within sixty days) from any decision of the Deputy Minister as to tariff classification, value for duty, or eligibility for drawbacks.[43] The revision of 1948[44] provided for appeal by an importer only, but that of 1950[45] permitted an appeal by "any person who deems himself aggrieved" by a decision of the Deputy Minister.[46] Application may be made to appeal from an order of the Tariff Board on a matter of law to the Exchequer Court within thirty days of the order; appeal from the Exchequer Court to the Supreme Court is governed by the general regulations concerning appeals to this court.

In Canada the privileges of the producer or manufacturer of a directly competing domestic product differ in some respects from those of his United States counterpart, discussed later in this chapter. Any person, of course, may make representations to the Department of National Revenue that any imported commodity is being classified or valued erroneously. After review and, if necessary, investigation by the Department he is informed that entry is being made in accordance with the law or that the law is now being enforced. No process exists in Canada as it does in the United States by which the domestic competitor can obtain information on which he may file a protest or appeal; and he cannot compel a formal decision of the Deputy Minister from which he may appeal to the Tariff Board. On occasion, however, the Department has referred to the Tariff Board the contention of a domestic producer; and the Board has treated such referral as an appeal. If a domestic producer is dissatisfied with the assurance he

---

appeal tribunal, complaints of unjust treatment during this period were surprisingly few. Many importers (though not all) report that, while local officials were some-times over-zealous, higher authorities were, generally speaking, just and reasonable.

[43]It has not as yet been found necessary to determine judicially whether in general the Deputy Minister can be required to give a decision in any case of dispute; *Re Superior Separator Co. of Canada Ltd.*, [1954] 1 D.L.R. 406 at pp. 420–1.

[44]11–12 Geo. VI, c. 41.   [45]11–12 Geo. VI, c. 43.

[46]Except with respect to values fixed by order in council under section 43. Prior to 1948 *any* interested person might appeal a value fixed under section 43. The revision of 1948 eliminated appeal from a value so fixed. I am informed that a domestic producer cannot secure a decision of the Deputy Minister except by becoming an importer.

receives, or if his contention is not agreed to by the Department or submitted to the Board, he may obtain judicial review only by importing the commodity, securing a decision by the Deputy Minister, and appealing to the Board on the grounds that he has been treated too leniently. (In the United States this procedure has not been permitted since 1913.) If he wins his case before the Tariff Board on a matter of appraisal the Department, generally, will apply the decision only to the shipments directly in question; but a decision as to classification may be applied more widely. The decision of the Board concerning the classification of ethylene glycol mixtures, mentioned in chapter VI below, was obtained through appeal by a domestic producer.

In 1948 the Tariff Board Act, too, was correspondingly amended.[47] The Board itself was reconstituted in 1949 and resumed its activities. It has not used the powers given it to make special procedural regulations. In appeals under the Customs Act, notices of the date of public hearing are mailed to those directly concerned, published in the *Canada Gazette*, and circulated to names on the Board's mailing list. Generally speaking, the Board hearings are public but, as the Tariff Board Act requires, confidential information is "not . . . made public in such a manner as to be available for the use" of a business competitor. In its reports the Board now describes briefly the circumstances of each case and gives the reasons for its decision as well.[48]

From January 1949 to June 29, 1953, there had been 107 appeals in customs disputes; 17 had been withdrawn and the Board lacked jurisdiction in 2 others. Of the 110 appeals with respect to sales tax and excise as well as customs, 49 had been allowed, 44 dismissed, 7 had been partly allowed and partly dismissed, 3 had been decided against both the Department and the appellant, and 7 were awaiting hearing or decision.[49] The proportion of successful appeals in these years, then, was considerably higher than in earlier periods.

Since resuming its activities, the Board has re-stated certain important principles and instituted certain practices. In refusing to rule on one appeal it pointed out once more that it had no authority to determine questions of law as distinct from questions of fact.[50] It has

[47]11–12 Geo. VI, c. 70.

[48]For an estimate of its importance by an importers' association see the letter from H. C. MacKendrick, General Manager of Canadian Importers and Traders Association, published in part in Wellington Jeffers' "Finance at Large," *Globe and Mail*, Jan. 1, 1952, p. 20.

[49]See Tables 4 and 5.

[50]"It has been held by the Supreme Court of Canada that the Tariff Board has not the authority to determine questions of law as distinct from questions of fact,

TABLE 4

APPEALS TO THE TARIFF BOARD UNDER PROVISIONS OF THE
CUSTOMS ACT AND THE EXCISE TAX ACT FROM APRIL 1, 1949,
TO JUNE 24, 1953[a]

	Appeals officially registered	Appeals officially withdrawn	Appeals in which Board had no jurisdiction
Tariff classification	89	16	1
Excise tax	15	2	
Sales tax	11	4	
Value for duty	11	1	
Class or kind	7	1	1
Excise and sales tax	3		
Total	136	24	2
Less cols. 2 and 3	26		
Decisions	110		

[a]Courtesy of the Tariff Board of Canada.

TABLE 5

TARIFF BOARD OF CANADA, STATUS OF DECISIONS,
APRIL 1, 1949, TO JUNE 24, 1953[a]

Appeals allowed	49
Dismissed	44
Part allowed and part dismissed	7
Decisions contrary to Department and appellant	3
Pending public hearing or decision	7
Total	110

[a]Courtesy of the Tariff Board of Canada.

refused, too, to hear an appeal which did not arise from a decision of the Deputy Minister in accordance with routine procedure prescribed by the Act.[51] "He, [the Deputy Minister] makes his decision in accordance with the provisions of that section [s. 48] which provides

---

even though in reaching decisions it must take cognizance of the law. Accordingly the Board declares that a decision in this appeal is not within its competence." A-155, T.B.C. 200, March 16, 1950. The relevant facts were not in dispute, but only the law defining goods shipped on consignment.

[51]A-184, T.B.C. 288, Feb. 6, 1951.

for an entry of goods, an appraisal by a Dominion Customs Appraiser and a review of such appraisal by the Deputy Minister." It has followed the practice, where the meaning of an item is not clear, of seeking the intent of the legislators at the time when the item was introduced, although recognizing that, when technological changes occur, the language of the law is to be read in its present sense.[52] When the phrasing of an item has become obsolete the Board has, on occasion, included in its ruling a suggestion that the Minister of Finance consider whether a study should be made with a view to changing the classification to correspond with the changes in technology.

Many of its practices seem eminently fair to importers. In consonance, apparently, with an early decision of the Exchequer Court,[53] the Board has held that where there is serious uncertainty concerning the interpretation of a tariff item the construction should be in favour of the importer.[54] Again, on one occasion, the Board held that it could not hear evidence purporting to show that the value fixed by the Minister (under section 43) was too low.[55] Though the Board is not empowered to order a refund of duty on account of hardship,[56] it has suggested, more than once, that the Deputy Minister draw to the attention of the Minister of National Revenue the circumstances surrounding the decision under appeal in order that he might consider the possibility of recommending a refund of the duty. For the most part these suggestions have been made when the importer has taken elaborate but unsuccessful precautions to be assured in advance of the rate of duty that would be charged[57] but has, in fact, been charged a higher rate. From these cases it appears that even under Canadian procedures it is occasionally difficult to be perfectly certain that a

[52]A–182, T.B.C. 197, Feb. 6, 1951, and A–176, T.B.C. 223, Dec. 1, 1950.

[53]*The Queen* v. *J. C. Ayer Company*, Exchequer Court of Canada, 1885. "Notwithstanding the Act provides that customs laws shall receive such liberal construction as will best insure the protection of the revenue etc., in cases of doubtful interpretation the construction should favour the importer."

[54]A–133, T.B.C. 179, June 9, 1949, and A–134, T.B.C. 177, June 14, 1949. Some careful reasoning may be required to bring this principle into harmony with section 60 of the Customs Act.

[55]On an appeal by an association of domestic manufacturers concerning values fixed in D.N.R., *Appraisers' Bulletin*, Misc. no. 39 (rev., Feb. 29, 1949). An importer, who became a party to the appeal, contended that the official values were too high but did not convince the Board. A–158, T.B.C. 202, March 27, 1950.

[56]A–132, T.B.C. 181, May 25, 1949.

[57]The wording of the ruling in A–132, T.B.C. 181 is typical.

firm decision as to classification has been obtained before the goods are actually imported or even at the time of entry. On the other hand, it is possible for the Government to introduce consideration of equity where strict interpretation of rules would result in unreasonable hardship. The procedure of the Board is relatively quick and informal and decisions usually follow reasonably soon after the appeal. Appeals from the decision of the Board to the Exchequer Court have been rare. However, it has been suggested occasionally that it is anomalous that the same body should advise concerning the writing of the Customs Tariff and hear appeals on issues that involve its interpretation.

7. ADMINISTRATIVE DISCRETION AND APPEAL—UNITED STATES

The discretionary powers granted the administration are much more narrowly limited in the United States than in Canada. Much of the procedural protection is written into the statutes and administrative appeals are less important.[58] However, Congress has empowered or required the administration to change rates of duty or to prohibit entry under carefully specified circumstances; often the amount of the change is limited and the procedure which must be followed is prescribed in detail.[59] Under the "flexible provisions" of the Act, the President is required to proclaim changes in rate of duty, or in classification, or in basis of value reported by the Tariff Commission to be necessary to equalize the cost of production of foreign and domestic producers.[60] During the twenties this provision was used, chiefly, to raise rates of duty;[61] after 1934 it was little used, partly because of objections of foreign producers to investigation by United States officials[62] and partly because the Trade Agreements Act exempted from its provisions any article mentioned in a trade agreement.[63] Recently, however, there have been a few investigations.[64] When the

[58]". . . some of the worst features of so-called administrative protectionism are not administrative at all but legislative. . . ." Bidwell, *Invisible Tariff*, p. 18.

[59]For discussion of the constitutional status of the Trade Agreements see Larkin, *Trade Agreements*.

[60]U.S. Tariff Act, s. 336. The Tariff Commission may not recommend a change in rate in excess of 50 per cent; and the President is required to proclaim the change specified "if in his judgment" the investigation has shown the change necessary to equalize differences in costs.

[61]Larkin, *Trade Agreements*, p. 4.

[62]Smith, *Customs Valuation in the United States*, pp. 21–3.

[63]U.S. Trade Agreements Act, 1934, s. 2 (a).

[64]Recent applications include dental burrs (dismissed), filberts (dismissed),

Tariff Commission finds that the importation of any article involves
unfair methods of competition, the President has power not frequently
used in recent years[65] to exclude it from entry. The Commission may
grant a re-hearing, and an appeal from its decision may be taken on
a matter of law to the United States Court of Customs and Patent
Appeals. The President's decision after receiving the final report of
the Commission is conclusive.[66] The President may also prohibit
importations or impose additional duties on imports from a country
which discriminates against the United States[67] though this power
has not been used.[68] The Secretary of the Treasury has power, after
investigation has proved injury or potential injury to domestic producers, to apply anti-dumping duties. He is required, too, to apply
countervailing duties to offset foreign export bounties, public or
private, on dutiable imports.[69] The Customs Simplification Bill of 1951
proposed that countervailing duties should similarly be restricted to
cases in which domestic interests were being endangered or seriously
injured. This provision met with opposition and was dropped from
the bill presented in 1953.[70]

Most of these administrative powers only permitted, or were often
used to bring about, increases in duty.[71] Much more important in
recent years have been the reductions in duty resulting from negotiations under the Trade Agreements Act which gives the President
powers to grant limited reductions of duty after receiving advice from
the Tariff Commission and certain other governmental agencies.[72]
These reductions are granted to all countries; but the President may
exclude from their benefit any country which discriminates against
United States commerce. Australia and Germany were thus "black-
listed" for a time; and the prospect of being excluded may have
influenced Canada to lessen her discrimination even before the negoti-

---

grape wines (dismissed), almonds (no finding). Parks, *United States Administration of its International Economic Affairs*, p. 15.

[65]*Ibid.*, p. 157. An exclusion order against certain cigar lighters is still quite
active.

[66]U.S. Tariff Act, s. 337.   [67]*Ibid.*, s. 338.

[68]Bidwell, *Invisible Tariff*, p. 127.   [69]U.S. Tariff Act, s. 303.

[70]U.S. House, 82nd Congress, 1st Session, H.R. 5505, s. 2 (c). Compare
Radcliffe, "The Tariff Act of 1930 as *not* Amended."

[71]Of the 38 changes in duty proclaimed under the flexible cost equalization
provisions, s. 336, in the eight years (1922-9) following its introduction, only five
were reductions. Between 1930 and 1938, however, lower rates resulted from
25 recommendations and higher rates from 22. Bidwell, *Invisible Tariff*, pp. 121-3.
From 1930 to 1953 there resulted 29 increases and 33 decreases.

[72]U.S. Tariff Act, s. 350.

ation of the United States–Canada Agreement in 1935. Products of Communist countries are at present required by statute to be excluded from the benefit of reductions in duty resulting from trade agreements.[73]

Recent extensions of the Trade Agreements Act have provided for upward "flexibility" of rates reduced by negotiation. The Trade Agreements Extension Act of 1951, for example, which extended the trade agreement powers of the President until 1953,[74] provides for the reduction of a concession under the escape clause of the General Agreement. If the Tariff Commission finds that a "product upon which a concession has been granted . . . is, as a result, in whole or in part, of the duty or other customs treatment reflecting such concession, being imported in such increased quantities, either actual or relative, as to cause or threaten serious injury to the domestic industry producing like or competitive products" it is required to advise the President to withdraw, suspend, or modify the concession. On receipt of such a recommendation the President is empowered to make such adjustments in the rates of duty, impose such quotas, and make such other modifications as are found necessary. If he does not act within sixty days he is required to submit a report stating his reasons.[75] The very careful wording of this section reflects an intense struggle[76] between extreme protectionists and their opponents but it also illustrates not unreasonably the detailed limitations characteristically placed on administrative action in the United States. A considerable number of applications have been made under the escape clause but relatively few have been granted. The Tariff Commission dismissed without formal investigation 14 of the 21 original applications. Of the 15 investigations completed to November 28, 1952, the Tariff Commission recommended modification of the concessions in 5 cases and the President acted only in 3 cases.[77] However, a quota was imposed,

[73]By the Trade Agreements Extension Act of 1951 the President was required to withdraw the concessions from communist countries, though the Secretary of State contended that the provision would not appreciably promote the purpose intended, that such action as could usefully be taken had been taken already, and that the complete statutory withdrawal proposed would be diplomatically embarrassing. Evidence of Dean Acheson, U.S. Senate, *On H.R. 1612*, pp. 8–9.

[74]In 1951 the Trade Agreements Act was amended and extended to 1953; in 1953 it was extended to July 1954; and in 1954 to July 1955.

[75]Trade Agreements Extension Act of 1951, s. 7.

[76]See U.S. Senate, *On H.R. 1612*, in many places; e.g., testimony of Dean Acheson (p. 7), and statements on behalf of the United States Council of the International Chamber of Commerce (pp. 594–7).

[77]Women's fur felt hats and hat bodies, hatters' fur, and dried figs.

on one of the commodities investigated, by an amendment of the Defense Production Act.[78] Though few concessions have been withdrawn under the escape clause, it should be noted that even an application for an investigation is likely to be sufficient to discourage foreign producers from attempting to enter the United States market or from attempting to expand their sales in the United States until the outcome is known. In addition it burdens those who wish to import with the trouble and expense of making representations to the Tariff Commission.[79]

An import quota may be established under section 22 of the Agricultural Adjustment Act when found by the Tariff Commission to be needed for the support of an agricultural programme;[80] and, in the case of a perishable agricultural commodity, the President may take whatever action is necessary to meet an emergency, even action inconsistent with the provisions of the General agreement.[81] Import quotas are also imposed by certain other legislation. The President has been required, also, under specified conditions to reinstate certain duties temporarily suspended by Congress, e.g., the duties on lead and zinc.

In addition to these explicit powers, changes occur in the administrative rulings of the Treasury which may, from time to time, change the treatment accorded to particular articles.

However, except in the case of dumping duties, administrative findings or rulings resulting in higher rates of duty apply only to goods entered, or withdrawn from warehouse, for consumption after the expiration of ninety (thirty in the case of countervailing duties) days after publication of the notice of the change.[82] Only in the case of a

[78]*Bell Report*, pp. 62–3.

[79]For a proposal to provide penalties for frivolous applications see Radcliffe, "The Tariff Act of 1930 as *not* Amended."

[80]Parks, *United States Administration*, pp. 115, 158; *Bell Report*, p. 41.

[81]Trade Agreements Extension Act of 1951, s. 8. These amendments were made in spite of Secretary of Agriculture Brannan's statement that power to withdraw concessions was not needed. See U.S. Senate, *On H.R. 1612*, pp. 58–63.

[82]The Customs Administrative Act of 1938 added the following provision to s. 315 of the Customs Act of 1930. "No administrative ruling resulting in the imposition of a higher rate of duty or charge than the Secretary of the Treasury shall find to have been applicable to imported merchandise under an established and uniform practice shall be effective . . . prior to the expiration of thirty days after the date of publication in the weekly Treasury Decisions . . . but this provision shall not apply with respect to anti-dumping duties." See Levett, *Customs Administrative Act of 1938*, p. 12. Extended to ninety days by T.D. 53093, Aug. 29, 1952.

collector's appeal for reappraisement and in very limited circumstances in the case of a domestic producer's protest can a judicial decision result in the application of higher duty to goods already cleared through customs. Both administrative and judicial decisions resulting in lower duties are applied retroactively to open transactions.

Since, in the United States, many procedures are defined in detail by the statutes, and administrative discretion is narrowly circumscribed (when it exists at all), appeals may be taken to the courts from almost any kind of executive or administrative action or decision. Appeal may be carried to the Customs Court without a prior decision by the Secretary of the Treasury. As a consequence administrative appeal is relatively unimportant, while judicial appeal is important and frequent.

Over the years an elaborate and specialized system of judicial appeal has been gradually developed. Changes in it have been made partly to secure uniformity in judicial decisions on customs matters, partly to relieve the ordinary courts from the congestion caused by customs cases, and partly to increase or diminish the power of the domestic producers to intervene in customs administration.

Before 1875, in disputes concerning classification (rate and amount of duty) importers were allowed to bring action in the Circuit Court of the district against the Collector of Customs, who was held nominally liable. The Tariff Act of 1875 not only authorized the Secretary of the Treasury to examine and reliquidate duties but provided that no suit for the recovery of duties could be maintained in any court except from his decision (unless the decision was delayed more than ninety days); but the Act of 1890 relieved the Secretary of these duties.[83] With respect to valuation, other methods of appeal had been developed. In 1823 provision was made for a second appraisal by an *ad hoc* board composed of local appraisers and private merchants. After 1851, when four travelling appraisers were appointed to promote uniformity between ports, it was provided that each board should include one travelling appraiser. As the number of appeals increased, this procedure became "not only ineffective but productive of serious abuses, scandal and contention."[84] In 1890, accordingly, a Board of General Appraisers was established to hear appeals and protests from the decision of the local officials. Originally an appeal was allowed from a decision of the Board to the Circuit Court of the district in which the dispute arose; and that Court had power on application

[83]Futrell, *History of Customs Jurisprudence*, p. 134.

[84]Treasury Dept., *Annual Report*, 1889, p. xxiii; quoted in Futrell, p. 87, who outlines this whole history. See also Bidwell, *Invisible Tariff*, pp. 33–8.

to refer the matter back to one of the Board to take further evidence. Under special circumstances an appeal might be taken to the Supreme Court. Appeals to the Circuit Court were numerous; dockets became crowded and there was much delay; at one time the average life of a customs appeal *after leaving* the Board of Appraisers was estimated by the Secretary of the Treasury to be four and a half years. In 1909 the Court of Customs Appeals was established and given exclusive jurisdiction in the review of decisions of the Board of General Appraisers; provision for review of special cases by the Supreme Court was continued. With added functions the Court of Customs Appeals became the Court of Customs and Patent Appeals. In 1926, the Board of United States Appraisers, whose nine members were appointed for life, became, by a change in name, the United States Customs Court.

Historically the appraiser has been responsible for determining the value of imports and the collector for deciding the rate and amount of duty. Accordingly, the process of appeal for reappraisal has come to differ from the process of protesting classification and other matters. If the final appraised value is higher than the entered value or if it will affect the classification of the merchandise, the collector notifies the importer who may file an appeal with the collector within thirty days; the collector must forward this appeal to the United States Customs Court; he may himself file an appeal on any appraisal within sixty days of appraisal. It is to be noted that an appeal cannot be made prior to appraisal; and appraisal is not completed until the appraiser is satisfied that he has sufficient information; as noted earlier, in difficult cases this may require several months or even years.[85] In the first instance appeals are heard by one judge of the Customs Court but his decision may be reviewed, on appeal within thirty days, by a division of three judges. From the decision of the reviewing division, appeal on questions of law only may be taken to the Court of Customs and Patent Appeals. Under certain circumstances appeal may be taken to the Supreme Court.[86] From a collector's decision with respect to classification, rate of duty, and other matters except valuation, the importer may file a protest with the local collectors within sixty days

[85]"Returns of invoices have been withheld for as long as three years, and it is not uncommon for such returns to be delayed for six or eight months or a year." U.S. Senate, Finance Committee, 75th Congress, 3rd session, *On H.R. 8099* (Customs Administrative Bill of 1938), p. 89. Quoted in Bidwell, *Invisible Tariff*, p. 34.   [86]U.S. Tariff Act of 1930, as amended, s. 501.

after liquidation of the entry. The form of the protest is prescribed and the validity of a protest has been the subject of a number of cases.[87] On receipt of the protest the collector is given ninety days to review his decision and, if he so decides, change it and refund the excess duties collected. If he does not change his decision, the protest is heard and decided by the Customs Court; thence an appeal may be carried to the Court of Customs and Patent Appeals.[88] Certain decisions of that Court, on permission, may be reviewed by the Supreme Court of the United States. Appeals to the Supreme Court, however, are infrequent.

It will be observed that statutory provisions for administrative review are narrowly limited, once the entry has been liquidated. There is no provision for administrative review of a final appraised value even though it is admittedly in error. The Customs Bureau will not appraise merchandise, though it frequently settles disagreements between field officers as to the principles to be applied in determining an appraised value, and thus prevents discrimination between importers at different ports in the valuation of their imports. Also, the Customs Bureau frequently settles differences between importers and field officers as to the valuation before an appraisement is completed. There is no statutory provision for an importer to appeal to the Customs Bureau even in other matters. The provision that a collector on receipt of a protest may review and revise his decision, and the encouragement given the importer to present fully any information bearing on appraisement, offer an excellent opportunity for consultation with local officials. However, in the United States, these opportunities, though they result in a large volume of consultation, have not prevented the litigation of a very large number of disputes.

The Attorney General's Advisory Committee comments at length on this outcome. The deficiencies of informal settlement are attributed in part to attempts to be more than fair with the importer in the matter of accepting protests which give no clear indication of the reasons for a protest or the goods to which it relates.[89] The protest is often filed by the importer's attorney, while the importer himself does not appreciate the point at issue and frequently refuses to discuss the facts with customs officials.[90]

[87]Futrell, pp. 112–16.   [88]U.S. Tariff Act of 1930 as amended, ss. 514, 515.
[89]A.G. Com., Mon. 27, pp. 146–8.
[90]*Ibid.*, p. 151. Customs attorneys undertake a large proportion of cases on the basis of a contingent fee.

The refusal or inability of importers to cooperate with the Protest Section is a real barrier to the proper consideration of protests. It has been the experience of reviewers that their most satisfactory decisions are made when the importers involved have been helpful. . . . In fact, the highest percentage of allowed protests occur in cases where the importers are not only ready to assist, but also volunteer information before being approached by the reviewer.[91]

When informal discussions of complaints occur they have provided an excellent means for ascertaining the true facts as well as narrowing the area of conflict between the importer and the government. Relatively few protests have been taken in connection with entries which have been subject to discussion prior to liquidation.[92] However, the importers have often entered the merchandise under a tariff item which they believed to be acceptable to the collector and 80 per cent of the protests have related to entries in which the collector had accepted the rate of duty claimed on the entry and was unaware that a dispute was in prospect.[93] The Attorney General's Committee considered these defects so important for subsequent litigation that it recommended not only that the importer be required to state the classification he considered appropriate on his entry form but that he subsequently be bound, as in valuation, by this entered rate; and that he be subjected to an additional duty, subject to appeal to the Treasury and the Customs Court, if the rate found to apply were higher than the entered rate. On this point it would appear that the Attorney General's Committee, as was perhaps to be expected, was more concerned with convenience in litigation than with reasonable treatment of the importer.[94]

The Customs Simplification Act of 1953 extends to some extent the power of the administration to order refund of duty even after liquidation. It remains to be seen how broadly these powers are interpreted. The number of protests received by collectors and the number granted by them are shown in Table 6. The *Annual Report* of the Treasury Department attributes the increases in both appeals and protests in 1949 and 1950 to "the system of dual currency invoked (and continued to be used) by many countries with resulting confusion as to the true value of merchandise for customs purposes." The decline in the number of protests and appeals in 1951, despite the increase in the number of commercial entries, is attributed to the simplification of customs procedure and to the efforts made by importers to ascertain correct values before entry of their merchandise.

[91]*Ibid.*, pp. 151–2.   [92]*Ibid.*, p. 127.
[93]*Ibid.*   [94]*Ibid.*, pp. 157–8.

TABLE 6

PROTESTS AND APPEALS FILED WITH COLLECTORS, UNITED STATES 1948–1953[a]

Protests	48	50	51	52	53
Filed with collectors by importers	9,567	17,759	12,268	19,534	32,549
Allowed by collectors	422	3,104	596	1,060	1,960
Denied by collectors and forwarded to Customs Court	7,660	13,029	10,989	14,259	20,387
Appeals for reappraisement filed with collectors	5,156	16,495	15,644	14,129	9,244

[a]Treasury Dept., *Annual Reports on the State of Finances*, fiscal years ending June 30, 1949–53.

"Though provisions for administrative review are not considerable, provisions for judicial review are frequently used. The right to sue before the Customs Court applies to practically every legal controversy between an importing tax-payer and his government. The fact that certain administrative officers have made a ruling does not prevent appeal—including the legality of all orders and findings entering into the same."[95] The *Annual Reports* of the Attorney General of the United States list seven representative types of claims heard by the Customs Court: (1) The value of the imported merchandise found by the appraiser is higher than the actual market value on the date of exportation. (2) Merchandise is more specifically described under another paragraph which provides for a lower rate of duty than that under which it was classified. (3) Rate and amount of duty is assessed in violation of a treaty and hence illegal or excessive. (4) The President has unlawfully changed a rate under the "flexible provisions" because he or the Tariff Commission did not follow required procedure. (5) "Collector has refused, as provided by law, to refund" duties by drawbacks. (6) The law under which the duty or tax has been assessed is unconstitutional and void. (7) The importer undervalued his goods unintentionally and should be relieved of the penalty duty.[96]

In consequence of the rigidity of the statutes and the meagre results of administrative review of appraisements, some 5 per cent of dutiable entries in the United States are appealed to the courts whereas in Canada, where the statutes are less detailed and where appeal to the

[95]Futrell, p. 18; Tariff Act of 1930, s. 514.

[96]U.S. Attorney General, *Annual Report for the Year Ending June 30, 1935*, p. 109, report of the Assistant Attorney General, J. R. Jackson, in charge of the Customs Division.

TABLE 7

U.S. CUSTOMS COURT—TOTAL CASES,[a] 1949–1952

Fiscal year ending June 30	Pending at beginning of fiscal year	Filed during fiscal year	Disposed of during fiscal year	Pending at end of fiscal year
1949	97,501	20,055	18,603	98,953
1950	98,953	29,642	14,250	114,345
1951	114,345	25,803	15,943	124,205
1952	124,205	29,328	7,414	146,119

[a]Information from Office of Assistant Attorney General in charge of Customs for 1949–51, and Administrative Office of U.S. Courts, *Annual Report of the Director*, 1952, Table G.1; includes classification cases, reappraisement cases (except appeals on remand or rehearing), applications for review, and petitions for remission of additional duties.

At the close of the fiscal year ending June 30, 1953, this Court had pending before it 158,422 cases of various types. At that time there were in excess of 200 test cases or issues being litigated before the Court.

TABLE 8

NUMBER OF CASES BEFORE U.S. CUSTOMS COURTS, FISCAL YEAR ENDING JUNE 30, 1952[a]

	Pending beginning of fiscal year	Filed during fiscal year	Disposed of during fiscal year	Pending end of fiscal year
Classification cases	75,109	14,205	6,322	82,992
Appeals for reappraisement	48,931	14,977	961	62,947
Applications for review	106	67	81	92
Petitions for remission of Additional duty	59	79	50	88
Appeals pending on remand and on rehearing	58	7	2	63
Total U.S. Customs Court	124,263	29,335	7,416	146,182
U.S. Court of Customs & Patent Appeals (Customs)	24	55	41	38
Grand total	124,287	29,390	7,457	146,220

[a]Data from Administrative Office of U.S. Courts, *Annual Report of the Director*, 1952, Tables G.1 and G.2.

Tariff Board is granted only from a decision of the Deputy Minister, the proportion is negligible. Table 7 shows the numbers of cases filed in the United States Customs Court; and Table 8, the composition of the cases before both customs courts of the United States in 1952, including remands, reviews, and appeals. It should be noted that a single judicial decision may dispose of a considerable number of cases, sometimes several hundred, which have been consolidated for trial or are disposed of on the basis of stipulations.

In the United States, domestic producers of competitive products have been granted more power than in Canada of intervening in customs administration. Powers granted in 1922 were continued by the Act of 1930 though they were limited by the Customs Administration Act of 1938 and, from 1934 until 1951, by the Trade Agreements Act. When a United States producer, manufacturer, or wholesaler believes that too low an appraised value is being attached to an imported article "of a class or kind" which he sells, he may complain to the Secretary of the Treasury and submit the information on which he bases his belief. The Secretary of the Treasury must transmit the complaint to the appraiser at each port through which the article is imported and require him to report with his reasons his appraisal of each entry of the article. If not satisfied with the appraisals at any port, the Secretary is required to instruct the collector to file an appeal with the United States Customs Court. In this case, (or if the local appraiser appraises at higher than the entered value on the basis of information furnished by the United States manufacturer and the importer appeals) the United States manufacturer becomes an interested party in the hearing of the case. If, on being notified, he is not satisfied with the action of the Secretary, he may file an appeal himself, in the same way and with the same rights as though he were an importer.[97] Thus, the American producer or wholesaler has all the rights of administrative appeal of the importer. If he is not successful in influencing the appraiser in this way, or in inducing the Secretary of the Treasury to instruct the collector to appeal on his behalf, he may still appeal in the same way as an ordinary importer. Domestic manufactures have not used (or perhaps needed to use) this right of appeal. There has been only one such proceeding since 1922, and it was not successful.

A domestic firm may also protest the classification accorded imports of competing merchandise. On written request the Secretary of the Treasury is required to state the classification and rate of duty imposed on the specified import. If the domestic dealer believes the proper rate is not being assessed, he may file a complaint with the Secretary,

[97]U.S. Tariff Act, 1930, s. 516a.

giving the reasons for his belief. If the Secretary decides that the classification should be revised, he must so notify collectors; in any event he
must notify the complainant of his decision. If the complainant is
dissatisfied with the action of the Secretary, he may file notice that he
wishes to protest the classification; whereupon the Secretary must
publish notice of his decision and of the complainant's desire to protest, furnish the complainant with information concerning particular
entries sufficient to allow him to protest them, and require the local
collector to notify the complainant when the first of these entries
is liquidated. The complainant may then file a protest in the
same way as an importer.[98] It has been decided, however, that a
domestic producer can protest only the classification and the rate of
duty, not the amount of the duty;[99] also that a trade association is not
an interested party.

The Tariff Act of 1930 originally provided that the liquidation of any
entry, made more than thirty days after the publication of the complainant's desire to protest, was to be suspended until the proper
classification was finally determined. Since a decision by the courts
ordinarily required a year and might require three or even more,
importers were left in doubt as to the amount of duty they would have
to pay over long periods of time and, if the trade continued, with
respect to many shipments. They complained, moreover, that domestic
interests filed a multitude of protests simply to create uncertainty and
discourage importation.[100] The Customs Administrative Act of 1938
gave some protection against these abuses. It provided that the imports
should be classified in accordance with the decision of the Secretary
until some court had decided otherwise; however, liquidation of duties
on goods entered or withdrawn after the decision was published was

[98]*Ibid.*, s. 516b.

[99]*E. C. Miller Cedar Lumber Co.* v. *U.S.*, (1936) 24 C.C.P.A. (Customs)
272,282 (T.D. 48701); appeal from U.S.C.C., T.D. 48161.

[100]In requesting revision of the Customs Administrative Act in 1938 the
Treasury Department submitted the following statement: "Existing law thus in-
vites domestic manufacturers, producers and wholesalers competing with domestic
importers to initiate proceedings without real hope of ultimate success in the
knowledge that a barrier may be maintained against foreign competition for as
long as the proceedings may be kept alive. Thirty-two complaints have been filed
with the Secretary under sec. 516(b) but not one has been sustained in the
courts." U.S. House, 75th Congress, 3rd session, *On H.R. 8099*, p. 14; quoted by
Larkin, *Trade Agreements*, p. 35. Larkin comments: "By simply starting litigation
under this provision the importer's goods might be held up for years, or released
only under such burdensome restrictions as would make importation unprofitable"
(p. 35). See also testimony of Winthrop Brown, Dept. of State, in U.S. Senate,
On H.R. 1612, pp. 1218–19.

to be suspended until the matter was finally decided. It provided as well that actions of this sort were to be given precedence over other cases by both customs courts; and that decision was to be hastened in every reasonable way. Moreover it has long been provided that the Customs Court may determine that an appeal or a protest was frivolous and may then assess a penalty against the claimant.[101]

The Reciprocal Trade Agreements Act of 1934 provided that, if an agreement had been concluded concerning any article, a domestic producer might not protest its classification; nor might he circumvent this provision of the law by importing the article himself and then, as an importer, protesting that it should be dutiable at a higher rate.[102] With the negotiation of trade agreements and the amendments of 1938 the ratio of protests to total cases filed with the Customs Court fell substantially; from more than 96 per cent in 1932 and 1933 to 86 per cent in 1939 and 1940.[103] On other articles, however, domestic interests, it appears, continued to enjoy statutory provisions for access to central administrative authorities that are not required by statute to be provided to importers on matters of classification (as well, of course, as on matters of valuation.)[104] In 1951 the clause that restricted the power of domestic interests to protest was struck out of the Trade Agreements Act.[105]

In appeals to the Customs Court the appellant is handicapped by certain provisions of the Tariff Act. He is under the burden not only of proving that the classification proposed by the collector is wrong but also that the classification he proposed is correct.[106] Similarly, in reappraisement proceedings the value found by the appraiser is presumed to be correct; and the burden of proof rests on the party who challenges it. The appraiser, of course, is prohibited from finding a value arbitrarily; but if in fact he does so while claiming that it is legally based, it may be very difficult to prove that the value should be some other exact amount. The appraiser is not required to disclose which of the bases of valuation he has used in his appraisal.

[101]28 U.S.C. 2641.

[102]See *Fletcher* v. *United States,* T.D. 48684; on appeal (1937) 25 C.C.P.A. 195; cited by Futrell, p. 64.

[103]I am indebted to S. Kaliski for devising and carrying out this test while analysing the relevant statistics.

[104]The power of domestic interests to appeal concerning valuation apparently was not used frequently.

[105]P.L. 50, 1951. The administration was opposed to the change. See testimony of W. Brown, U.S. Senate, *On H.R. 1612,* pp. 1218–20.

[106]For recent cases see *G. T. Grant Company* v. *United States,* 38 C.C.P.A. 57, and *Joseph E. Seger & Sons, Inc.* v. *United States,* 30 C.C.P.A. 150, C.A.D. 227.

The United States customs courts, like the Canadian Tariff Board, accept the principle of law that cases of real doubt should be resolved in favour of the importer.[107] In several cases, however, in which this principle has been applied by the Customs Court, the Court of Customs and Patent Appeals by superior energy or ingenuity has found a method of resolving the doubt. Since resolution of the doubt could not favour the importer the higher of the disputed rates has then been found to apply.[108]

The work of the Customs Court is often facilitated by arranging that one of a multitude of similar cases be chosen as a test case, while the remainder are suspended to await the outcome of the test case. Even after such an issue has been decided, however, the Supreme Court has held that, in certain circumstances, a new case may be advanced by the government or by an importer.[109] If the customs authorities intend to bring a new case, local officials are instructed to apply the judgment of the court only to the entries actually adjudicated. It is not applied to shipments subsequently received, and suspended cases may remain suspended until the new test case is decided. Canadian exporters complain that this practice may delay final decision almost interminably. The practice is considered sufficiently important (and presumably defensible) that it was recognized as legitimate by a clause in the General Agreement[110] and the Havana Charter.[111] That this procedure is taken into account by other countries is illustrated by the history of the customs treatment of nepheline syenite, which is considered to be in competition with feldspar produced in the United States. This history illustrates as well the role of the courts and of trade agreements in determining the customs treatment of imports into the United States. Ground nepheline syenite first entered the United States in 1936 as a manufactured mineral at 30 per cent *ad valorem*. In the trade agreement with Canada, effective 1939, the duty on both ground feldspar and nepheline syenite was reduced to 15 per cent subject to a tariff quota of 50,000 tons annually. Importers appealed the classification[112] and it was decided in 1940 that nepheline syenite was manufactured sand, and entitled to entry free of duty. The Treasury, however, instructed customs officials not to follow this decision. Importers again protested and in 1942 the Customs Court affirmed its original ruling.[113] In 1946

---

[107]See e.g. 38 C.C.P.A. 107, *United States* v. *Kling Chee Fur Corporation*.
[108]See Futrell, pp. 116–19.
[109]See *United States* v. *Stone & Dower*, 274 U.S. 225, cited by Futrell, p. 143.
[110]Art. 10, 3(b).   [111]Art. 38, 3(b).
[112]4 U.S.C.C. 86, C.D. 293.   [113](1942) 9 U.S.C.C. 170, C.D. 685.

the Treasury issued special instructions[114] to admit nepheline syenite free of duty under paragraph 1775 because it had come to its attention that one of the ports was not applying the 1942 decision.

At the hearings in 1951 on the bill to extend the Trade Agreements Act, domestic producers of feldspar objected to being excluded from making protest. Since the Customs Administrative Act of 1938 prevented domestic interests from harassing the importers by causing liquidation of entry to be suspended, they argued, the right to protest should be returned to domestic interests.[115] Even though the United States courts had decided the matter, Canada insisted at Geneva that duty-free entry for ground nepheline syenite be confirmed in the agreement.[116] The paragraph relating to sand was bound free of duty and a special note was appended promising that ground nepheline syenite would continue to be classed under this paragraph for the duration of the agreement. In estimating the effectiveness of this note it should be recalled that, though the Trade Agreement Act does not empower the administration to change the classification of an article, it does empower it to "proclaim . . . such continuance, and for such minimum periods, of adjusting customs or excise treatment of any article covered by foreign trade agreement." In the past the administration has sometimes continued for several years an erroneous classification because of a note of this kind in a trade agreement[117] but the courts have not yet been called upon to decide on the administration's interpretation of the effect of, and authority for, such notes.

Even when no new case is prepared, however, the final decision may be long delayed. The long history of the litigation concerning the treatment of the British purchase tax has become notorious. The story of the valuation of Canadian firebrick products is recounted in a later chapter. These cases, however, are by no means unparalleled. In thirteen of the twenty-five published customs decisions of the United States Court of Customs and Patent Appeals reported in full during the year ending March 31, 1951, for example,[118] the date of the disputed entries is mentioned. One of these decisions related to shipments entered in 1935, sixteen years before, and five to shipments

---

[114]T.D. 51462 (1).

[115]Testimony of Edwin G. Martin, U.S. Senate, *On H.R. 1612*, pp. 156–65.

[116]Can., Banking & Commerce, *G.A.T.T.*, 1948, p. 76. See G.A.T.T., Schedule XX, item 1775.

[117]T.D. 52576 (1) corrects an erroneous classification that had been thus continued for several years because of a similar note.

[118]38 C.C.P.A. (Customs). These cases are extreme rather than usual since the date of entry is more likely to be significant in ancient than recent cases.

made more than ten years before; the remaining eight decisions related to shipments imported between 1940 and 1945.[119] One of the three cases recorded in the memorandum of decisions in the same volume related to merchandise imported in 1936. These rough statistics confirm the general impression that in difficult cases the amount of the duty may not be known until many years after the merchandise has been imported. Such delays have not been unusual in the past although the war seems to have delayed certain appraisals. Concerning the number of cases pending in 1939 the Attorney General's Committee remarked: "Although the volume of cases is considerable, it is said that there are no more than 300 major issues involved in all pending protest litigation, and that the decision of a number of test cases would result in a prompt clearing of the Court's docket. The factor remains, nevertheless, that most cases are not decided until many months, and frequently several years, after the filing of protests."[120]

After 1938 the number of protests filed fell sharply (though the rate of turnover had also fallen) and the number of classification cases pending was reduced from more than 200,000 in 1938 to 76,000 in 1950. However, the number of protests in 1952 increased by almost 50 per cent and the number of cases pending increased to nearly 83,000. Appeals to reappraise may last even longer than disputes concerning classification; they "have lasted ten years . . . the average is probably two and a half to three years."[121] This period is in addition to the delay between entry and appraisal. The number of reappraisement cases pending increased from some 11,000 in 1938 to 15,000 at the beginning of 1949; and since 1949 has risen even more rapidly to nearly 63,000 at the end of 1952. Some of this increase in volume is attributable to disputes concerning the valuation of imports from countries which maintain multiple exchange rates; and Congress failed to pass the proposals of the Simplification Bills which were designed to facilitate the conversion of currencies for duty purposes. The reasons for delay are not primarily attributable to the inadequacy of the judicial facilities or personnel but to the fact that the tariff items and many other provisions of the Tariff Act (those with respect

[119]The dates are 1935, 1; 1936, 2; 1937, 1; 1939, 1; 1940, 1; 1942, 1; 1943, 2; 1944, 2; 1945, 2.

[120]A.G. Com., Mon. 27, p. 140, footnote 229. There have been complaints that these delays complicate the administration of the estates of deceased importers and customs brokers.

[121]Testimony of W. R. Johnson, U.S. House, On H.R. 1535, p. 61.

to valuation among others) require that a decision be based on a great number of factual details difficult to determine, and even more difficult to interpret. Speed of proceedings is affected by other factors too. The unwillingness of attorneys to proceed too quickly,[122] for example, and the desire of domestic interests to prolong uncertainty of the importer may favour delay; or the desire of the appraiser to be perfectly fair to the importer by allowing him plenty of time to produce evidence to support his contentions.

The complicated relationships between customs duties, import taxes, commercial agreements, and litigation in the United States is exemplified in the long series of disputes concerning the measurement of imported lumber. Lumber imported into the United States is subject to an import tax under the Internal Revenue Act as well as to any duty prescribed in the Tariff Act.[123] It has been decided that, in the absence of statutory provision to the contrary, customs duties are to be applied to the imported article "in the form and condition as imported." It is an accepted principle that the units of measurement mentioned in Acts imposing internal taxes are to be interpreted as having the meaning commonly given to them in commercial usage in the United States. Planed, finished, or tongued and grooved lumber is said to be commonly quoted and sold commercially in units of gross board measure; that is, the lumber is referred to as containing the same number of thousand board feet as the rough lumber from which it was manufactured. The relevant paragraph of the Tariff Act contains a specific provision that gross board measure is to be used; but no similar provision was contained in the relevant section of the Revenue Act of 1932.

The use of gross board measure in assessing the Revenue Act duty was contested in 1932.[124] In November and December of that year two shipments of dressed lumber were entered at Port Huron. Both the duty and the tax were assessed on the gross measure of the lumber. The importer appealed from the assessment of the import tax and was sustained by the Customs Court on October 28, 1935. The Court of Customs and Patent Appeals upheld the lower court decision on October 6, 1936.[125] The Court held that the provision for taking rough measure as a basis of appraisal of duty under paragraph 401 of the Tariff Act was definitely limited by the phrase "for the purposes of

[122]See e.g. testimony of John G. Lerch, U.S. House, *On H.R. 5106*, p. 71.

[123]See U.S. Revenue Act of 1922, s. 601 (c) (6), and U.S. Tariff Act of 1930, pars. 401 and 1803, for example.

[124]*Myers* v. *The United States*, T.D. 47964.   [125]24 C.C.P.A. 156; T.D. 48640.

this paragraph" and was not applicable to any subsequent act of Congress. It held that Congress had specifically indicated its intention that gross board measure should not be used in assessing the import tax by omitting the clause prescribing it which had appeared in comparable provisions of several successive Tariff Acts; also, that the provision in the relevant section of the Revenue Act of 1932 requiring that the tax be levied, collected, assessed, and paid, in the same manner as the duty imposed by the Tariff Act was merely an administrative provision intended for the convenience of the Customs, and in no way affected the amounts of duty to be collected.

On October 15, 1937, the Court of Customs and Patent Appeals denied a government motion to reopen the case to hear the evidence to the effect that, in commercial practice in the United States prior to 1932, no deductions from board measure were made on account of planing and so forth. The Court based its decision on the grounds that it was the clearly expressed intent of Congress to confine the use of gross measure to the Tariff Act paragraph; and that evidence concerning commercial practice was therefore irrelevant.[126] On April 18, 1938, the Customs Court decided a similar case based on another Myers shipment; the issue was identical with that involved in the first case and was similarly decided.[127] Meanwhile certain domestic interests apparently had not been satisfied with the Treasury's procedure on a related matter. In July, 1934, the Bureau of Customs received an inquiry from a domestic producer of lumber in the State of Washington about its practice in assessing lumber less than one inch thick, and specifically whether it was assessed as if it were an inch thick. On August 22, 1934, the firm was advised that[128] the lumber was not so being assessed for purposes of the import tax or the import duty. Under the provision of the Tariff Act which grants domestic producers the right to appeal with respect to the classification of imports,[129] the domestic lumber company took exception to the method of assessment in use and stated its belief that lumber ordinarily produced by resawing, to a thickness of less than one inch, bevel sidings or boards, and items which may be produced by surfacing lumber the rough size of which is below 1 inch thick should be assessed as if fully 1 inch thick; the company contended that it had long been commercial practice in the United States so to compute footage in selling such lumber.

Since the Treasury had made a careful investigation in 1933 which

[126]T.D. 49210.
[128]In accordance with T.D. 46250.

[127]T.D. 49530.
[129]U.S. Tariff Act, s. 516 (b).

failed to reveal any such accepted practice and since it had received no further information since that time, it declined to change its practice; but it gave notice on April 5, 1935, that all entries or withdrawals after thirty days from publication would be subject to the court decision should the company enter a protest.[130] On October 14, 1935, the Miller Company filed notice of its intent to protest and, upon being given information as to entries, protested the classification and rate of duty on a consumption entry dated Blaine, Wash., June 14, 1935, and liquidated September, 1935. On November 23, 1935, the Treasury ordered all collectors to suspend liquidations of all unliquidated entries of merchandise in question imported or withdrawn after the expiration of thirty days from the publication of the notice of April 5.[131] However, on August 6, 1936, the collectors were notified that they might liquidate any such merchandise entered on or after January 1, 1936; the Canadian trade agreement became effective on that date, and under the Trade Agreements Act, merchandise mentioned in a trade agreement was not subject to the provisions that allowed a domestic producer to protest.[132]

On November 30, 1936, the Court of Customs and Patent Appeals upheld the Customs Court's decision denying the manufacturer's right to protest.[133] The Court held that the Tariff Act gives an American manufacturer the right to protest the classification and the rate of duty, not its amount; he may not protest the collector's findings as to the quantity imported unless such findings affect the rate of duty. The Court denied that the rates in question were so affected.[134] In 1938 the Internal Revenue Act was amended to require, provisionally, the use of the gross measure when assessing the import tax, by adding to the relevant section: "In determining board measure for purposes of this paragraph no deduction shall be made on account of planing, tonguing and grooving." This provision was to become effective, "1) on the sixtieth day after enactment, unless it is in conflict with any international obligation of the United States; 2) if so in conflict then on the termination of such obligation otherwise than in connection with the undertaking by the United States of a new obligation that continues such a conflict."[135] In drawing this amendment to the attention of collectors, the Treasury announced that, after careful consideration of the Canadian and Cuban agreements, it saw no conflict between them and the new provision and, therefore, considered it applicable as from July 27, 1938.[136]

[130]T.D. 47621.   [131]T.D. 48036.   [132]T.D. 48470.   [133]T.D. 48161.
[134]T.D. 48701.   [135]U.S. Revenue Act, 1938, s. 704.   [136]T.D. 49662.

On October 31, 1940, the Customs Court upset this contention of the Treasury.[137] The plaintiff had imported planed lumber on August 1, 1938. Both the duty at 50¢ per M and excise import tax at $1.50 per M were assessed on the gross number of board feet, admittedly 2,564,098; and not on the net, admittedly 1,900,399. The rate of duty was not contested, but application was made for a refund of the tax on the difference between the net and the gross board measurements. The Court pointed out that the Canadian Trade Agreement was signed on November 15, 1935, eighteen days after the first Myers' decision; that the American negotiating party, therefore, must have been aware of the current state of the law on the matter; hence, since the agreement specified that only taxes and duties in force at the time of the signing shall be levied, and since Congress showed that it did not intend to abrogate the agreement, the gross footage provision was ineffective and the taxes were to be refunded.[138] The Treasury changed its ruling on this matter to conform with the Court's decision and, in a Treasury decision dated March 28, 1941, declared as well that the conflict was continued by the 1938 Trade Agreement with Canada. Therefore, shipments of lumber, planed, grooved, or tongued, entered or withdrawn on or after January 1, 1941, were to be subject to the import tax according to the net quantity imported.

The General Agreement reduced the import charges on certain lumber items but provided that lumber, planed, tongued and grooved, and so forth, was to be assessed for import tax according to gross and not the net measurements;[139] on this occasion, Canadian exporters complained that United States port colletcors seemed to be aware of the unfavourable change in regulations concerning measurement before they were aware of the favourable change in rate of duty. This impression may well have arisen from the admirable practice of the Treasury of giving notice in advance of a change in a well-established practice.

In this series of cases, the importers of tongued and grooved lumber, by appeal to the courts, were eventually able to obtain more favourable treatment than the Treasury decision had prescribed. Final decision required about five years in the earlier case; and two years in the later one. However, in addition, a domestic lumber company was able to delay liquidation of entries of lumber siding for some two years.

Whatever the reasons, it is apparent that even elaborate provision

[137]*Seaboard Lumber Sales Co. Ltd.* v. *United States*, 5 U.S.C.C. 161, C.D. 391.
[138]The Court reaffirmed this decision in *M. V. Jenkins* v. *United States*, U.S.C.C. Abs. no. 44656 of Oct. 31, 1940.   [139]G.A.T.T., Schedule XX, Part I, item 3424.

for appeal to independent tribunals is not sufficient to secure prompt and just treatment for the importer if the statute, as interpreted by the courts, prescribes difficult administrative procedures and clumsy definitions. Indeed, if domestic competitors are provided with avenues of appeal as good as, or better than, those granted the two parties directly concerned in the payment and receipt of duty, it is no longer clear whether the appeal facilities are the more effective in protecting the importer from arbitrary administrative action or in subjecting him to the persecution of competing domestic interests. The prospect that the amount of duty payable on an article not formerly imported will not be known for several, perhaps for many, years is a substantial deterrent to attempts to develop exports to the United States. The importer must refuse to import, or narrow his market by charging a price based on an estimate of the worst treatment possible, or take the risk of heavy losses.

The choice between arbitrary speed and ultimate justice is a difficult one. Other things equal, the more strenuous the attempt to lessen administrative discretion by prescribing in the statute the details of administrative procedure, the more numerous are the possible grounds for appeal; and the more frequent the appeals the less probable it becomes that the administration will be able to state quickly and finally the treatment that will be accorded any article; or to make dependable declaratory rulings. If the statute is less detailed, more scope is left to administrative discretion; resort to the courts is more and more restricted and surprises may arise from arbitrary changes in administrative interpretation. How far should immediate certainty be sacrificed to ultimate justice?

For the United States, the Attorney General's Committee issued a general warning as to the limitations of control by judicial review:

Yet judicial review is rarely available . . . to compel effective enforcement of the law by the administration. . . . the courts cannot, as a practical matter, be effectively used for that purpose without being assimilated into the administrative structure and losing their independent organization. To assure enforcement of the laws by administrative agencies within the bound of their authority, reliance must be placed on controls other than judicial review—internal controls in the agency, responsibility to the legislature or executive, careful selection of personnel, pressure from interested parties, and professional or lay criticism of the agency's work.[140]

---

[140]A.G. Com., *Final Report* (1941), p. 76. The passage quoted is not specifically related to customs administration; but see p. 183: "In respect of the activities of the Customs Bureau, the committee's recommendations in Chapter III relating to informal methods of adjudication and in Chapter VII relating to rule making are applicable. Special attention is called to the Committee's recommendations in Part C, Chapter 5 relating to declaratory rulings."

The seriousness of the dilemma and the appropriate methods of solution may be different in different countries. In countries where a system of parliamentary government works moderately well, satisfactory results may be obtained, perhaps, with less detailed statutes and less frequent appeals. Appeal should be permitted, of course, on purely administrative and legal questions to a tribunal independent of the officials who must administer the regulations and collect the duty; but proceedings should be speedy and the decision final—even if sometimes not perfectly just.[141] Recent proposals and agreements for reforming customs practices have stressed the importance of making adequate provision for appeal to tribunals independent of the enforcing agency.[142] It is to be hoped that the current emphasis on appeal as a "means" will not obscure the "end," which must surely be to ensure reasonably prompt and equitable determination of the amounts of duty chargeable on imports.

In the United States, limiting the time allowed for appraisal and liquidation of entry might decrease delays; but it might result in more severe decisions, and a higher proportion of protests and appeals. It is not clear that similar difficulties would result in Canada from limiting the time during which the importer can be required (unless fraud can be proven) to file an amended entry.

In the United States, a great deal of uncertainty could be removed by denying competing domestic interests the right to bring an appeal from the decision of the administration to the Customs Court. If this were done, the customs administration would be able in most cases to state for the importer a rate of duty and a basis of valuation for any imported article even before the shipment arrived, or on the basis of a sample shipment. It would be legally possible, too, for it to continue this treatment a reasonably longer time after publishing notice of a change.[143] It would appear, however, that simplifying customs tariffs and customs administrative requirements might also do much to lessen the number of disputes and delays arising from them. Proposals for improvements in classification and in valuation are discussed in the next three chapters. Other administrative practices also from time to time have afforded intentional or unintentional protection: these are considered in chapter VIII.

[141]On the whole difficult problem see Dawson, *The Government of Canada,* chap. XIV.

[142]G.A.T.T., art. x, ss. 1(b) and 1(c), and Havana Charter, art. 38, ss. 3 (b) and 3 (c).

[143]Now thirty days after final decision on protest by a domestic producer.

V

CLASSIFICATION

> I found that, however simple the plan on which a protective
> policy started, it was drawn on irresistibly to become intricate,
> and to lend its chief aid to those industries that were already
> strong enough to do without it.
>
> ALFRED MARSHALL

1. NUMBER AND OCCASIONS OF CLASSIFICATION DISPUTES

CLASSIFICATION must give rise to some problems even when a
tariff is quite simple; and the number of problems, the extent of the
uncertainties, and the delays and costs which result from them, can
be increased almost without limit by increasing the complexity of the
tariff structure or the ambiguity of the items, whether by accident,
ineptitude, or design. In fact, as has been noted above, both Canada
and the United States have complicated tariffs. To some extent the
wording of the tariffs has been designed to attract imported articles
into items or paragraphs that impose a high rate; to some extent as
well, especially in the United States, domestic producers have used
their right (limited between 1934 and 1951) to harass the importers
with litigation or the threat of litigation concerning the classification
of competing imports.

No exact measure is available of the number of surprises occasioned
by customs classification, still less of the total burden borne by importers and consumers or by exporters and producers, or of the amount
of trade prevented by the costs and difficulties of classifying imports
and by the possibility that they may be classified so as to subject them
to an unexpectedly high rate of duty. A consideration of the number
of appeals to judicial or quasi-judicial bodies, however, suggests that
the effects are not negligible. The number of classification appeals
filed in the United States in certain years is shown in Table 9. During
the three years 1949 to 1951 inclusive, on the average, 4,278,000
import entries were filed per year in the United States. During the
same period the number of classification protests per year filed with

the United States Customs Court averaged 11,238, nearly three protests of classification per thousand entries. In addition, on the average, 1,426 formal protests per year were allowed by collectors of customs.

TABLE 9

CLASSIFICATION CASES, U.S. CUSTOMS COURT[a]

Fiscal year	Cases pending beginning of year 1	Cases filed during year 2	Cases disposed of during year 3	Cases pending close of year 4	Ratio col. 1 to col. 3.[b] 5
1932–34 (Average)[b]	226,714	66,959	77,759	215,915	2.9
1938–40 (Average)[b]	202,482	43,837	56,574	189,745	3.6
1947	105,433	6,627	15,293	96,767	
1949	81,962	10,020	15,777	82,992	
1950	76,205	12,971	12,421	75,109	6.6
1951	76,755	10,722	12,368	76,775	
1952	75,109	14,205	6,322	76,205	
1953	82,992	20,723	10,212	93,503	8.1

[a]U.S. Attorney General, *Annual Report*, 1932–40, and Administrative Office of U.S. Courts, *Annual Report of the Director*, 1947–53.
[b]Computed from data given in above sources.

An indication of the time required to secure a decision in classification cases filed with the Customs Court is given by the "turnover" of cases on hand for decision. On the average, during the years 1949 to 1952, for example, the number of cases pending at the beginning of the year has been between six and seven times the number of cases disposed of during the year. This is considerably higher than the pre-war ratio. However, on the average, fewer protests of classification have been filed on post-war years.

In Canada, during the period 1949 to 1952 inclusive, 2,624,000 import entries were filed on the average each year, while from April 1, 1949, to June 24, 1953, only 96 appeals were registered with the Tariff Board on matters of classification, including appeals from "made in Canada" rulings. Of the total of 136 appeals filed with the Board during this period (including all classes of customs appeals and also appeals concerning excise tax and sales tax) only seven decisions were pending as of June 24, 1953. The insignificant number of appeals to the Tariff Board in Canada, however, is not comparable with the number of protests filed with the Customs Court in the United States. In Canada, a very large number of disputes are settled informally on appeal to the Deputy Minister of National Revenue. In Canada, too, refunds can be secured on disputed entries on the basis of a favourable decision of the issue by the Tariff Board provided that a protest in writing has been filed with the Department (not the Board) within the prescribed period; such protests are not recorded as cases pending before or decided by the Board. In the United States, on the other hand, nearly all protests are filed with the Court and each protested entry is counted as a case even though a single judicial decision may decide a large number of protests which have been consolidated for trial or are disposed of perfunctorily following a decision in a test case.

Given the tariff structure, classification difficulties seem to arise most frequently when new commodities enter international trade, or are produced by new methods; when items or rates of duty have been changed by tariff revision or trade agreements; and when trade takes a new direction and commodities enter different ports in large quantities, in competition with domestic producers. They may increase also when domestic producers are permitted to lodge protests or even when additions occur to the ranks of customs lawyers; or when changes are made in the upper levels of customs administration. They seem to occur most frequently in certain sensitive sectors of the trade, where the advantages of domestic and foreign producers are almost evenly balanced, having regard to the duty; or where a domestic industry or trade association is coming into existence or struggling against extinction.

In what follows, the disputes, delays, and obstacles to trade arising from classification procedures are illustrated principally from the experience of importers into Canada but also, in certain cases, into the United States. They are selected primarily to illustrate the sorts of difficulty encountered by Canadian importers; indeed, mention is made of nearly all the classification appeals to the Canadian Tariff Board since it was reconstituted. This emphasis has been influenced by the fact that the classification problems of importing into the United States have been more widely recognized, and much more thoroughly discussed in published works. As noticed above, classification disputes are many times more frequent in the United States; and examples are recounted here, in part to serve as a bench-mark with which to compare Canadian procedures and in part to illustrate the classification difficulties encountered by Canadian exporters to the United States. An attempt has been made to organize the Canadian examples so as to illustrate the kinds of items and the economic considerations that occasion difficulties rather than the legal principles involved in the judicial decisions. It will appear that certain types of difficulty exist under both tariffs, that some are relatively more common under Canadian procedures, others under those of the United States.

In Canada the customary avenues of appeal usually yield relatively speedy determination of disputes. To emphasize this fact the time elapsed between entry and final settlement is given in brackets where readily available; and it is readily available in almost every recent case appealed to the Tariff Board of Canada.

2. COUNTRY OF ORIGIN: POINT OF PRODUCTION

Though the United States no longer has a simple unilinear tariff it appears that some of the kinds of protection afforded by Canada's three-column tariff have no exact equivalents there. The requirement, that to be accorded the more favourable rates the goods must be shipped direct from the British or Most-Favoured-Nation country of origin, for example, gives special protection to Canadian ocean ports and transportation facilities; the United States protects her shipping by other methods which, though important, are not considered in this study.

An extension of the concept of "British content" has been used in a few items of the Canadian tariff to give additional incentives to Canadian (and British) manufacturers to use Canadian (and British) products and to develop Canadian processing. Item 438c, for example, provides for the entry of certain parts for use in the manufacture or repair of motor vehicles (and certain other goods) free of duty under the Preferential Tariff and at the rate of $17\frac{1}{2}$ per cent under the Most-Favoured-Nation Tariff. However, free entry is provided under the Most-Favoured-Nation Tariff as well for such of them as are not made in Canada, when used as original equipment by a manufacturer of passenger automobiles, provided a specified proportion of his cost is incurred in the British Commonwealth; the required British content varies from 40 to 60 per cent depending on the output of the importer. Different percentages and outputs are prescribed for the parts when used as final equipment for trucks and certain other vehicles. Paradoxically, a reduction of duties of this kind increases the incentive of the manufacturer to make sure that a sufficient proportion of his manufacturing is done in Canada.[1]

Finally procedural difficulties and disputes have arisen concerning the meaning of phrases designed to encourage direct shipment from point of production to Canada without intermediate processing. Since 1906, tariff item 137 has permitted free entry of certain kinds of molasses, under the British Preferential Tariff, "when imported direct by ship from the country of production, or from any British country, *in the original package in which it was placed at the point of production, and not afterward subjected to any process of treating or mixing.*" In 1948 a shipment of molasses from the British West Indies was entered under this item; but a Canadian molasses company objected to the classification on the grounds that, before being put in cans, the molasses had been transported in wooden puncheons from the particular farm, plantation, or storage at which it had been produced. In dismissing the appeal and confirming free entry the Tariff Board held that "the requirement of this item is met if 'point of production' be read as meaning 'country of origin' and that the tins constituted the 'original package.'" (Dismissed; nine months.)[2]

Under a complex customs tariff a single importation frequently gives rise to several sorts of problems. The Canadian case of the cotton-embroidered linen pillow cases, for example, involved problems relating both to country of origin and to composition of the article. In October 1932, after the conclusion of the Ottawa agreements, "articles wholly of flax or hemp such as sheets, pillow cases, table cloths and napkins . . ." were admitted free under the Preferential Tariff, but item 548 prescribed a Preferential rate of 25 per cent for articles "composed wholly or in part of vegetable fibres but not containing wool not otherwise provided for." At the same time, under the Intermediate Tariff, the articles in question, when wholly of linen, were

---

[1]This procedure was devised in the 1930's on the occasion of a reference to the Tariff Board regarding the motor industry. See evidence of W. J. Callaghan, Commissioner of Tariffs, Can., Banking & Commerce, *Torquay*, pp. 171–2. I have not discovered many items that provide for entry, free or at reduced rates, based on the proportion of factory costs of a foreign producer incurred in the purchase of British, including Canadian, products though there seems to be no reason, except fear of retaliation or difficulty of administration, why Canadian products might not, in this way, be given protection in a foreign market; see, however, item 280b which provides temporarily free entry for certain hydrogenated oils produced from fish, seal, or whale oil, or tallow wholly of Canadian origin.

[2]A–132, T.B.C. 182.

dutiable under item 540b at 30 per cent plus 3½ cents per pound; while articles composed of cotton and linen were dutiable under the mixed fibre class at the lower rate of 30 per cent plus 1½ cents per pound.[3] Canada imported cotton-embroidered linenware both from British and from non-British countries. Naturally importers wanted to enter the British embroidered linenware free as composed wholly of linen and the non-British articles under item 548 as articles of cotton and linen. However, importers of linen pillow cases, embroidered with cotton, found that their imports were classified under item 540b, when imported from countries entitled to the Intermediate rate, on the grounds that the value of the cotton embroidery was negligible. In September 1933 the Tariff Board issued a ruling, to come into effect a month later, that cotton-embroidered linenware was not entitled to enter under item 540b. This would have denied free entry to the British articles; however, it was provided, by an order in council to come into effect on the same date as the ruling of the Tariff Board, that embroidering the articles mentioned in item 540b with cotton would not deprive them of free entry under the British Preferential Tariff if the embroidering was done in a country enjoying the benefits of the tariff.[4] (Later similar provision was made to allow free entry to handkerchiefs even though their borders were corded with cotton.)[5] Meanwhile customs officials continued to classify cotton-embroidered linen pillow cases subject to the Intermediate Tariff under item 540b, presumably either because they interpreted the order in council as indicating the interpretation of the item for goods subject to the Intermediate Tariff as well as those entitled to the Preferential, or because they wished to prevent importers from circumventing the duties by a change which could be made easily and inexpensively.

In January 1948, in conformity with the Geneva agreements, the rates on both items were reduced, but the Intermediate rate on the pure linen item was reduced below that on the vegetable fibre item.[6] Cotton-embroidered linen pillow cases began to be classified as textile articles of vegetable fibres, presumably because there was now no reason to suppose that cotton embroidery would be applied merely to attract the higher rate. When importers objected to this change in practice they were advised, if they wished, to appeal for refunds of

[3]Changed to 30 per cent Jan. 1, 1939, under the second Canada–United States trade agreement and later reduced further; see note 6 below.

[4]Can. Customs Tariff, item 812.   [5]Sept. 1, 1937, tariff item 813.

[6]For certain price ranges at least. The intermediate rate in 548 was reduced to 25 per cent, and in 540b to 20 per cent plus 3¢ a lb.

the higher duties incurred by the former practice. However, imports of cotton-embroidered linenware from non-British countries had not been large in the three preceding years for which applications for refund might have been made and the importers preferred to take the position that the embroidered linenware should continue to be classed under item 548. In February 1949 provision was made for admission of linenware free of duty under the Preferential rate in item 540b even though embroidered or hemmed or hemstitched with cotton threads in a country enjoying the benefits of the Most-Favoured-Nation Tariff.[7] In May 1950 the Most-Favoured-Nation rate on pillow cases, table-cloths, and certain other articles under item 548 was further reduced so that presumably on these articles there is now little difference in rates prescribed by the two items.

Procedural problems concerning country of origin have long been recognized, whether they arise from differential rates of duty, or from valuation or marking regulations. If procedural protection is to be avoided the procedures prescribed should not, in the first place, increase the obstacles to international division of labour imposed by the differential rates themselves; nor, in the second place, divert shipment from the cheapest or most advantageous route.[8]

Regulations requiring direct shipment, it is clear, contravene the second of these principles. The Havana Charter and the General Agreement both prohibited the introduction of new regulations that discriminated against goods which passed through third contracting countries, as compared with those which did not; but neither required modification of existing regulations.[9] The implications of the first of the principles stated above are not equally clear. Basing its recommendations on the 1930 proposals of the Economic Committee of the League of Nations, the International Chamber of Commerce has recommended that "when the manufacturing process has taken place in more than one country, the country of origin should be the country in which the last manufacturing process has taken place, provided that the process is economically justified and important. An 'important' manufacturing process should be one which effects a substantial change in the nature of the product."[10] It was recommended that un-

---

[7]Can. Customs Tariff, item 812b.

[8]See Hawkins, *Commercial Treaties and Agreements*, p. 51.

[9]Havana Charter, art. 33, s. 7; and G.A.T.T., art. 5, s. 6. For changes in the Canadian definitions of direct shipment for purposes of valuation see chap. VI.

[10]League of Nations, Economic Committee, *Report to the Council of the Work of the 35th Session*, p. 12. International Chamber of Commerce, *Resolutions*

loading and reloading, unpacking and repacking and cleaning should not affect the origin of the goods whether or not carried out under customs supervision.

3. RIGIDITY OF CLASSIFICATION: TREATMENT OF NEW COMMODITIES

A complex tariff structure would produce classification problems even if international trade were completely static. In fact, of course, the content of international trade changes continually; new articles keep entering into trade, and old articles are being changed in ways that cannot be predicted. Even if tariff structures were simple the classifying of such articles would now and then occasion uncertainty, costs, and disputes. The governmental organization of the United States hinders frequent and piecemeal adjustment of the tariff items, though the Trade Agreements Act permits specialization through negotiation. Canadian practice is more flexible; from time to time new items have been introduced and old items revised. However, in both countries it has been necessary to adopt certain general principles of interpretation. These often have the effect of solving disputes by applying the higher rate.

Each of the tariffs is inclusive: it purports to prescribe a rate of duty (or free entry) for every permissible import. Each contains a general basket item for non-enumerated articles; articles, that is to say, which can not be included in any other item. The use of this general basket item is limited by provisions prescribing the methods to be used in fitting articles into the other classes. These provisions have been amplified, especially in the United States, by departmental and judicial rulings. Unless otherwise provided, an article is classified under that item which refers to it most specifically. If it is actually named in a particular paragraph, for example, it is dutiable at the rate prescribed by that paragraph; if not, it is dutiable under an item which describes it in preference to the general basket item. In Canada it has been decided that a class relating to goods n.o.p. "of a class or kind not made in Canada" is more specific than a corresponding basket item not so restricted.

The United States Tariff provides that a non-enumerated article composed of two or more materials is dutiable at the rate at which it would be chargeable if composed wholly of the component material of chief value. Since the rate prescribed for non-enumerated items is,

---

Adopted by the 9th Congress, p. 6. Also I.C.C., *Invisible Trade Barriers,* p. 9. Quoted in Hawkins, *Commercial Treaties,* p. 51.

for the United States, relatively low this provision often results in the application of a rate higher than that prescribed by the general non-enumerated item. The United States Tariff includes also a provision for classifying an article by "similitude." Any non-enumerated article which is similar to any enumerated article, "either in material, quality, texture, or the use to which it may be applied," is to be dutiable at the same rate as "the article which it most resembles in any of the particulars before mentioned." If it is equally similar to more than one enumerated article dutiable at different rates, it is to be charged the highest of these rates.[11] So strictly has the similitude rule been applied that nylon yarn was at one time classed as similar to wool if there was a crimp or crimple in it and as similar to silk if there was not.[12] It is clear then that the similitude rule may be interpreted to make the rate of duty depend on characteristics of an imported article which would not ordinarily be mentioned in an invoice or even in a catalogue. Until 1950 the Canadian Customs Act contained a provision concerning similitude though it made no reference to similarity of texture.[13] The Act still provides that if an article is "enumerated in the tariff under two or more names or descriptions and there is a difference of duty, the highest duty provided" is to be collected.[14]

4. CLASSIFICATION AND TRADE AGREEMENTS

On the whole, classification anomalies are more enduring under the United States procedures. The flexibility introduced by the Trade Agreements Act extends only, within the prescribed limits, to rates and not to classification. Indeed, one of the provisions of the General

[11]U.S. Tariff, par. 1559. This higher rate rule is seldom if ever used.

[12]See statement by Harry S. Radcliffe, on behalf of National Importers' Association, U.S. House, *On H.R. 1535*, p. 272. On protest, the Customs Court held that the resemblances were superficial and that spun nylon yarn was to be classed under par. 1303 as "Spun yarn of rayon or other synthetic textile," dutiable at 6¼¢ per lb. and 22½ per cent *ad valorem. Holeproof Hosiery Co. v. United States*, 27 U.S.C.C. 176, C.D. 1366, Oct. 23, 1951. By emphasizing the use of "means" instead of "shall mean" the Court was able to conclude that the enumeration of synthetic textiles given in par. 1303 was intended to include only the synthetics known in 1930, and was not intended to exclude other synthetics developed later.

[13]Customs Act, ss. 58, 59; both repealed, 1950, c. 13, s. 4. For a Tariff Board decision turning on these sections see A–202, T.B.C. 236, July 3, 1951. A mixture of cottonseed oil and hydrogenated soya bean oil was held to be similar to and dutiable as, cottonseed oil n.o.p. at 17½ per cent, m.f.n., rather than as a non-enumerated article at 20 per cent (allowed; two years, seven months).

[14]Customs Tariff Act, s. 50. It has seldom been necessary to make use of this rule or the similar rule in the U.S. Tariff Act.

Agreement for escape and adjustment seems specially designed to fit the legislative inflexibility of the United States Tariff and the dangers of unexpected changes by judicial interpretation. Article 11, section 5, provides, in part, for prompt negotiation with a view to compensatory adjustment if one contracting party considers that a product is not receiving from another the treatment contemplated by a concession in the agreement, and if the other contracting party agrees that this is so "but declares that such treatment cannot be accorded because a court or other proper authority has ruled to the effect that the product involved cannot be classified under [its] tariff laws . . . so as to permit the treatment contemplated."

Difficulties of this kind may be illustrated from the experience of Canadian exporters. Under an early trade agreement with Canada the duty on "tennis racket frames, valued at $1.75 or more each, . . . wholly or in chief value of wood" was reduced from 40 per cent to 20 per cent.[15] Subsequently a shipment of racket frames imported from Canada was classified as articles not specially provided for, wholly or partly manufactured of rattan, bamboo, osier, or willow under paragraph 409, dutiable at 45 per cent. The Customs Court decided that the frames in question would have been classified under paragraph 409 prior to the agreement; and that since the President had no power to change the classification of an item, or reduce the duty by more than 50 per cent, the item in paragraph 412 on which duty was reduced to 20 per cent could not have included tennis rackets of the type in question![16]

As was noted in chapter II, the United States has subdivided her tariff items to achieve bargaining results substantially similar to those achieved through discriminating between countries. This process has made it necessary to distinguish between imported articles which are almost identical; and most trade agreements have been followed by a burst of protests and litigation. Specialization has also permitted the United States to restrict her concessions very narrowly. The minute subdivisions introduced into the paragraphs relating to hops and ply-wood are examples of the many instances in which this process has affected producers in Canada and in other countries as well.

5. CONTAINERS AND PACKAGING

In Canada usual coverings, containers, and packaging are not dutiable if the contents enter free or subject only to a specific duty.

[15]Reported in T.D. 49752.

[16]*Chamberlain Importing Co.* (*Los Angeles*) v. *United States*, (1944) 13 U.S.C.C. 323.

Unless they are separately shown and valued in the invoice they are subject to the same *ad valorem* rate of duty as the contents. If they are separately shown and charged on the invoice, item 710(b) provides for entry free of duty under the British Preferential Tariff and at rates of 7½ per cent and 20 per cent under the Most-Favoured-Nation Tariff and the General Tariff respectively. In 1954, after an importer's successful appeal to the Tariff Board, this item was amended to exclude usual containers not customarily charged separately in the home market, thus explicitly confirming a practice followed by the Department of National Revenue during much of the period since 1908. Unless the relevant tariff item directs otherwise, however, containers capable of holding liquids used to contain imports dutiable at a specific rate are dutiable as though imported separately, as are unusual containers. In the United States, usual containers are included in the value of the contents and subjected to the same rate of duty *ad valorem*. Unusual containers are subject, in addition, to the rate which would be applied if they were imported empty; they are, therefore, dutiable twice over. In some paragraphs of the United States Tariff the classification and rate of duty depend on the value of the commodity and in these cases the cost of the containers may also affect the rate of duty. However, it has been decided that the cost of containers entitled to free entry as United States products returned or subject to a separate rate of duty (not including unusual containers) is excluded in determining a rate of duty dependent on value.[17]

6. SIMPLE OVERLAPPING AND AMBIGUITY

Many classification disputes or uncertainties result from simple overlapping: from overlapping meanings of ordinary terms, from overlapping uses of articles, or from the fact that the basis of classification varies as between different classes. Is an ash-tray, combined with a music box, an ash-tray or a music box or neither? Doubtless some will be tempted to decide that the producer and importer of such a monstrosity deserve that it be classified in that basket item which bears the highest of all rates in the tariff. However, this example illustrates the difficulty of foreseeing and certainly providing for oddities or innovations. In fact one of the most pervasive and important effects of tariff procedures is that they impose special costs on innovators and innovations, not only with respect to the type of article but with

[17]T.D. 48025; T.D. 22462; T.D. 22490; C.D. 1235. See also *Maynard and Child Inc.* v. *United States*, (1950) 24 U.S.C.C. 215.

respect also to methods of production and channels of trade. This effect occurs even when procedures and delays are not specially designed to produce it.

A number of such "simple" classification disputes are bound to occur. Those listed below illustrate the need for clarity in such matters; the difficulty of securing it, if the tariff structure is complex; and the need (and difficulty) of providing means by which an importer can secure a binding declaration as to classification before the article is imported. Though many of the examples have been drawn from the reports of the Tariff Board of Canada, these "simple" cases are even more numerous in the United States. Where reported, the time which elapsed between entry of the goods and settlement of the dispute is indicated in brackets. It will be apparent that the Canadian decisions have usually been reached in a matter of weeks or months; in the United States decisions have often taken years, sometimes more than a decade.

Some Canadian importers, brokers, and port officials seem for a period to have been uncertain with respect to the classification of jugs and teapots. The item which admits china and other tableware free under the Preferential rate excludes teapots, jugs, and similar articles "of the type commonly known as earthenware." At some ports it was the custom to enter the higher priced teapots free and to call the cheaper ones earthenware, while at other ports all or nearly all teapots were considered dutiable. Similarly, at one time, china and semi-porcelain mugs and jugs were allowed to enter as tableware not subject to duty; however, when certain ornamental mugs and jugs began to be imported from England and elsewhere they were admitted free at some ports and charged duty at others. When the discrepancy was brought to the attention of Ottawa officials all ornamental mugs and jugs were made dutiable and the customs memorandum concerning such articles was revised.[18] Character and Toby semi-porcelain jugs then began to be classed under the dutiable item (288). On appeal, the Tariff Board declared them to be entitled to free entry except those with a capacity less than one fluid ounce (five weeks).[19]

Are trays kitchen hollow-ware? Or are they articles of iron or aluminum? "For ten years before 1947 aluminum trays were classified as manufactures of 'aluminum' and steel trays as 'manufactures of steel.'" In November 1947 they were ruled to be "hollow-ware," as

[18]Can., D.N.R., *Customs Memo.*, Series D, no. 50; T.D. & R. 27, rev. Jan. 28, 1950.   [19]A–159, T.B.C. 209, March 27, 1950.

being capable of holding a liquid. When some manufacturers produced aluminum trays with open ends these were ruled to be "manufactures of aluminum." On June 9, 1949, the Board ruled on an appeal[20] from a decision of the Department of National Revenue "that certain dust-pans, step-on or refuse cans, trays, cake covers and trays, and match safes" were manufactures of steel dutiable at 25 per cent under the Most-Favoured-Nation Tariff rather than hollow-ware of steel dutiable at 20 per cent. After commenting on the difficulty of applying a term such as hollow-ware which has had a vague and changing meaning the Board held that "in cases of serious uncertainty as to the correct classification the benefit ought to be given to the importer," and ruled that four of the five articles, including trays, were hollow-ware. As a consequence the Department of National Revenue declared trays in general to be hollow-ware. Now it happened that, whereas the Most-Favoured-Nation rate on steel manufactures was higher than the rate on steel hollow-ware, the Preferential rate on aluminum hollow-ware was higher than the Preferential rate on manufactures of aluminum, and an appeal was carried to the Board from a ruling of the Department that certain aluminum trays were hollow-ware. Here the Board was faced with a dilemma that lurks in all complex tariffs based on multiple criteria. If it adhered to its decision to give the benefit of "serious uncertainty" to the importer, it would be forced to declare that while iron trays were hollow-ware, aluminum trays were not; and incidentally that the Department of National Revenue had been mistaken in supposing that all trays, whether of iron or aluminum, either were hollow-ware or were not hollow-ware. In the event, the Board dismissed the appeal on the aluminum trays but appended a final paragraph: "Impressed by the necessity for a revision of the tariff items relating to 'Hollow-ware', the Board desires to draw the attention of the Minister of Finance to this case, aware though it is of the difficulty attaching to such revision because of the fact that some of the tariff items involved are included in schedules to Trade Agreements" (eleven months).[21] Administratively this problem arose from an ambiguous word, but a more fundamental source of difficulty was the complex tariff structure which reflected unresolved conflicts between different purposes and interests. Before a dictionary of tariff terms can be generally accepted for tariff purposes such differences must be resolved.

Lest it be supposed that the Canadian Tariff is peculiarly ambiguous or schizophrenic it should be noted that in the Tariff of the United

[20]A–133, T.B.C. 179. [21]A–142, T.B.C. 194.

States the term hollow-ware is used; and there are a dozen different hollow-ware items distinguished on the basis of material content and attracting different rates of duty (ranging in 1953 from 7½ per cent to 65 per cent, neglecting the specific elements in the compound rates);[22] and the relationship between the duty on hollow-ware of a particular metal and that on articles of the same metal may change with changes in relative prices of the different metals.[23]

Buttons and fasteners may be ornamental as well as useful. Formerly in Canada difficulties were encountered in knowing when buttons became so elaborate as to be classed as ornaments which attracted a higher rate of duty. More recently an appeal to the Tariff Board was allowed from a decision that a particular type of pearl snap fasteners was jewelry. (Time elapsed from entry to declaration, four months.)[24] Apparently, then, in Canada, it has been easier at times to gain support for high import duties on items whose wording suggests ornaments, jewelry, toys, or other fripperies than on items whose wording suggests staid usefulness. In the United States such items seem to have been worded intentionally so that they apply much more widely than superficially they appear to do. Some of these items have become notorious, for example those relating to toys, and to embroideries, fringes, and articles wholly or in part thereof.

In certain items of the Canadian Tariff the term "separation" is considered to have a narrow rather than a broad meaning. Screens used for the sifting and grading of sand and gravel were declared dutiable as "machinery of a class or kind made in Canada" and not as "machinery for the concentration or separation of ores metals and minerals." Though screening is "separation" in a literal sense the Board considered that "in the process of recovering minerals of value the word 'separation' . . . refers to the division of minerals into various constituents primarily on the basis of composition and value rather than size."[25]

In Canada, agricultural implements and machinery are admitted free of duty, and the Tariff Board has been called upon to distinguish implements and machinery from other forms of apparatus "such as silos or milking stalls." Recently it has allowed appeals to admit certain cattle stocks (four months), calf chutes (ten months), cattle squeezes and livestock oilers[26] (nine months) as agricultural machinery or agricultural implements n.o.p.

[22]U.S. Tariff, par. 339.   [23]See U.S. Tariff Act, pars. 310, 311, 339, 397.
[24]A–229, T.B.C. 258.   [25]A–183, T.B.C. 229, Feb. 6, 1951.
[26]A–253, T.B.C. 274, 275, 276, and 281, allowed.

Frequently appeals with respect to "simple" ambiguities are related to more complicated problems as well. Recently importers have been testing out the breadth of the classes relating to "vehicles" following a decision of the Tariff Board concerning rubber tires, originally entered as parts of "an excavating and transporting scraper" under item 422a at 10 per cent, which the Department sought to classify as "rubber tires for vehicles . . . fitted or not" (named in item 618b and dutiable at 25 per cent). In the course of several hearings the Department produced evidence that the tires were advertised, sold, and used as general purpose vehicle tires but it also argued further (presumably because they were imported fitted to a scraper) that the scraper itself was a vehicle as defined in the Customs Act; and that this definition contained in the Customs Act was applicable to the Tariff Act unless inconsistent with the context. It was argued that, formerly, this broad definition of vehicle in the Customs Act (and the corresponding definition of vessel) had been supposed to apply to the conveyance used in transporting imported merchandise into Canada. The Board upheld the ruling of the Department that the tires were dutiable separately as rubber vehicle tires. At the same time it expressed the belief that the persistence of this wide definition in the Customs Act would modify the scope of a great many items of the tariff (twelve months, dismissed).[27] A number of appeals followed. The Board declared, for example, that a road grader is not a vehicle (three months),[28] nor is a portable belt conveyor (thirteen months)[29] nor a power shovel (eighteen months).[30]

Though the declarations of the Board on these subsequent appeals were not published until several months after the articles to which they relate were entered, it is not to be supposed that the articles were imported in the expectation that they would be classed as vehicles and accorded the corresponding rates of duty. All three of these subsequent appeals relate to articles entered prior to September 1951 while the declaration of the Board in the original "vehicle" case was not made until January 9, 1952,[31] and the third hearing at which the

[27]A–221, T.B.C. 247, dismissed. [28]A–236, T.B.C. 264, dismissed.
[29]A–242, T.B.C. 268, dismissed. [30]A–242, T.B.C. 269, dismissed.
[31]These vehicles appeals include:

Declaration no.	Ap. no.	Date of declaration	Date of entry
A–221	247	Jan. 9, '52	Jan. 4, '51
			Jan. 6, '51
A–236	264	June 3, '52	March 5, '51
A–242	268	Sept. 16, '52	Aug. 8, '51
A–242	269	Sept. 16, '52	Feb. 10, '51

Department presented arguments concerning vehicles occurred on December 17, 1951. In 1952, item 618b of the Tariff Act was rewritten to omit reference to vehicles and prescribe free entry for tires wholly or in part of rubber, if for replacement on agricultual implements; otehwise they are dutiable at 20 per cent, 22½ per cent, and 35 per cent.

Canadian legislative flexibility with respect to the tariff items is illustrated by the treatment of overhead carrier systems. In January 1952 the Tariff Board declared that painted iron rails for an overhead carriage system were not "railway rails of iron or steel," dutiable under item 387 at $5.00, $7.00, or $8.00 per ton, as the importer contended; nor manufactures' articles or wares of iron or steel, as the Deputy Minister of National Revenue had decided, dutiable under item 446a; but that they were iron or steel sections, further manufactured than hot rolled or cast, dutiable under item 388d at 20 per cent, 30 per cent, or 40 per cent.[32] However, the Customs Tariff Amendments of 1952 included an item "388 g. Rails (tracks) of iron or steel, other than railway rails, further manufactured than hot rolled . . . free, 12½ per cent, 35 per cent."

A number of other Canadian disputes which involved relatively simple interpretation of language may be mentioned. The Tariff Board dismissed an appeal against a ruling that classed certain soap flakes as common or laundry soap (and not toilet soap) on the grounds that "the products in condition as imported are sold as laundry soaps, advertised as laundry soap and used as laundry soaps and therefore are, in fact laundry soap" (three and a half months).[33] Soya bean meal though compressed in pellets is still soya bean meal (eleven and a half months).[34] A telechron timer is a clock movement and not part of a wireless radio apparatus (two years, three months).[35] Aneroid altimeters, though calibrated in feet and inches, were declared admissible as "aneroid barometers, engineering," rather than as "philosophical . . . photographic, mathematical and optical instruments, n.o.p."[36] (seven and eight months, allowed). Sauerkraut, though the end product of fermentation of cabbage, is still a vegetable; and canned sauerkraut is a "canned vegetable" admissable under tariff item 89 and not a vegetable pickled or preserved in salt brine or oil or in any other manner n.o.p.[37]

Difficulties encountered in the United States in classifying relatively simple articles may be illustrated from the customs treatment of

[32]A–223, T.B.C. 255, Jan. 22, 1952.   [33]A–167, T.B.C. 214, July 10, 1950.
[34]A–213, T.B.C. 249, appeal allowed.   [35]A–254, T.B.C. 282, appeal dismissed.
[36]A–192, T.B.C. 235.   [37]A–128, T.B.C. 162, May 11, 1949.

"pickets" and "sticks" of wood. Of the four principal paragraphs in the free list relating to forest products in the rough, 1805 relates to "pickets, palings, hoops and staves," 1803 includes, among other articles, "firewood, handle bolts, shingle bolts," and 1806 sticks of certain woods "not otherwise provided for, in the rough or not further advanced than cut into lengths suitable for sticks for umbrellas, fishing rods or canes." By an early Treasury decision sawed strips of white pine 4 feet in length and one inch square were admitted free of duty as pickets although imported to be turned into rollers.[38] A letter to the collector of customs at Detroit in 1933 reaffirmed this decision and extended it to such sticks of varying length.[39] In 1948, however, this decision was repealed[40] and sticks to be converted into shade rollers were held dutiable as pine lumber, under paragraph 401 of the Tariff Act and subject as well to an import tax under the Internal Revenue Code. Pickets, it was then said, as used in the manufacture of fences, are generally wider than they are thick, and often have pointed ends.

Prior to 1932 certain other rectangular blocks or sticks of wood 21 inches long and 1½ inches square, designed to be turned into handles for billiard cues, had been admitted free under paragraph 1803 as "handle bolts"; and other "rough turned hardwood sticks" 5 feet long and 1⅛ inches in diameter had been admitted free as "sticks" under paragraph 1806. In that year both these articles were ruled dutiable at 10 per cent under paragraph 406 relating to "oar blocks, heading blocks, and all like blocks and sticks, rough hewn or rough shaped, sawed or turned." Thirty days' notice of the change was given.[41] In 1950, however, the United States Customs Court ruled that a shipment of 20,000 pieces of "Brazilian Sawed Brauna" was admissible free of duty under paragraph 1803 rather than dutiable under paragraph 406 on the ground that "paragraph 406 was intended to cover only wooden articles completely finished or so advanced that one can tell from the shape that it has been dedicated to the making of a finished article of the character therein named."[42] In the same year, for similar reasons it held that certain rough turned wooden dowels were not dutiable at 5 per cent under paragraph 406 as the collector had ruled, nor free as sticks of wood under paragraph 1806 or as sawed lumber under paragraph 1803 as the importer had contended. Subsequently a customs decision was published which classi-

[38]T.D. 20243, cited in U.S., *Digest of Customs and Related Laws* (1935).
[39]T.D. 46515 (1) June 23, 1933.   [40]T.D. 52510, May 1948.
[41]T.D. 45887, Sept. 19, 1932.
[42]*Hunter* v. *United States*, 21 U.S.C.C. 139, C.D. 1143.

fied them as wood, unmanufactured, n.s.p.f., dutiable under paragraph 405 at 10 per cent.[43]

In the United States such "simple" problems of classifying tariff items have frequently arisen after reduction of rates of duty by trade agreements. Under the United States–Canada Trade Agreement a rate of 17½ per cent was conceded by the United States under paragraph 353 on "cooking stoves and ranges having an electric element or device as an essential part." A sample shipment of a small electric cooking stove from Canada was entered at that rate. A month later a carload was shipped, cleared at that rate, and delivered to the shipper. Several months later notice was received that they were dutiable at 40 per cent as household utensils under paragraph 339; several thousand dollars was collected in additional duties. Similar trouble was encountered with electric kettles. When power chain saws, produced in British Columbia, began to be exported, delays and disputes ensued arising in part from problems of classification. A shipment entered in October 1945 was classified as "machines n.o.p." dutiable under paragraph 372 at 27½ per cent. A protest that the shipment was properly dutiable as "saws" at 15 per cent under paragraph 340 as amended by the Swedish Trade Agreement was dismissed by the Customs Court and, on appeal, by the Court of Customs and Patent Appeals in a decision given in May 1950. (Four years, six months.)[44]

7. Parts, Components, and Entireties

In this section two problems are illustrated; they are logically distinct but a single shipment may require a decision on both. In the first place decisions must be made as to what constitutes a particular article (for example a tractor) mentioned or described in the tariff (an entirety), as distinct from attachments, equipment, or (in some cases) components that must be treated as distinct articles and entered under a different tariff item or paragraph. In the second place it must be decided how customs entireties are to be treated when imported knocked down as complete sets of parts or when imported as repair parts. Of course, a shipment of knocked-down equipment may include not only the complete sets of parts for a machine (say a tractor) but also attachments or equipment which must be entered separately as distinct articles; and a shipment of merchandise intended for the

[43]*Superior Dowel* v. *United States*, 25 U.S.C.C. 292, Abs. 54751, Oct. 16, 1950; and T.D. 53142.

[44]*Geo. S. Bush & Co. Inc.* v. *United States*, C.A.D. 435, 38 C.C.P.A. 30.

repair of an item of equipment may include not only articles which are identifiable as parts for a particular type of equipment but other articles, such as bolts, nuts, chains, and bearings, which must be entered separately. In both tariffs the narrowness of the meaning of parts has at times surprised importers and exporters.

Some 225 items in the Canadian Tariff refer to parts, using some 22 different wordings; and of these, 25 of the items and 6 of the wordings relate in some fashion to parts n.o.p. In a declaration in September 1952 relating to pressed-on industrial solid tires (consisting of a steel rim covered as to its outer surface with cured-on rubber) imported for use on high-lift fork lift trucks (but which could be used on other vehicles) the Tariff Board gave detailed consideration to the relative priority ("supersessiveness") to be accorded to certain forms of the provisions as to parts ("parts of" or "thereof," and "parts therefor") as compared with other items in the tariff. It concluded, though one of the three members presented a dissenting opinion, that since among other reasons the tires in question were not provided for by name (*eo nomine*) in any other item in the tariff at the time the goods were entered, they were dutiable as a part of the lift truck rather than as manufactures of steel n.o.p. at a higher rate. It is interesting to note that after the date of the entries in question but even before the Board's declaration, Parliament had enacted a new tariff item which made specific provision for these industrial tire replacements.

The Tariff Board has been called upon to decide a number of other appeals relating to parts and wholes. Buff sections, generally used (and used up) on automatic polishing machines (but not part of their equipment when shipped from the factory) were held not to be part of the machines (four months, allowed).[45]

Favourable decisions were given in appeals to have wooden television cabinets and plastic radio cabinets classed as parts of radio receiving sets (three months, seven months),[46] at 27 per cent instead of, respectively, as wooden furniture at 25 per cent and as plastic furniture at 27½ per cent.[47] Incidentally, the parallel uncertainties encountered by importers of cabinets in the United States is exemplified by a Treasury decision (not to take effect until thirty days after publication) that wooden sewing machine cabinets were to be admitted at 25 per cent as manufactures of wood, rather than at 20 per cent as furniture.[48]

An appeal was dismissed which sought to have certain tractor covers

[45]A–266, T.B.C. 291.   [46]A–220, T.B.C. 281.
[47]A–220, T.B.C. 251, Dec. 21, 1951.   [48]T.D. 52431, March 14, 1950.

entered free as tractor parts rather than at 25 per cent as textile "manufactures of vegetable fibres but not containing wool, n.o.p." (three and a half months);[49] as was an appeal to have half-tracks for a tractor classed as tractor parts (three months and two months).[50] This last case illustrates the operations (and the rare difficulties) in the Canadian procedure of giving classification rulings prior to importations. The importer had obtained a ruling nearly a year before the first entry, that the half-tracks were entitled to entry free of duty, and apparently he had not been apprised of any change in the departmental procedure. The Board called the circumstances of the case to the attention of the Minister of National Revenue "in whom lies complete and final discretion as to whether or not remission is warranted."

On the other hand automobile wireless aerials were held to be neither parts of radio receiving sets nor of automobiles but electric wireless or radio apparatus (three years, five months).[51] In support of this interpretation the Board referred to the definition of radio apparatus contained in section 2(h) of the Radio Act.[52]

A hay drier, which, incidentally, also stores hay, was declared eligible for entry as an agricultural implement rather than as comprising a machine n.o.p., an electric motor, and a manufactured article of iron n.o.p. (eleven months).[53] A self-unloading deep box, dutiable at 15 per cent if entered as a part for farm wagons, was declared an entity and allowed free entry (seventeen months).[54] Multiplex aerial mapping equipment was also declared an entity entitled to enter under the general basket item (711) rather than as a number of separate articles under terms bearing higher rates of duty (two years, three months).[55]

Machines or equipment operated by an attached or built-in motor have sometimes occasioned classification problems not unlike those involved in classifying tires. Is the motor a part of the machine and dutiable at the same rate or is it to be classed separately as an electric motor (at 15 per cent, 22½ per cent, 37½ per cent) or as machinery of iron or steel (at 10 per cent, 22½ per cent, 35 per cent)? A larger discrepancy in rates occurs in special cases which provide for free entry of the apparatus or machine; for example, agricultural machinery, or scientific apparatus, and mechanical equipment of a kind not made in Canada imported by educational institutions and public hospitals. In such cases, if the mechanical equipment including the motor is

[49]A–229, T.B.C. 259.   [50]A–227, T.B.C. 257.   [51]A–211, T.B.C. 248.
[52]2 George VI, c. 50.   [53]A–265, T.B.C. 287.   [54]A–246, T.B.C. 273.
[55]A–204, T.B.C. 244.

judged to be an entity, the whole apparatus enters free; but if the motor is judged to be a separate article it may be held dutiable as being of a class or kind made in Canada.[56] Similar problems have arisen with respect to other motor-powered equipment. The Board has decided, for example, that a lift truck powered by an internal combustion engine was not, as the appellant contended, a tractor (free) to which a completely separate machine had been attached, but a composite machine dutiable as machinery.[57] In 1948 Parliament settled this problem so far as it relates to farm machinery by creating a new item, 409q, which provides that the motive power is to be dutiable as part of the machine in the "farm machinery" items of the Tariff.[58]

In both Canada and the United States, difficulties arise from the complexities of the provisions relating to parts and entireties. In both countries, typically, importations which consist of all and only the parts necessary to assemble one or more complete articles recognized as customs entities are entered as entireties subject to the rate of duty applicable to such complete sets of parts.[59] Repair parts on the other hand are, or may be, classified differently; in a shipment of repair parts such items as bolts and nuts and ball or roller bearings must be entered as distinct items at the rate specified by the tariff item which names them (unless they are so specialized that they can be used only as part of the machine in question). This requirement increases the cost and trouble of documentation and may unpleasantly surprise the inexperienced shipper as to the rate of duty too. In Canada, however, the surprise is sometimes pleasant, for the rates on ball and roller bearings, or certain parts of them, are lower than the rates on machin-

[56]I was informed of a problem case of this sort, relating to an importation by the University of British Columbia through the port of Vancouver, which involved an interchange of correspondence with Ottawa officials. When, later, I mentioned the case to a group in Toronto, without mentioning the port or university, I was told by a University of Toronto official that a decision had finally been reached to allow the University of Toronto to import the whole article free of duty. This illustrates the fact that the same sort of problem frequently arises simultaneously at different ports and receives similar treatment. It is true, however, that communication with Ottawa is more convenient for some ports than for others.

[57]A–168, T.B.C. 211, July 12, 1950. The difficulties resulting from complex machines are not restricted to agricultural implements nor to parts-and-wholes problems; see A–128, T.B.C. 168, in which an index desk with sorting reels is classified as a desk, the reels being hand operated.

[58]The benefit of the doubt was given by the Tariff Board to an appellant whose grain-loading equipment was entered earlier. A–134, T.B.C. 177, allowed.

[59]In Canada some tariff items do not yet include complete sets of parts at the same rate as the entirety.

ery, n.o.p.; in the United States they are higher. The requirement that bearings be separated from the machinery in order to enter at the lower rate has caused some complaint from Canadian importers. In both countries the rate of duty on bolts and nuts appears to be higher than the usual rates on machinery but it is impossible to be perfectly certain since, in the United States, a specific rate is prescribed; and in Canada a compound *ad valorem* and specific rate.[60]

Even when the shipment consists of all and only the items required to assemble an item as it is sold to the public problems arise as to what is to be considered part of the customs entirety and what are distinct articles. In Canada, for example, all parts of tractors, when entered as a complete set of parts, including nuts, bolts, and bearings, enter free of duty; but wrenches and grease-guns must be entered separately even when imported with a complete set of parts. Clevises are classified as tractor parts if the importer or his agent presents a declaration that they are for use as tractor parts and will be used for that purpose only; occasionally an importer of clevises suspects that a competitor is using such clevises for other purposes.

The judicial interpretation of the United States Tariff Act in respect to such items as nuts, bolts, and bearings imported as repair parts for a particular agricultural machine is illustrated by the decision of the United States Court of Customs and Patent Appeals in *United States v. F. A. Freeman and Sons*.[61] Paragraph 1604 of the United States Tariff provides for free entry of "Agricultural implements: . . . mowers . . . and all other agricultural implements of any kind or description not specially provided for, whether in whole or in parts, including repair parts: provided, that no article specified by name in Title I shall be free of duty under this paragraph." In a shipment of articles to be used in the construction or repair of mowers, the collector classified various balls, roller bearings, chains, bolts, rivets, and nuts, under the dutiable

[60]For the United States see C.A.D. 177 (weekly T.D., July 17, 1941). The relevant items are as follows. In Canada: item 427b, ball and roller bearings and complete parts thereof n.o.p., free, 17½ per cent, 35 per cent; item 427, iron machinery n.o.p., 10 per cent, 22½ per cent, 35 per cent; item 430, nuts and bolts of iron and steel, 25¢, 50¢, 75¢ per hundred lbs. and 7½ per cent, 17½ per cent, 25 per cent. In the United States ball and roller bearings and parts were dutiable at 8¢ a lb. and 35 per cent, par. 321 (reduced by 1953 to 4¢ a lb. and 17½ per cent); machines n.s.p.f., 27½ per cent (by 1953, 13¾ per cent); steel nuts and bolts, $\frac{9}{10}$¢ and 1¢ a lb., par. 330 (reduced at Geneva to $\frac{9}{10}$¢ and $\frac{5}{10}$¢).

[61]C.A.D. 177, 29 C.C.P.A. 103, June 9, 1941, Ap. from C.D. 353. Both courts cited *United States* v. *American Express Co.*, Ct. Cust. Ap. 483, T.D. 40693.

paragraphs which named these articles. The importer protested the classification and was upheld by the United States Customs Court which argued in part that "To uphold the government would be to defeat the intent of Congress since all metal parts named *eo nomine* in 1604 are also named under Title I." On appeal, however, this decision was reversed with respect to all the items except the wrist pin nuts which, having a special thread, were usable only on M & O wrist pins on McCormick mowers.

Occasionally in the United States tariff the transferable part determines the rate of duty to be attached to the whole article. A complicated paragraph (329) that relates to chains imposes *ad valorem* duties as high as 40 per cent on some items, and on others specific duties up to 4 cents a pound with the proviso that "all articles manufactured wholly or in chief value, of chain shall not be subject to a lower rate of duty than that imposed upon the chain from which it is made."[62] (Time, four years and one month.)

Technology changes frequently; and its progress has increased the number of standardized, interchangeable parts as well as the number of complex entireties. If a complicated tariff structure is maintained, it will probably be impossible to eliminate completely disputes concerning parts and wholes, or entities and entireties. However, in Canada, such disputes form a relatively high proportion of the total number; and it may be possible to reduce them. It appears, for instance, that the number of different wordings in the provisions relating to parts might with advantage be reduced and the meanings clarified.

In Canada, these disputes have arisen chiefly from uncertainty as to the extent of the "holes" in a tariff structure that is not unusually high. They are to be distinguished from those arising from the trick classes (or jokers) in the United States Tariff which impose rates that are extraordinarily high, even in a tariff that contains many high rates. It should not be forgotten, however, that the complexity of the Tariff of Canada (as well as that of the United States) arises in part from the desire to give protection; and some of the Canadian disputes concerning entities are more intimately related to this motive than to any ambiguity of phrasing. In some of these disputes the distinction between distinct entities and complex entireties cuts across the distinction between items that relate to articles "of a class or kind not made in Canada" to which we may now turn.

[62]Certain of these rates have been reduced at Geneva and Torquay.

8. Of a Class or Kind not Made in Canada

Certain tariff items prescribe low rates of duty or free entry for the articles described when "of a class or kind not made in Canada."[63] These items relieve Canadian importers from the higher rates prescribed in other items until such time as an article, being produced in Canada in substantial quantities, is held no longer to qualify for entry under the lower rate. When such a decision has been reached, three weeks' notice is given before subjecting the imports of the article to the higher rates: though introduced to relieve importers this arrangement, in fact, holds forth the prospect that a higher protective duty will become effective when the article is made in Canada. Section 6 of the Customs Tariff, too, imposes dumping duties on imported goods "of a class or kind made or produced in Canada" if sold for export to Canada at a price less than their fair market value. For the purposes of the Tariff Act, it is provided that "goods shall not be deemed to be of a class or kind made or produced in Canada unless produced in substantial quantities"; and the Governor in Council is given power to define such quantities as a percentage of the normal Canadian consumption. In point of fact, an order in council of 1936[64] provides that an article shall not be deemed to be of a class or kind made or produced in Canada unless the domestic production will supply 10 per cent of the normal Canadian consumption of that article. However, the Minister of National Revenue is empowered to make regulations necessary for carrying out the dumping section, and *for the purposes of the dumping section* it is provided that goods may be deemed to be "of a class or kind not made in Canada where similar goods of Canadian production are not offered to all purchasers on equal terms having regard to the custom and usage of trade." Accordingly, articles which are not freely offered for sale might be regarded as being of a class or kind not made in Canada for purposes of the dumping duty but of a class or kind made in Canada for purposes of tariff classification.

Many of the classification decisions concerning "class or kind" depend on whether, for the particular articles being considered, that phrase is held to refer to a wide or to a narrow range of goods. Since the Canadian market is small many domestic producers find it convenient to concentrate on producing a relatively few sizes, styles, patterns, or types. In some industries the Canadian output is a rela-

[63]In the 1952 amendment to the Customs Tariff, some of the amended items are worded "when of a class or kind made in Canada." See, e.g., item 438(b).

[64]P.C. 1618, July 2, 1936.

tively small proportion of the total Canadian consumption even of the exact types of an article produced in Canada. In more firmly established industries the domestic output forms a large proportion of Canadian consumption of the exact types produced and, in some, a substantial proportion even of a broader class which includes other substitute products.

Under these circumstances the importer is interested in seeing that the classification adopted is fine enough that less than 10 per cent of the grades and types of article he is importing are made in Canada; the domestic producer on the other hand will gain from a grouping that will include as many as possible of the immediate substitutes for his product while still showing that at least 10 per cent of the Canadian consumption of these commodities taken together is produced in Canada. In a moderately well-established industry, domestic producers as well as importers may be ready to accept a classification that distinguishes between articles that are commonly regarded as belonging to one class. However, the fragmentation of commodities is limited eventually by the possibilities of devising physical criteria which, when communicated to port officials, will enable them to discriminate between the articles which are and those which are not entitled to be treated as belonging to a kind not made in Canada. In well-established industries domestic producers may favour a broader grouping which will include competing substitutes which are not made in Canada at all.

Since the war the Tariff Board has considered arguments as to the meaning of the phrase "class or kind," as to the power of the Department to subdivide subdivisions of commodities, and as to the reasonableness of the criteria used by the Department of National Revenue. In allowing an appeal from a decision that certain models of Mossberg .22 calibre rifles were of a class or kind not made in Canada the Board cautiously remarked: "Dictionary definitions of the word 'class' indicate that it is used both for very broad and for very narrow designations, but *in the context* in which it is used in tariff item 441e it appears to be more or less synonymous with 'kind.' " Consequently, in interpreting this item the Board has taken cognizance of the more precise designation "kind." Auto-loading rifles are of a kind not made in Canada.[65] In one appeal concerning fork lift trucks neither the importer nor the domestic producer disputed the need for fragmentation of items but attention was directed to the ambiguity of nominal manufacturer's capacity rating, which had been used by the Depart-

[65]A–155, T.B.C. 206.

ment of National Revenue to distinguish those lift trucks which were, from those which were not, of a class or kind produced in Canada. The Board suggested a revision of the relevant Customs Memorandum in the light of the information newly made available but suggested to the Minister of Finance the desirability of including in the tariff an item referring by name to fork lift-trucks.[66] Later, after giving qualified approval in one decision[67] to a less ambiguous method of measuring the capacity of lift trucks the Board remarked on another appeal: "That a perfect method . . . has not yet been discovered, no one familiar with the complexities of the problem would deny."[68]

Meanwhile on a reference from the Deputy Minister of National Revenue a domestic producer contended that the Department was not empowered to subdivide subdivisions of machinery and that all power cranes or power shovels constitute an indivisible class which is made in Canada.[69] In justifying its attempt to ascertain the intention of the legislature, the Board noted "that the phrase 'class or kind' when applied to the words 'all machinery . . . n.o.p.' has no plain and obvious meaning but rather is extremely flexible in its connotation," and again, "Indeed it is difficult to conceive any precise terms which would be suitable for differentiating the various and differing 'machinery' dutiable under tariff items 427 and 427a." Among other reasons the Board advanced the argument that sections 6(10) of the Customs Tariff Act appeared to contemplate counting of pieces of machinery; and that "similarity sufficient in degree to make sense of the counting must pre-suppose a reasonable degree of narrowness in the grouping or classification." Accordingly, it gave the opinion "that in classifying power cranes and shovels on the basis of nominal dipper capacity the Department of National Revenue (Customs and Excise) has acted within powers." But the Board did not suggest that this basis of classification was necessarily the only basis on which power cranes and shovels could be classified; or that the classification currently in use is necessarily correct.

It is clear then that the multitude of Made-in-Canada Regulations include many and fine distinctions. Some of these are based not only on differences in physical characteristics but also on the use to which the article is to be put. Silk and artificial silk fabrics, for example, of a kind not made in Canada, when imported by manufacturers for use exclusively in manufacturing neckties, scarves, or mufflers in their

[66] A–212, T.B.C. 246. [67] A–235, T.B.C. 246.
[68] A–264, T.B.C. 286, dismissed. [69] A–260, T.B.C. 272, March 18, 1953.

own factories are admitted under tariff item 564 at 17½ per cent, 15 per cent, and 29 per cent respectively under the three columns. It has been decided that some types of fabrics which are made in Canada are suitable for scarves and mufflers but not for neckties. Accordingly a certain fabric may be accepted "as of a kind NOT MADE IN CANADA when used in the manufacture of neckties, but as MADE IN CANADA when used for scarves and mufflers."[70]

The items relating to goods not made in Canada necessarily impose a substantial administrative burden on the Government, on certain importers, and indeed on domestic producers. But the size of this burden and the way in which it is shared between the Government and private individuals is determined, of course, by the detailed provisions of the item, and by the methods used in administering it and in communicating changes in the regulations.

It seems possible that as Canadian manufacturing industries develop, and come to need protection less, they may be able, nevertheless, to narrow and perhaps even close the gaps in the protective tariff by obtaining a broader grouping of articles in determining made-in-Canada status.[71] Such an anomaly may perhaps be partly avoided by separating new items from the broad group and providing for them lower rates than those prescribed in the n.o.p. item for that class of goods when made in Canada; but it is not to be expected that this will be done automatically or easily. Even this process will have the unwelcome effect of increasing the number of items in the tariff schedule.[72]

The United States Tariff in general does not grant the administration the power of deciding that certain imports are competitive with domestic products while others are not and classifying them so that they attract different rates of duty. In some of the paragraphs relating to coal tar derivatives, however, an analogous provision appears. The *ad valorem* rates prescribed in those paragraphs are to be applied on the American selling price of any similar competitive article manufactured or produced in the United States; but if there is no such similar competitive article then the rate is applied to the United States

[70]A–182, T.B.C. 197, Feb. 6, 1951.

[71]The scope of anti-dumping duties may be similarly broadened; see, for example, the transfer of all remaining toys to the class made in Canada: D.N.R. Series D, no. 51, M.C.R. 146, File no. 86550, Dec. 13, 1952.

[72]For opposition to "blanket rulings" on goods of a class or kind made in Canada see evidence of V. C. Wansbrough before Can., Senate, Trade Relations, no. 7, May 6, 1953, p. 166.

value of the article. A similar competitive article is defined, for this purpose, to be one which accomplishes substantially equal results when used in substantially the same manner.[73]

The application of these items requires a multitude of administrative decisions: a decision with respect to each size, shape, and style of certain machines, for example, that a foreign producer sells in Canada. Each of these decisions is communicated to the customs authorities of the ports from which an enquiry has come. Other ports are not informed of the decision unless it is considered to be of general interest. The local port officials, then, are not aware of some of these decisions until at least one importer shipping through that port has obtained a ruling from Ottawa, or a certified copy of the ruling from a port which has received it. However, it is reported that Ottawa officials deal promptly with requests for a ruling. If a ruling has already been given concerning that particular machine, a reply is usually sent from Ottawa by return mail; if not, the delay, of course, is longer; the delay is necessarily longer in ports that are farther from Ottawa than in those close at hand. Clearly these "not-made-in-Canada" items impose extra administrative costs and they require the use of broad administrative discretion. Unquestionably they lessen the impact of the protective duties in some respects (though they also make a greater amount of protection possible—or palatable). Ironically, by complicating the tariff and helping to make it unintelligible, they may in some cases increase the uncertainties and the financial burdens of the importers they are designed to benefit.

9. Specific Use

The Canadian Tariff in particular abounds in "specific use" or "end use" items designed to reduce duties on articles imported by Canadian manufacturers or others, to be used for specified purpose. Though they afford relief to those who enjoy their benefits they also complicate the tariff and occasion procedural expenses and difficulties.[74]

The Tariff Board which, as part of its duties, advises the Government, on request, concerning classification and rates of duty, has recently enunciated "the principle that it is not advisable to dilute such protection as may be suggested by singling out particular users of that material for preferred treatment" and it noted that in the field

[73]U.S. Tariff, pars. 27(c) and (d); and 28 (c) and (d).

[74]Items of this kind appeared even in very early Canadian tariffs. Nova Scotia objected to items based on specific use shortly after Confederation. Can., Commons, *Sessional Papers, 1868,* vol. 9, no. 86, correspondence; cited in Gordon Blake, "Customs Administration," p. 255.

of plastics such items would occasion prohibitively great administrative difficulties.[75] However, in spite of the administrative problems involved and the expense both to the Government and importers, these items are so flexible and convenient in other ways that they continue to increase in number.

Of the two following examples, one illustrates the routine costs which tend to diminish the usefulness of such concessions, and the other the surprises and negotiations that arise from them. When the items relating to cotton lace and embroidery were subdivided to allow their entry at a lower rate when used by manufacturers, importers who sold chiefly to manufacturers, but also to retail stores, were placed in a difficult situation. After trying in vain to obtain permission to enter all their imports of this type at the lower rate they were finally permitted to pay the lower rate when the shipment arrived, provided that they made amended entries quarterly to cover that part of the shipment which was subsequently sold to the retail stores. This involved the importers in the trouble and expense of keeping special stock records to show precisely what part of each shipment was sold to manufacturers and what part to others; in addition it involved making amended entries and paying broker's fees several times on one shipment. Again, item 326e allows articles of glass, not plate or sheet, designed to be cut or mounted, to be admitted free of duty under the Preferential and the Most-Favoured-Nation Tariffs. A Canadian manufacturer began importing forms for sanding in the belief that these also would automatically be admitted duty free since the purpose of the cutting and sanding is approximately the same. His belief was based in part also on the circumstance that the Department of National Revenue which collects customs as well as other taxes had ruled, not long before, that sanded glass articles as well as cut glass ones were subject to the 25 per cent luxury excise tax. However, entry at the lower rate was not automatically granted. This is an interesting example of a narrow interpretation of the limits of a customs item defined by specific use, and also of the differences in the breadth of the classes as between two Acts administered by the same Department.

Many tariff items introduced by order in council are based on specific use; these reductions are often temporary, and are sometimes designed to reduce the duty only on one or two shipments imported by an industry which, the Government considers, ought in the public interest to be thus assisted.

Specific use items are often used, too, to lessen the burden of pro-

[75]See T.B.C., Ref. 109, *Inquiry Respecting So-called Plastics.*

tective duties on certain classes of consumers or importers. Though imports under these items are relatively small in total value they include articles of many kinds, ranging from supplies for foreign embassies to settlers' effects, and from exhibits for trade fairs to educational or surgical equipment or apparatus for educational institutions or hospitals. The Canadian Tariff, for example, provides for the free entry of scientific apparatus and many other kinds of imports when imported by a hospital or an educational institution; other items relate to articles of "an international educational, scientific or cultural character"; others to articles used by religious and charitable institutions. Most of these items are easily recognizable; and they may give even more stimulus than intended to the forming of cultural or scientific organizations. It is said, for example, that some years ago an individual imported a telescope. His claim that it should enter free as an instrument used for scientific purpose was allowed only after an astronomical club had been formed to use it.

The Tariff of the United States contains relatively few items based on chief use, end use, or the status of importers; those that exist sometimes occasion difficulties. Agricultural implements not specified by name in the dutiable list are admitted free of duty under paragraph 1604, on the basis of chief use in the United States. However, a Canadian who exported fruit graders encountered considerable difficulty and delay because, he believes, some of the graders were sold to agricultural colleges and to other institutions, instead of to farmers. Certain chemicals are dutiable at one rate when not suitable for medicinal use and at another when suitable; and animals imported for breeding purposes are admitted free of duty. Books and certain other items are admitted free of duty when imported by the United States or the Library of Congress or by "any society or institution organized solely for religious, philosophical, educational, scientific or literary purposes" as well as certain items for the use of public hospitals. Certain leathers are subject to a lower rate "if imported to be used in the manufacture of footwear";[76] other specific end-use items are molasses not to be commercially used for the extraction of sugar for human consumption and patna rice cleaned for use in the manufacture of canned soups.[77]

Like other holes in the tariff such items unquestionably give relief to certain importers and consumers but the cost of administering them and of conforming with the regulations governing them is part of the costs of a protective tariff. It may be worth repeating too that the additional complexity they occasion lessens in some degree their general ameliorative effects.

[76]U.S. Tariff, par. 1530(c).   [77]U.S. Tariff, pars. 502 and 1752.

10. GOODS RETURNED AND CONTAINERS

Item 709 of the Canadian Tariff provides for the free reimportation of goods, including containers, which have been produced in Canada, or entered for consumption in Canada and subsequently exported. However, if a draw-back or refund of duty has been granted on exportation a duty equal in amount is collected. To qualify for entry under this item, goods must be reimported within five years. Substitution of containers may be permitted if evidence is produced of exportation of an equal number of similar containers. Goods may not be entered under this item if they have been advanced in value or condition while abroad. By exception, however, a few other items provide for free entry of Canadian products that have been further processed abroad. Item 280b, for instance, provides temporarily for free entry of certain hydrogenated oils produced from materials of Canadian origin, when imported for use exclusively in Canadian manufactures.

In both tariffs provision is made for free entry of goods under a number of other special circumstances. These provisions of the United States Tariff have recently been amended to allow the Treasury to simplify some of the more complicated procedures formerly prescribed, and to forego collection in certain cases where the costs to the Treasury would greatly outweigh the revenue.[78] Of these miscellaneous provisions for free entry only that concerning American goods returned will be discussed here. The United States Tariff contains a paragraph granting free entry to goods produced in that country and returned without having been advanced in value; and to substantial outer containers that have been previously exported from the United States.[79] However, unless they are admitted free under some other paragraph, such imports which have been exported with benefit of drawback of duty, or remisssion or refund of internal revenue tax, are subjected to current duties, not to exceed any drawback, remission, or refund that had been received on exportation plus the current internal revenue tax. The Treasury is empowered to prescribe regulations as to proof of identity and compliance with the conditions; in fact decisions of the Customs Courts have required the Treasury to impose strict conditions of proof, including costly, and sometimes impossible, verification from the customs documents relating to the article when last exported. It

[78]The Customs Simplification Act of 1953 contains liberalizing amendments with respect to American goods returned (s. 8), articles for non-commercial exhibitions (s. 9), supplies and equipment for vessels and aircraft (s. 11), and administrative exemptions (s. 13).

[79]U.S. Tariff, par. 1615.

has been held, since the grant of free entry by Congress was limited, that the limitations must be strictly followed.[80] The determination of the exact amount of drawback allowed on metal drums returned has been "a terrific problem" to the United States Customs[81] as well as to the importers.

The Customs Simplification Act adds a number of sentences to the paragraph concerning American goods returned, to provide that "when, because of the destruction of customs records or for other causes it is impracticable to establish whether a drawback was allowed" or to determine its amount, the goods are to be assessed a duty equal to the amount of the estimated drawback and internal revenue tax allowable or refundable at the rate applicable on the date of importation; further "in order to facilitate the ascertainment and collection of the duty the Secretary of the Treasury is authorized to ascertain and specify the amount of such duties applicable to articles or kinds of articles," and to exempt from assessment of duty "articles excepted from the grant of free entry under the paragraph if the collection of the duty involves expense and inconvenience to the government disproportionate to the probable amount of such duty."[82]

In the past, with narrow exceptions, provision was not made for original free entry of containers in bond.[83] However, the Customs Simplification Act of 1953 amended the clause that allowed containers for compressed gas to be entered in bond pending re-export;[84] so that it now permits original free entry in bond for filled, reusable "containers or other articles in use for covering or holding merchandise (including personal or household effects) during transportation, and suitable for reuse for that purpose."[85]

The provisions of the Customs Simplification Act of 1953, however, do not appear to be sufficiently broad to allow easy division of processes between Canada and the United States. The problems are illustrated by the case of a Canadian manufacturer who exported a

[80]*Maple Leaf Petroleum Limited* v. *United States*, 5 C.C.P.A. (Customs); T.D. 48976, cited by Hadley S. King representing the Association of the Customs Bar, New York, in U.S. House, *On H.R. 1535*, p. 436. Collectors of customs, however, are authorized to waive compliance with the regulations as to proof of self-evident and certain other facts in these cases.

[81]Evidence of W. R. Johnson, House, *On H.R. 1535*, p. 98. See also the *Bell Report*, pp. 53–4.

[82]Customs Simplification Act of 1953, s. 7.

[83]See *Bell Report*, pp. 53–4.

[84]U.S. Tariff, s. 308(7).

[85]Customs Simplification Act of 1953, s. 10(e).

car of agricultural machinery parts including, in certain of the parts, ball bearings which had been imported from the United States. In order to secure free entry for these ball bearings they would have had to be removed from the parts, identified, and entered separately. On later shipments the exporter arranged with the United States manufacturer to deliver the bearings direct to his customers in the United States.

11. TECHNICAL DIFFERENCES; PURITY; DEGREE OF ADVANCEMENT

Whether the words of a tariff item are given their commercial or trade meaning, or whether, in the absence of a clear-cut meaning in the industry, inquiry is made more directly to the intent of the legislators, a considerable amount of more or less technical information is often required concerning the exact composition of the imported articles or their physical and chemical properties or their degree of advancement in the industrial process or the methods used in producing them. One group of cases relates to the degree of purity that is required, or the amount and type of admixture that is permissible without removing the substance from a particular item. This problem is sometimes, though by no means always, related to the degree of advancement of the substance in a manufacturing process. In such cases the number of classes and the intricacy of the class boundaries is associated with the attempt to give protection to almost everyone in an industry.

The uncertainty that may be associated with such technical considerations is illustrated by the experience of Canadian importers of cocoa and chocolate paste. The tariff provides that cocoa paste, not sweetened, in blocks or cakes, may be entered at 3 cents per pound, except under the general tariff; and cocoa paste, sweetened, in blocks weighing not less than two pounds, at 4 cents a pound. Preparations of cocoa or chocolate, not otherwise provided for, however, have been dutiable at 2½ cents a pound plus 20 per cent *ad valorem* (2½ cents plus 10 per cent under the Preferential Tariff).[86] A Canadian importer, having received orders for chocolate paste, consulted the local customs, and was informed (by some strange chance, in writing) that the sweetened paste was admissible at the rate of 4 cents a pound. On the basis of this information he ordered a large shipment which was duly entered at the quoted rate. Later, in 1947, after the paste had all been sold, he received notice that required the classification to be changed

[86]Changed by 1953 to 10 per cent under the Preferential and 20 per cent under the Most-Favoured-Nation Tariff. See tariff items 20, 21, 23.

to preparations of chocolate and demanding many thousand dollars in additional duties. The importer found that the change in classification was required because the various pastes imported contained either flavouring or milk or both. In spite of the importer's contention that nearly all chocolate pastes contained flavouring and a homogenizer the customs authorities adhered to their decision to collect the higher rate and the importer appealed to the Tariff Board. At that time the Tariff Board was inactive but when it was reconstituted and resumed activities the appeal was heard, and was dismissed in a declaration of August 26, 1949. However, since the importer had taken pains in advance to ascertain the rate of duty that would be applied, and may have been misled by the information he obtained, the Board suggested that consideration be given to the possibility of refund or remission under the provisions of the Financial Administrative Act. Since this appeal had to wait for the Tariff Board to resume its activities the time between entry and decision is considerably longer than is usual. On the same date the Board dismissed another similar appeal concerning chocolate liquor slabs and made the same recommendation.[87]

Degree of finish was also involved in a Tariff Board decision concerning importations of certain soap bases. The Board ruled that they were not dutiable as toilet soap as claimed by the appellant since they required further processing; and not as "common soap" as the Customs contended, since no special category of soap seemed to attract this designation; but as soap n.o.p. (eight months).[88]

The difficulty of drawing the line between chemical mixtures can be seen by comparing the outcome of the last two appeals with that of the appeal by an importer from a customs decision that paperine was dutiable as "a chemical preparation, dry, compounded of more than one substance n.o.p." under tariff item 220a (15 per cent, 20 per cent, 25 per cent) rather than as "a preparation having the quality of starch" under item 39(ii), (per lb., 1 cent, 1 cent, 2 cents). Paperine consists of precooked starch, 82.8 per cent, and small but precisely determined amounts of three other chemicals; it is used in the manufacture of paper as a beater size. The Board accepted the argument of the appellant that the added chemicals merely keep the starch from

<hr />

[87]A–137, T.B.C. 166 and 184, Aug. 26, 1949.

[88]A–166, T.B.C. 207, July 10, 1950. The tariff items involved were: 228(i), toilet soap. n.o.p., 15 per cent, 22½ per cent, 32½ per cent; 228(ii), soap n.o.p., 15 per cent, 20 per cent, 32½ per cent; 229, soap, common or laundry, per 100 pounds, $0.50, $1.50, $1.50.

lumping in the beater and permit it to work more efficiently, and rejected the contention of Customs that the starch and other chemicals had been manufactured into a distinct chemical product by a delicate processing (eight months—to twenty-one months; allowed).[89] This decision allowed the variant import to be included in the named class, while the other two excluded it, presumably because in this case item 220 referred not only to starch but to "preparations having the quality" of starch.

12. OBSOLETE DISTINCTIONS

It is a general rule of statutory interpretation, applicable to tariff laws as well as other laws, that the meaning of a statute is fixed as of the time of its enactment. Items which are differentiated by fine distinctions with respect to the stage of advancement, degree of purity, and other matters too, often become obsolete quite rapidly. These vestigial remnants of a former technology complicate the tariff and, being without current meaning, occasion surprises—sometimes even to customs officials themselves.

The Tariff Board of Canada, for example, recently allowed an appeal by a Canadian chemical company against a decision of the Deputy Minister that an ethylene glycol blend was admissible free of duty as "ethylene glycol, imported by manufacturers for use in the manufacturing of anti-freezing compounds."[90] The Board held that the meaning of the tariff item was unambiguous; and that it had been intended to refer to the reasonably pure substance which had been used for making anti-freeze when the item was inserted in the tariff, before satisfactory anti-freezing compounds had been developed that contained mixtures of ethylene glycol with other glycols. In an addendum one of the members concluded from the evidence that the same ethylene glycol as used in the trade did not generally, at least as yet, include such mixtures. Apparently the customs authorities had attempted to interpret the name flexibly to correspond with changing technology, but this decision of the Board, on appeal by a domestic manufacturer, upset their interpretation. (Eight months, allowed.)[91]

On a request from the Deputy Minister of National Revenue for a ruling as to the kinds of mineral wax that were dutiable as paraffin the Board declared that the Tariff Board report of 1936[92] showed the intent of the legislators when the tariff item was adopted and that the practice of Customs accorded with that meaning as was required by

[89]A–239, T.B.C. 254, June 24, 1952.
[91]A–258, T.B.C. 284, March 12, 1953.
[90]Tariff item 208h.
[92]T.B.C., Ref. 84, 1936.

the law. The Board pointed out that it had no power on an appeal under the Customs Act to suggest changes in the tariff item though changes in technology had probably made revision necessary. Interested parties were advised to direct their request to "another level of the administration." [93]

Equally fine (and obsolete) technical distinctions are used in determining classification in the United States. "Standard newsprint paper" enters the United States free of duty; but to qualify as standard newsprint, paper must conform with the strict technical requirements of the customs definition. It must be in rolls more than 15 inches wide; it must not contain more than 6½ per cent ash; it must not weigh more than 35 pounds per ream; and its surface must be rough so that it does not test higher than 50 per cent when examined by a venerable and obsolete instrument known as a glarimeter.[94] Except for the width, which was inserted in the law by amendment in 1944, these specifications are required by the legal principle stated at the beginning of this section; they serve to define the grades of paper that were chiefly used in the United States in printing regular editions of newspaper immediately before the enactment of the Tariff Act of 1930. It is apparent that unchanging tariff classifications may discourage technological advance.

Fine distinctions between tariff items may become obsolete also because of changes in market conditions. The United States for the most part has avoided formal discrimination between different nations yet one technical distinction which now seems to have lost its protective significance was left to discriminate, unintentionally but in fact, between fishermen in Newfoundland and Canada; when Newfoundland joined Canada international was changed to interprovincial discrimination.

The United States Tariff Act of 1922 applied a higher duty to dried salted groundfish than to wet salted groundfish and made the dividing line 43 per cent moisture content. The two classes were originally introduced to protect the New England fisheries and to allow United States

[93]A–176, T.B.C. 223, Dec. 1, 1950. The relevant items are: 225, wax, vegetable n.o.p. and mineral, 5 per cent, 7½ per cent and 10 per cent; 272b, paraffin wax n.o.p., 15 per cent, 17½ per cent, and 25 per cent; 272c, paraffin wax, when imported exclusively for use in the manufacture of candles, 10 per cent, 12½ per cent, and 25 per cent; changed by 1953 to 272b (ii), free, free, 25 per cent. Since 1936, mineral waxes whose melting point was less than 139.1 F. had been considered paraffin.

[94]See report of address by D. W. Ambridge, President, Abitibi Power and Paper Co., "Some Plain Talk on U.S. Tariffs," *Financial Post*, Oct. 24, 1953, p. 21.

to import fish, at the lower rate, which were wet enough that they could be filleted in the United States. As it turned out Newfoundland fisheries, in their colder climate, could produce salt fish with 43 per cent moisture content which had the keeping qualities required in Puerto Rico, while the Nova Scotia fisheries could not. Meanwhile the New England fisheries trade became almost entirely occupied in producing fresh fish. Thus the moisture content chosen as the dividing line between the tariff classes had lost significance for the United States fisheries and served merely to exclude Nova Scotia fish from the Puerto Rico market while allowing the Newfoundland fish in. The Nova Scotian fishermen protested. When Newfoundland joined Canada the discrimination was transformed, again quite unintentionally, into a protection in the Puerto Rican market of fishermen in one section of Canada against those in another. At Geneva an equal reduction of ⅛ cent a pound was made on wet and dry fish; and this, of course, did not satisfy the Nova Scotia fishermen. The mirth-producing potentialities of this conundrum are clear but, more seriously, it may be difficult now for Canadian fishermen to speak with one voice on this matter unless the duty is removed entirely.[95]

13. COMMERCIAL USAGE

The usage of the trade may help to decide questions as to classifications that turn on technical differences or degree of finish. The Tariff Board of Canada declared that various processed castor oils were admissible free of duty as "castor oil . . . for use in the manufacture of paints and varnishes,"[96] rather than dutiable under the general item for unenumerated commodities. The Board held that the term castor oil, as used in the trade, included these processed oils; though one member of the Board dissented, on the grounds that the processed oil was referred to in the trade as dehydrated castor oil and that it was a different article, the product of a highly complicated industrial processing.[97] (Five months to fourteen months.)

The wording of a tariff item, however, may be sufficiently specific to make commercial usage irrelevant; as is illustrated by the United States classification of boarded leather. Side upper leathers (including grains and splits) and leather made from calf or kip skins are ad-

[95]Can., Banking & Commerce, *G.A.T.T.*, no. 7, May 11, 1948. See evidence of F. W. Zwicker and H. R. Kemp.

[96]Item 278e, by O.C. May 1, 1942, D.N.R., Series D, no. 47–62. Cancelled Feb. 6, 1951.

[97]A–171, T.B.C. 215, Aug. 28, 1950.

missible into the United States at a lower rate than "leather of all kinds, grained, printed, embossed, ornamented or decorated . . . or by any other process made into fancy leather."[98] Boarded leathers which form a large proportion of the upper leathers used in the United States for duty purposes are classed with the fancy leathers though they do not resemble them in quality or use. In a case decided by the Court of Customs and Patent Appeals witnesses agreed that the boarded leather in question was not fancy leather but disagreed as to whether or not it was grained leather: one holding that grained leather was leather embossed to resemble grain leather; another, that boarding accentuated the natural grain and that boarded leather was therefore grained leather. In deciding that boarded leather was grained leather and dutiable at the higher rate, the Court of Customs and Patent Appeals held that commercial usage with respect to the meaning of the term "fancy" was irrelevant since Congress had *eo nomine* stated what was fancy for the purposes of the paragraph.[99]

14. METHOD OF PRODUCTION

Logically it might be expected that commodities would be classified in such a way that those articles which were precisely substitutable in use would be placed in the same class; but classification problems in fact are frequently decided by information concerning the processes used in producing the import. Use and method of production, of course, are often related, and the problems of apportioning protection between different processes favour the use of classes based on degree of manufacture.

The process of production, moreover, sometimes provides the most readily available evidence as to the identity of the imported article. The Canadian Tariff Board declared, for example, that zincy-lead dross, being the residue from a smelting furnace, was not entitled to free entry as an ore but, in dismissing the appeal, suggested to the Deputy Minister of National Revenue that a refund might be justified since in two previous rulings of the customs authorities residues from smelting furnaces had been deemed admissible as ores of other metals (seven months).[100] Tariff item 681a now provides for entry of such residue free of duty.

The products of secret or unusual processes sometimes occasion

---

[98]U.S. Tariff, pars. 1530(b)(4) and 1530(d).

[99]*United States* v. *John B. Stetson*, 12 C.C.P.A. 3, April 12, 1933, cited in *Rubin Bros. Footwear* v. *United States*, C.D. 895, 13 U.S.C.C. 209, Nov. 15, 1944.

[100]A–139, T.B.C. 191 (1), Sept. 21, 1949.

disputes in Canada, or, in the United States, resentment at being required to disclose trade secrets. A reclaiming oil was declared dutiable as a product of petroleum (per gal. ⅓ cent, ⅓ cent, 1 cent) rather than of asphalt (free, 10 per cent, 10 per cent) when a technical witness for the appellant gave some, though not complete, information concerning the process of manufacturing, which the customs expert complained most manufacturers of reclaiming oils kept closely guarded as a secret.[101] In 1952 a new item (269c) was inserted in the Tariff admitting free of duty plasticizers or reclaiming agents of petroleum origin for reclaiming rubber.[102] The classification now depends on use rather than the exact process used.

The secrecy surrounding the process used in producing certain pine pitch products, entered in 1947, seems to have occasioned some difficulty both to Canadian customs officials and, on appeal, to the Tariff Board. The importer appealed from the customs ruling that they were dutiable as belonging in the non-enumerated class and not, as claimed by the importer, admissible free of duty under item 585, as pine pitch or pine tar: but the appeal was dismissed on the ground that "there is a marked difference between tall oil and tall oil pitch." (Two years, five months, dismissed.)[103]

In another appeal, a gloss, produced by treating naphtha-resin solution with lime by an unusual process, was declared to be admissible not as resin in liquid form but under the basket item for chemical preparations (seven and ten months, dismissed).[104]

Changes or differences in method of production which apparently do not affect the imported product at all, or not significantly, may nevertheless occasion change in classification and occasion delays, uncertainty, and losses. A Canadian importer of nets, laces, and embroideries began to import cotton bobinet from the United States instead of from overseas. He cleared a small shipment at the rate of 27½ per cent plus 3½ cents per pound. Later he arranged to import a large shipment of some twenty thousand yards and based his price on the rate of duty he had been accustomed to pay. When the shipment arrived the customs officials decided the net was made on a knitting machine rather than on a bobinet machine and accordingly classified it as knitted goods, subject to a duty of 35 per cent plus 25 cents per pound. Ottawa authorities confirmed this decision, which is of course in itself, literally and technically, quite reasonable. Two points in this case should be noted, however; in the first place the

[101]A–234, T.B.C. 241, May 26, 1952.   [102]S.C., 1952, c. 23.

[103]A–153, T.B.C. 171, Feb. 22, 1950; and Can., D.N.R., Series D, no. 47–253, May 19, 1948.   [104]A–188, T.B.C. 227, Feb. 23, 1951.

goods made by a bobinet machine cannot be distinguished from those made on a Rachael knitting machine without the use of a magnifying glass or a microscope to investigate precisely how the weaving is done; in the second place it shows that, even in Canada, the importer is not invariably able to depend on the results of sample shipments. It only becomes worth while to make a detailed investigation when larger shipments arrive. It is also to be supposed that domestic producers of the same or substitute products are likely to be stimulated to see that the authorities treat these products as strictly as tariff prescribes only when they begin to arrive in fairly substantial quantities. In this case the importer did not object primarily to the classification itself; he did object to its being applied unexpectedly so that he was misled by his past experience.

The Canadian Customs' treatment of lace, net, and embroidery made on a knitting machine furnishes one of the few cases in recent years in which the Canadian Customs failed to generalize a liberalizing decision of the Tariff Board. In 1947 the Dress Manufacturers' Guild of Toronto appealed successfully from a decision that "material described as lace" was properly dutiable under tariff item 568 as knitted goods n.o.p. dutiable at 35 per cent and 25 cents per pound under the Intermediate and Preferential Tariffs.[105] The customs authorities applied this ruling only to the particular fabric on which the Board had ruled, and continued to class certain other lace-like fabrics as knit goods if they had been made on knitting machines. In deciding a later appeal concerning one of these other fabrics the Board noted the argument that the fabric in question might be held to qualify for inclusion in both classes and that it should therefore be charged at the higher rate. However, it allowed the appeal on the grounds that the article, being lace, was dutiable in the class in which it was named rather than in the other class that referred to a group of items not otherwise provided for. (Three years, four months, allowed.)

In this declaration, the Board remarked:

The necessity of an appeal to the Board in connection with each separate fabric in a category covering hundreds of such no doubt constitutes a hardship for the trade; on the other hand, the administrative authorities have found it increasingly difficult, in the absence of any definition in the Customs Tariff of 'lace', to make rulings as to classification otherwise than on an ad hoc basis, the more so that established precedent in departmental practice had been disturbed by the Board's ruling on Appeal No. 159. Obviously, definition of 'lace' and 'laces' . . . would appear to be desirable and indeed imperative in the interest of efficient administration of the tariff schedule.[106]

[105]A–125, T.B.C. 159, Feb. 28, 1947.   [106]A–128, T.B.C. 160, May 11, 1949.

In the United States Tariff some items of the well-known embroidery paragraph distinguish, confusingly, between the products of different sorts of machines, as do certain of the knit-goods paragraphs.

The relationship of trade agreements to classification problems can be illustrated by an earlier example from this field. The principal lace items of the Canadian Tariff now include embroidery as well at the same rate; but the Canada–France Trade Agreement reduced the rate on cotton lace not otherwise provided for, and the reduction was not at that time extended to embroidery. A Canadian importer received a shipment of goods from Switzerland which was classified as lace and entered at the lower rate of duty. A second shipment, however, similar to the first, except that the textile between the stitchings was burned instead of cut out, was classified as embroidery. The importer, believing that both shipments should have been classified the same way, appealed to Ottawa. His judgment that both shipments should be treated similarly was confirmed; the higher rate of duty was applied to both.

With the disruption of trade in natural rubber during the war, synthetic products were substituted in substantial amounts and in many items for the natural rubber. This change occasioned classification problems. Paragraph 1537b of the United States Tariff imposes a duty of 10 per cent *ad valorem* on automobile, motor-cycle, and bicycle tires composed wholly or in chief value of rubber. But, in response to enquiries, the Bureau of Customs gave the opinion that synthetic rubber tires would probably be dutiable at 30 per cent as articles or wares composed wholly or in part of carbon,[107] and that heavy truck tires if classed under the component of chief value (rayon) would be dutiable at 65 per cent plus 45 cents a pound.[108] Canadian authorities were faced with the same problem and in 1944 a new subsection was inserted in the Tariff Act defining "rubber" to include synthetic rubber.[109]

15. BIOLOGICAL TECHNICALITIES

A group of classification difficulties that turn wholly or in part on technical biological considerations may be illustrated from the treat-

[107]U.S. Tariff, par. 216. Reduced by 1953 to 15 per cent.

[108]Under par. 1312, reduced by 1953 to 27½¢ a lb. and 35 per cent. The United States duty on synthetic rubber and manufactures, not in part of carbon (par. 1558, unenumerated) was reduced at Geneva from 20 to 10 per cent.

[109]". . . (n) rubber includes synthetic rubber which may be defined by regulations prescribed by the Minister." Amendment to s. 2, S.C., 1944-5, c. 6, assented to, Aug. 18, 1944.

ment of certain lumber items imported into the United States from Canada. Presumably the sensitiveness of certain United States interests to lumber imports has played a part in complicating the documentary requirements and occasioning expensive litigation in this field. The first Canada–United States Trade Agreement reduced the duty on lumber from $1.00 to 50 cents per 1,000 board feet and the import tax, collected under the Internal Revenue Code, from $3.00 to $1.50.

In 1938 Northern white pine, Norway pine and Western white spruce were exempted from the Internal Revenue tax.[110] The exemption of Western white spruce gave rise to two problems: one of distinguishing lumber made from white spruce from that made from Engelman spruce; and the other of distinguishing between Western white spruce and other kinds of white spruce. These problems are considered in turn.

In British Columbia white spruce and Engelman spruce grow in the same areas within altitude ranges which, though different, overlap. The lumber from the two kinds of trees is very similar. It is said that the only single method of distinguishing between the trees themselves is by the shape of the cone scales; that some trees are atypical; and that hybridization may occur.

When lumber from Western white spruce was exempted from the import tax in June 1938, the Treasury issued regulations that, concerning lumber claiming exemption as Northern white pine, Norway pine, or Western white spruce, a declaration must be filed made by "the shipper or other person having actual knowledge of the facts as to the species of lumber comprising the shipment."[111]

In addition, in 1939, it was required that customs invoices of lumber shipments for which exemption was claimed "must set forth that the lumber is not Engelman spruce,"[112] but in 1943 this additional requirement was limited to lumber claimed to be exempt as Western white spruce.[113] In 1947 the rulings requiring additional information concerning shipments of Western white spruce were consolidated in an omnibus regulation which required that the declaration should not only contain a statement of the species but should set forth as well all the pertinent facts on which that statement was based, including the location and the altitude of the stand where the lumber originated.[114]

[110]S. 704(c) of the Revenue Act of 1938 amended s. 601 (c)(6) of the Revenue Act of 1932 to exclude Northern white pine, Norway pine, and Western white spruce.

[111]T.D. 49643 (8), June 29, 1938.   [112]T.D. 50006, Nov. 1, 1939.
[113]T.D. 50835, March 18, 1943.   [114]T.D. 51770, Oct. 15, 1947.

That the actual enforcement of the regulations occasioned the shippers considerable uncertainty, and involved them in much more expense than the mere provision of the additional documents, may be shown by summarizing the experience of shippers of lumber from two neighbouring timber berths in British Columbia. From 1942 to 1946 shipments of lumber grown on these berths were entered as Western white spruce. In 1946, however, this classification was challenged. Penalty notices were received demanding additional payment of more than $100,000 and charging that the shipments had consisted of lumber made from Engelman spruce. In addition to the financial uncertainties, trouble and expense were involved in collecting and presenting evidence and retaining counsel. A year later the Treasury decided in favour of the shipper and a charge which had been laid of falsifying invoices was withdrawn.

This particular strand in the skein of Western white spruce controversies has a happy ending, if the end has indeed been reached. A law to extend the exemption from import tax to Engelman spruce was approved in September 1950 applicable to lumber entered after October 7, 1950.[115] Collectors of customs and others were advised of the amendment by Bureau letter no. 2713, dated October 4, 1950, and for purposes of permanent record the amendment was published in *Treasury Decisions* in January 1951.[116] The Treasury decision removing the requirements of distinguishing between the two types was published on December 6.[117]

The problem of distinguishing Western white spruce from other white spruce proved even more troublesome, and the results have been less satisfactory, at least to Ontario shippers. It has been argued, variously, that "Western" refers to the geographical region, that it refers to a subspecies, and that it is merely a trade name in common use in 1938.

In April 1939 the Bureau of Customs notified port officials that lumber was not to be classified as Western white spruce unless it originated in Manitoba or provinces farther west. Maps issued by the United States customs in 1942 showed certain stands of Western white spruce and the customs regulations concerning lumber claimed to be exempt from the import tax required a declaration of the geographical location of the stand from which the lumber was made.

In September 1939, a shipment of lumber from Hudson, Ontario, though invoiced as Western white spruce was, nevertheless, assessed

<hr>

[115]P.L. 852 (1950), s. 2, approved Sept. 27, 1950.
[116]T.D. 52658, Jan. 30, 1951.   [117]T.D. 52620, Dec. 6, 1950.

the import tax at the rate $1.50 per M. On protest, this assessment was upheld by the Customs Court[118] in 1946, one judge dissenting. The appellant having died, the administrator of his estate appealed, but the Court of Customs and Patent Appeals upheld the decision in a judgment given against the appellant on December 2, 1947, eight years and three months from the date of entry.[119]

In reaching their decisions the court studied the legislative history of the Revenue Act in question and concluded that Congress had not intended to confine the tax concession to white spruce from the prairie provinces but had intended to exempt whatever was at the time of the passage of the Act commercially known as Western white spruce without regard to its location or origin. However, no witnesses had contended that in 1938 commercial usage applied the term Western white spruce to lumber from Ontario. The United States Bureau of Customs, after giving notice, has ruled that Ontario white spruce lumber is not entitled to the exemptions accorded Western white spruce and Engelman spruce.[120]

16. Wholly or in Part

One of the principal bases of arrangement in the tariff of each country is the material of which the imported articles is composed. Most imported articles, however, consist of several "materials," especially if they have been manufactured or partly manufactured; and some (for example, wearing apparel or household furniture) are composed of a number of different sorts of manufactured material, some of which are themselves composite.

Two of the more common methods of classifying articles of mixed composition are indicated by the phrases "composed wholly or in chief part by weight, volume, etc. of . . ." or "wholly or in chief value of . . . ." Both these methods, of course, require information which may not be furnished on a commercial invoice or indeed made known to the buyer. It may not be known even to the manufacturer without special investigation. Moreover, changes in the relative prices of the materials may involve a change in the rate of duty applicable to an article classified by component of chief value. Similarly, changes in design and methods of production may effect the relative physical

---

[118]V. W. Davis v. United States, C.D. 1005, May 1946.

[119]Victor W. Davis Jr. Administrator v. United States, 35 C.C.P.A. 792, C.A.D. 374.

[120]U.S., Treasury Dept., Bureau of Customs, Circular Letter no. 2841, Federal Register, April 28, 1953, cited in Foreign Trade, April 4, May 9, 1953.

quantities of the different materials components. Of these two straight-forward methods of classification, the physical criterion of weight (or volume) is to be preferred, administratively, since it can usually be determined from the article itself; while to determine the component of chief value may require a time-consuming foreign investigation. More deceptive is the method which includes in a high-duty class articles that contain any of a particular material.

It is a difficult matter to classify an imported article that does or may include several different substances as between items which include such phrases "wholly," "wholly or in part," "in chief part by weight," and "in chief part by value." The Canadian textile items provide an example of this kind of complexity. It is not possible to summarize them briefly in their full complexity; but if attention is confined to the principal n.o.p. basket items, an oversimplified picture can be presented. Under the Preferential Tariff woven fabrics, if composed wholly of cotton or vegetable fibres, are dutiable at 17½ per cent; but if they contain any wool they may be dutiable at 22½ per cent plus 12 cents a pound; and, formerly, if they contained any synthetic fibre but no wool they were dutiable at 22½ per cent. Under the Most-Favoured-Nation Tariff, woven cotton fabrics are divided into three classes according to value, dutiable at different rates. Again, fabrics that contain any wool or rayon are dutiable at higher compound rates; and other rates are provided for fabrics in chief weight of silk, or composed wholly or in part of vegetable fibre not to contain wool, silk, or synthetic textile fibres.[121]

Clothing items are less numerous than those relating to textiles. However, since an article of clothing is often composed of a number of different fabrics any one of which may contain different fibres, the chances of complication are even greater. Formerly, garments not otherwise provided for entered at the lowest rate if composed *wholly* of cotton. If other fibres entered into its composition, but not wool, higher rates might be charged. If it was composed wholly, or in chief

[121]The 1953 resolutions contained a proposal that textile yarns and fabrics should not be held to be composed in part of any textile fibre unless it contained at least 5 per cent by weight of that material. However, only one item was amended. Item 561 provides for "woven fabrics wholly or in part of synthetic textile fibres or filaments not containing wool, not including fabrics in chief part by weight of silk n.o.p. . . . 27½ p.c.; 40 p.c. plus 40 cts. per lb.; 45 p.c. plus 40 cts. per lb." To it was added "woven fabrics containing five p.c. or less, by weight, of synthetic textile yarns or filaments are not dutiable under this item but are dutiable as though such fabrics were composed only of the remaining constituents." S.C., 1952–3, c. 31.

part, of silk or of artificial silk, still higher rates applied. Finally, if it contained wool the rates were highest of all. By 1950, however, this symmetry had been disturbed. Woven textile articles n.o.p. were subject to the highest rates under the Preferential and Most-Favoured-Nation Tariff if the component of greatest value was silk, but under the General Tariff if of synthetic fibres. They were dutiable at the lowest rate under the Preferential Tariff if the component of greatest value was synthetic fibre and under the Most-Favoured-Nation and the General Tariffs if wholly of cotton, or wholly or in part of vegetable fibres but not containing wool.

It is apparent that importers of garments or textile articles must be provided with a great deal of detailed information in order to classify their imports properly. If an exporter does not provide in his invoice information sufficient to allow the importer to classify the article correctly, delay and additional expense is inevitable. An unexpected thread of wool, for example, not only in the main parts of the garment but in the facing or decoration, may subject the entire article to a different classification.[122] It is not surprising that Canadian importers of textiles and clothing quite generally claim that it is very difficult to forecast the laid-down cost of their imports. Since, in the staple lines of textiles and clothing at least, price is an important consideration, the uncertainty arising from the complexity of the tariff structure hinders importation of these staple items; and the uncertainty is even greater with respect to expensive and unusual fabrics.

The United States textile items too are excessively complicated. The rate of duty in some classes, for example, varies with the number of the yarn or the weight of the cloth. Though the main principle of distinction between textiles of different fibres is the component chief value, special classes are provided with higher duties for cloth in chief value of cotton, for example, which contains any rayon or

---

[122]Fortunately the rates under item 548, which relates to clothing and other articles made from woven fabric composed wholly or partially of vegetable fibres but not containing wool, are identical with those of item 532, which relates to wearing apparel and woven fabric articles composed wholly of cotton n.o.p. Item 555 exemplifies the complexity of these textile items: "555. Clothing, wearing apparel and articles made from fabrics, and all textile manufactures, wholly or partially manufactured, composed *wholly or in part* of wool or similar animal fibres, but of which the *component of chief value* is not silk or synthetic textile fibres or filaments, n.o.p., fabrics coated or impregnated, composed wholly or in part of yarns of wool or hair, but not containing silk nor synthetic fibres or filaments." Reduced at Geneva to 25 per cent, 27½ per cent, 40 per cent, and 35¢ per lb.

wool. And if any fabric (with one minor exception) contains more then 17 per cent by weight of wool but is not in chief value thereof, *whether or not specifically provided for*," it is dutiable according to a formula that relates the amount of duty to the proportion by weight of the wool content. Some of the items, wool gloves and mittens valued at not more than $1.75 per dozen pairs, for example, bear rates of duty that are based on the American selling price of similar domestic articles.

Prior to 1938, paragraph 1115(b) applied a high rate of duty to bodies for hats *wholly or in part* of wool felt. The 1938 Customs Administration Act amended this paragraph by striking out "wholly or in part of wool felt" and substituting "wholly or in chief value of wool but not knit or crocheted nor made in chief value of knit, crocheted, or woven material." It is said that this change was made to avoid a ruling of the United States Court of Customs and Patent Appeals that, in order to be subjected to this high-duty paragraph as originally drawn, the hat bodies had to be made of material that existed as felt before being used to make hat bodies.[123]

The United States textile paragraphs are less important to Canadian exporters than certain other paragraphs almost equally tricky. A Canadian manufacturer of rubber products, for example, exported rubber bands to the United States. His earlier shipments had been cleared as manufactures of India rubber at 25 per cent. A later shipment in 1945, however, found to be made of synthetic rubber with carbon as a colouring matter, was classed as articles in part of carbon dutiable at 30 per cent. His export of rubber bands ceased completely. The United States duty on articles in part of carbon was reduced by the Geneva Agreement.[124]

The most troublesome kind of item relating to composite articles imposes a high duty on every article containing even a trace of a particular ingredient, even though the item in question is specifically mentioned by name in some other paragraph and there assigned a different rate of duty. Of such items the most famous is paragraph 1529 of the United States Tariff which prescribes rates of duty for laces, fringes, braids, embroideries, and a great many other types of ornament and finishings and for "fabrics and articles wholly or in part

---

[123]See Levett, *Customs Administrative Act of 1938*, p. 26.

[124]"On another 'basket item' articles or wares composed wholly or in part of carbon or graphite, the rate has been reduced from 30 p.c. to 15 p.c. This is the item under which many articles manufactured of rubber substitute are presently classed." Can., Banking & Commerce, *G.A.T.T.*, April 1948, p. 80.

thereof . . . *by whatever name known, and to whatever use applied and whether or not named, described or provided for elsewhere in this Act.*" The rate of duty originally prescribed was 90 per cent, but on certain items the rates have since been reduced under the trade agreements.

The operation of this clause is illustrated by the treatment of fringed rugs. Under the United States–Belgium Agreement of 1935 the duty on imitation oriental rugs wholly or in chief value of cotton was reduced from 35 per cent to 20 per cent. On May 9, 1941,[125] the United States Customs Court ruled that cotton rugs with ends finished by omitting the weft thread and allowing the warp to protrude are to be classified as articles composed in part of fringe and dutiable at 90 per cent under paragraph 1529a. Later it ruled[126] that "imitation oriental rugs wholly or in chief part of cotton," on which the duty was reduced, did not include rugs composed in part of fringe[127] since the latter are more specifically described in paragraph 1529.

However, even though this trick class imposed a 90 per cent rate of duty, it was at one time used by importers to obtain entry of oriental rugs at a lower rate than they would otherwise have had to pay. The manufacturers of rugs in the United States had obtained a duty on Oriental rugs of 50 cents per square foot but not less than 45 per cent of their foreign value. On the cheaper Chinese rugs the specific duty at times amounted to much more than 100 per cent *ad valorem.* Importers of Chinese rugs, accordingly, advised their shippers to have a small figure embroidered along the edge. Eventually these rugs were held by the Court of Customs and Patent Appeals to be admissible at the 90 per cent rate. Shortly after this decision, on the complaint of a Senator, Congress passed an amendment excluding embroidered rugs from the embroidery section. The rate on oriental rugs, however, was subsequently reduced by trade agreement.[128]

The specialization that results from the trade agreements may have a broader, more persistent effect on such trick classes than appears at first glance. At Geneva, for example, the rate on embroidered gloves was reduced from 90 to 70 per cent as a concession to China. When this concession was withdrawn from China in 1950 it was thought that the rate would return to 90 per cent, but the domestic manufacturers discovered (or feared) that the gloves might be classed as appliqued

---

[125]U.S.C.C., C.D. 498.   [126]U.S.C.C., C.D. 707.

[127]For other classification difficulties concerning imitation oriental rugs of cotton see Levett, "Reduction of Trade Barriers," p. 5.

[128]See *ibid.*, pp. 4–5.

wearing apparel of wool now admitted at 50 per cent. Moreover, withdrawal of the latter concession, they feared, would not restore the former rate since concessions had been made on other items that the gloves might be made to fit; by allowing the threads to extend from the cuffs they might be classed as fringed gloves, for example, and with a little net as articles of net.[129]

For Canadian exporters the embroidery class is less important than certain others like it. Paragraph 1539b of the United States Tariff imposes a compound duty on "laminated products (whether or not provided for elsewhere in this Act) of which any synthetic resin or resin-like substance is the chief binding agent . . .";[130] and on "manufactures wholly or in chief value of any of the foregoing or of any other product of which any synthetic resin or resin-like substance is the chief binding agent."[131] The effect of this item is illustrated by the treatment accorded a shipment of floor tile from Canada to the United States. As floor tile it would have been dutiable under paragraph 202 at 30 per cent, which amounted to about 5 cents per square foot. However, in manufacturing the tiles a synthetic resin had been used as a binder, and the tiles were reclassified under paragraph 1539 as manufactures wholly or in chief value of a product of which synthetic resin is the chief binding agent, with a duty of 50 cents a pound and 40 per cent *ad valorem*. Heavy additional duties were assessed.[132] Incidentally, articles containing synthetic resin or hydraulic cement are excluded from the 10 per cent duty prescribed by part (b) of paragraph 1501 relating to asbestos articles; but part (c) imposes a specific duty on articles in part of asbestos "if containing hydraulic cement or hydraulic cement and other material."[133] Asbestos articles containing synthetic resin might also be classified in paragraph 1501(d) were it not for the inclusive wording of paragraph 1539.

[129]U.S. Senate, *On H.R. 1612*, p. 206. Testimony of Edwin G. Martin, Attorney for Knit Handwear Association.

[130]Fifteen cents a lb. and 25 per cent *ad valorem*; reduced at Torquay to 7½¢ a lb. plus 12½ per cent. The Canadian Tariff has included items relating to certain laminated products but without the trick ("inclusive") wording. Item 237 (1), 15 per cent, 20 per cent, or 25 per cent and 237 (ii), 20 per cent, 25 per cent, or 30 per cent. Cancelled in 1952 on recommendation of the Tariff Board in the report on Ref. 109; and replaced by item 916 which prescribes a rate of 15 per cent under the Preferential and the Most-Favoured-Nation Tariffs.

[131]Reduced at Torquay to 25¢ a lb. plus 20 per cent.

[132]Chamber of Commerce, Joint Canada–United States Committee, *Customs Administration and Procedure between Canada and the United States*, p. 13.

[133]Reduced at Geneva to ³⁄₁₀¢ a lb. if not coated, impregnated, decorated, or coloured in any manner and ³⁄₈¢ a lb. if coated, decorated, etc. in any manner.

Another over-riding paragraph in the United States Tariff prescribes a duty, formerly 70 per cent, on imports of toys not specially provided for, and comparatively high rates even on the enumerated toys. This paragraph has occasioned Canadian exporters some unpleasant surprises. Canadian manufacturers of rubber goods, for example, report that many of their products, apparently provided for by name in some other paragraph, have been classed as toys and subjected to rates ranging up to 70 per cent.[134] The toy paragraph is especially likely to be used to apply high rates of duty to relatively cheap or simple types of an article which might be used by adults or by children. The cheaper kinds of mouth organ, for example, have been classified under this paragraph.[135]

Apparently it has not been thought necessary to introduce a general provision into most of these over-riding paragraphs to prevent their wording from attracting into them articles that would otherwise bear a higher duty still. But the jewelry paragraph (1527) which imposes high rates of duty, some of them compound, does provide that none of the merchandise it includes "shall be subject to a less amount of duty than would be payable if the articles were not dutiable under this paragraph." This proviso is made to apply even to the special items covered by trade agreements. Paragraphs that apply to every article that contains a specified ingredient even though the article is specifically named elsewhere are clearly trick classes. They are designed not only to give complete protection to the makers of the named product but also to the makers of any article that contains it. However, for the purposes of this study, classes of this sort are considered reprehensible not because they prescribe high protective rates of duty but because these high rates are well concealed; and even more because these classes are apparently designed to produce, and in any event must almost inevitably occasion, a multitude of losses and unpleasant surprises for importers of many articles for which lower rates of duty are provided elsewhere in the tariff clearly and specifically.

17. REMEDIES

The importance of uncertainties introduced into international trade by the classification problems posed by complex customs tariffs has

---

[134]The rates on certain types of toys were reduced by 1953. Toys n.s.p.f. were dutiable at 35 per cent; if of rubber 50 per cent.

[135]A.G. Com., Mon. 27, p. 126. "A small mouth-organ may be entered as a musical instrument but if it is of the class which is chiefly sold and used as a toy, it is dutiable as a toy."

been recognized for a very long time. To diminish it, many proposals have been made; a few have been adopted. The League of Nations undertook an ambitious programme in 1927, of preparing a scheme to unify customs nomenclature. The World Economic Conference of that year recommended that the Council: "take the initiative in drawing up an appropriate procedure for establishing, in liaison with the producing and commercial organizations concerned, a systematic customs tariff nomenclature in accordance with a general plan covering all classes of goods."[136] The difficulties of the project soon became evident. It involved consulting and securing preliminary understandings with representatives of innumerable groups of producers, syndicates, and cartels whose interests varied, and providing a draft acceptable to countries in different stages of industrial development, using different technologies, accustomed to different tariff practices, and pursuing different tariff objectives. It involved as well an attempt to develop methods of keeping the nomenclature abreast of technical developments. This project was revived from time to time, and some progress has been made. A standard nomenclature, for example, has been compiled by the Customs Study Union which has met in Brussels in recent years. It appears easier, however, to induce countries to adopt a standard nomenclature for statistical purposes than for the actual prescription of rates of duty, but, given the desire to make customs tariffs internationally intelligible, some such proposals may ultimately be more widely adopted.

Since many disputes concerning classifications are clearly associated with the complexity of modern tariffs, with their multitude of classes often distinguished by differences which for most other purposes are unimportant, there have been proposals to solve classification problems by drastic simplification of the tariff. The *Bell Report*[137] makes such a proposal with respect to the United States Tariff. It proposes that the Tariff be composed of four divisions or lists: the free list; the specific list restricted to basic agricultural and mineral imports; the *ad valorem* list consisting of four schedules subject respectively to rates of 10 per cent, 20 per cent, 30 per cent, and 40 per cent; and the extraordinary list, consisting of articles for which quotas or tariff quotas are prescribed, and articles which are found to require a rate of duty other than those provided in the *ad valorem* list for reasons

[136]See League of Nations, Sub-committee of Experts, *Report to the 11th Assembly.*

[137]*Bell Report,* pp. 43–5. This report gives an exceptionally clear and concise account of the problems arising from customs procedures in the United States.

of defence or to prevent serious injury from imports. It recommends that goods in the *ad valorem* list "that are of essentially the same character" be made dutiable at the same rate and included in one of the rate schedules. In order to avoid the difficulties encountered in framing the 1930 Act the *Report* proposes that Congress authorize the President, with the advice of a special commission and subject to prescribed limitations and standards, to proclaim the required modifications of duties, to proclaim reductions in tariffs in return for concessions made by other countries, and to renegotiate trade agreements on items which could not be consolidated in the revised tariff.

A drastic simplification of this sort would probably be more effective than any other type of reform in simplifying customs classification. Even more important, it would indicate that the country adopting it was willing to forego the clever subtleties condoned by protectionist public opinion. It may be that protectionist beliefs are still strong enough to prevent such reform even during a prolonged period of prosperity.

Less ambitious proposals suggest methods of giving piecemeal relief from classification uncertainties by changes in the wording of particular items, together with some consolidation of items; by changes in the laws and regulations governing the classification of non-enumerated items; and by changes in customs procedures relating to classification.

With respect to the wording of items, it follows from the example discussed above that a significant number of classification disputes and surprises might be avoided if certain types of item were excluded from tariffs either by unilateral action or by international agreement. These troublesome types which might well be outlawed include items or paragraphs that prescribe relatively high rates of duty and provide specifically that the article described by them shall be subject to that duty even though enumerated by name elsewhere in the tariff; items which are distinguished by small and unimportant differences such as those that read "comprised wholly *or in part* of . . ."; and items distinguished by methods used in producing the articles, especially where the exact methods are likely to be regarded as trade secrets. Similarly, if classification does refer to the composition of articles likely to be composed of more than several materials, the criteria relating to physical composition (proportion by weight or volume for example) is to be preferred to criteria which depend on the proportion measured by value.

The combined effect of the enumeration of characteristics with respect to which an unenumerated article may resemble enumerated ones, together with the proviso that when it resembles several enumerated articles it is to bear the highest rate attached to any of them, tends to attract unenumerated articles into high duty classes. In the United States the National Council of American Importers Inc. has proposed that provision requiring that the highest rate apply be repealed and that there should be substituted for it "the rate of duty applicable to the unenumerated article to which it is most closely related according to the practices of the trade for which it is destined."[138]

In both countries provision is made for publication of general rulings and for giving warning when certain types of changes in administrative regulations are in prospect. The Customs Administrative Act of 1938[139] amended the Tariff Act[140] to provide that no ruling which imposed a higher rate of duty than would have been imposed under a well-established and uniform practice was to be effective with respect to imports entered for consumption until thirty days after its publication in *Treasury Decisions*. This amendment codified an administrative practice that had developed even before 1938.[141] More recently, ninety days' notice of intention has been given and written representations invited.[142] This procedure is not applicable to changes required by statutory enactment, judicial decision, or presidential proclamation. Similarly in Canada, three weeks' notice is given when an article is being transferred from the list of articles not made in Canada to the list of articles of a class or kind made in Canada; however, no general rule concerning notice of changes has been formally adopted in Canada. It is greatly to be desired not only that sufficiently lengthy notice of change in procedural practice or law be given but also that importers and foreign exporters be given assurance that adequate notice will be given. Uncertainties are diminished still further when customs authorities make declaratory decisions, binding on all customs collectors, with respect to the classification of particular articles which it is proposed to import.

It has been possible to secure dependable decisions from Canadian customs authorities,[143] and the rare cases of misunderstanding or error have been called to the attention of the Minister of National Revenue

[138]U.S. House, *On H.R. 1535*, p. 272–8.   [139]S. 6.   [140]U.S. Tariff Act, s. 315.

[141]In the *Federal Register*, March 3, 1953, notice of intention to reclassify onion powder from par. 781, spices dutiable at 25 per cent, to par. 775, vegetables reduced to powder dutiable at 35 per cent; also Feb. 7, 1953, concerning the reclassification of certain varieties of mustard seed not used as spices.

[142]U.S.C.R., 1937, art. 82 as amended by T.D. 49658 (1938); cited in A.G. Com., Mon. 27, p. 126. Notice under s. 315 of the Tariff Act was extended from 30 to 90 days by T.D. 53093 of Aug. 29, 1952.

[143]Misunderstandings occur now and then even under this system, as is illustrated by two or three cases above, but they have not been numerous.

so that he might investigate whether refund of duty might equitably be recommended. Until recently, however, no provision was made for declaratory rulings by the customs authorities of the United States. Each port collector made his own classification subject to report to the Customs Information Exchange and eventual uniformity secured by agreement of the collectors, or, failing that, by a Treasury decision from which, of course, a protest might be carried to the Customs Court. In 1938 an amendment to the Customs Administration Bill was introduced in the Senate providing for the issue of "declaratory rulings" by the Secretary of the Treasury; but it met with much opposition and was rejected by the conference committee.[144] The Attorney General's Committee on Administration recommended that the advance opinions given by the collector in the port of New York (if necessary after reference to Washington for a ruling) be made binding and conclusive in the absence of appeal.[145] In 1949, the Import Advisory Committee of the Office of International Trade of the Department of Commerce recommended that provision be made to provide a definite classification of an article prior to importation within thirty days if the article had been previously imported, or within six months if it was a new article,[146] and the *Gray Report* recommended that "Every effort should be made . . . to give binding rulings; and, insofar as possible, to give these rulings promptly and in advance of importation."[147] In November 1950 the Bureau of Customs amended the Customs Regulations of 1943 by adding a new section to provide for obtaining decisions on tariff classification in advance of importation in commercial quantities, and to ensure that notice is published before such decisions are changed to impose higher duties. This decision was welcomed, though not without some skepticism, by Canadian exporters.

Pre-import decisions may diminish considerably the uncertainties and losses associated with classification if they can be obtained speedily and at little cost; and if they are binding for a sufficiently long period to make it reasonable for the foreign exporter to incur the costs of developing the protected market (or to provide productive capacity to supply it). At best, of course, the trouble of obtaining the ruling will remain. Moreover, it is difficult to see how even pre-import

[144]Levett, *Customs Administrative Act of 1938*, p. 12.

[145]A.G. Com., Mon. 27, p. 159.

[146]*Interim Report*. Compare the three-day period said by Canadian importers to be sufficient if a decision has already been given concerning the article.

[147]*Gray Report*, p. 80.

decisions can give the importer reasonable security in doubtful cases if competing domestic producers are allowed to contest the decisions of the customs authorities. It follows, accordingly, that domestic competitors should not be given the privilege of appealing from a customs decision to the Customs Court in the United States; nor to the Tariff Board in Canada; or at any rate that results of such appeals should not be allowed to upset pre-import decisions.

In both Canada and the United States it seems desirable that a reasonable time limit be set between the completion of entry of an article and the final determination of its classification by customs, subject to appeal. In Canada this would require that the power of the Department of National Revenue to demand an amending entry be restricted to a period long enough to allow for reasonably expeditious central checking; an exception, of course, might be made of cases in which the importer is charged with fraud. In the United States it would require the setting of a reasonable limit to the time allowed the collector to determine classification, as well as the current limitation of the period within which a protest may be filed. Both tariffs contain items in which the rate of duty depends on the value of the article. Accordingly, this proposal implies a limitation of the time allowed for valuation as well as for classification.

VI

VALUATION AND ANTI-DUMPING DUTIES
THE UNITED STATES

A Barrister, brought to arrange their disputes—
And a Broker, to value their goods.

The Hunting of the Snark

WHEN AN ARTICLE is subject to an *ad valorem* duty or a compound duty, its value must be fixed for duty purposes; and such value, equally with the tariff rate, determines the amount of duty payable on the imported article. The rates of duty, of course, are stated explicitly in the customs tariff; they are adopted by the legislature or proclaimed under powers granted by it; and they are open to the scrutiny of the public, even though the multiplication of classes makes modern tariff structures complex and difficult to understand. Valuations, on the other hand, cannot be stated thus explicitly in the tariff; they are governed instead by definitions and procedural instructions, statutory and administrative. The wording of these definitions and rules, and the way in which they are interpreted and applied, may have a decisive effect in determining the degree of protection given by the rates of duty prescribed in the tariff.

Anti-dumping measures, too, require valuation; and in Canada, particularly, and especially in the early 1930's, complementary modifications of the rules relating to valuation and those concerning dumping were used to increase very greatly the protection afforded by the customs duties. Accordingly, it is convenient to discuss these two topics in the same chapter.

The differences and similarities of valuation procedures as between Canada and the United States provide an excellent illustration of the effects of differences in size, political constitution, and commercial policies. The United States, with a long history of relatively high rates on dutiable commodities, has developed methods of discouraging undervaluation more elaborate than have been found necessary in Canada.

In the United States the meaning of the sections of the Tariff Act that relate to valuation have been precised and subtly interpreted by a long line of court decisions. There, constitutional separation of powers has militated against changes in the statute and has, for that reason, favoured changes in its application by judicial interpretation of its meaning. Even when the statute is amended its new meaning often must be determined by a succession of court decisions.

In Canada the party discipline resulting from responsible government has facilitated amendment of the statutes; and the breadth of the discretionary powers granted the administration has further limited the importance of judicial appeal.

In the United States the greater number of entries and of importers, and early difficulties of transportation and communication, have favoured decentralization. The appraisers at each port have been encouraged to make their own initial decisions in the light of information disseminated by the Customs Information Exchange of the port of New York and by the customs branch of the United States Treasury; co-ordination of these decisions comes later. In Canada the decentralization has been less complete.

There are, however, in the valuation procedures of the two countries, important similarities. Both countries are large and have widely separated ports of entry; both accordingly have adopted the policy of establishing, as the fundamental principle of valuation for duty, something that approaches the value of the commodity in the country of origin, rather than the laid-down value at the port of entry, which is the more usual (and higher) basis for customs valuation in other countries. However, there are often many prices for the same goods in a foreign market and sometimes it is very difficult or even impossible to ascertain the true market value of the commodity in the principal markets of the country whence exported. Accordingly, both countries have adopted rules and interpretations for determining this value. In addition, the United States requires certain imports to be appraised at the American selling price of competitive articles, while in Canada invoice value is a minimum, as once was cost of production.

Both countries, too, have required declarations by foreign exporters or producers, and by domestic importers; both have employed a staff to conduct foreign investigations; both have imposed penalty duties for undervaluation, though this practice was abandoned much earlier by Canada than by the United States; both have made use of official valuation of imports though this practice was abandoned earlier by the United States.

Though this study is concerned primarily with the period since 1921, many of the regulations and interpretations affecting United States appraisement were developed over a much longer period; the Canadian statutes and practices also are based on a long history which stretches backward to the pre-confederation tariffs of the colonies.

VALUATION IN THE UNITED STATES

A. DEVELOPMENT

In the period before the war of 1812 the United States Tariff was low and uncomplicated, and the basis for dutiable value was, generally speaking, the specific price charged by the exporter for the particular shipment of goods in the country of origin; plus a mark-up of 10 or of 20 per cent, intended to correspond roughly with the cost of transporting the merchandise from the country whence exported. However, the collector was empowered to appraise imported goods at their usual value if he suspected that the invoice value was fraudulently low. In the years following 1816, more onerous rates of duty were collected, and, the danger of fraudulent valuation being thus increased, changes were made from time to time in valuation procedure. For a time arbitrary minimum values were established for certain imports. Specific export price was replaced by foreign market value, temporarily in 1828 and finally in 1842.[1] The Act of 1842 defined dutiable value as the "market or wholesale price" of the imported merchandise, "at the time when purchased, in the principal markets of the country from which the same shall have been imported" to which were to be added all costs and charges except insurance. In 1851 the relevant date was changed from the period of purchase to the period of export.

Alternative methods of valuation have long been used in difficult cases. The Act of 1833, for example, included a cost-of-production formula, and under the Administrative Act of 1890 appraisers were instructed to make use of the cost-of-production declarations which, with consular attestation, were required on goods consigned to the United States by the manufacturer. United States value, a constructed foreign value reached by making specified deductions from the selling price of the imported article, was introduced in 1894. In order to

[1]This chapter leans heavily on the excellent history and analysis of United States customs valuation in Smith, *Customs Valuation*. See also Futrell, *History of Customs Jurisprudence*, and Bidwell, *Invisible Tariff*.

provide additional protection against exports from countries with depreciating currency, "export value" was introduced in 1921 and was made permanent in 1922, to be used in the absence of, or when higher than, foreign value. The Tariff Act of 1922 provided also that American selling price be applied to coal-tar products and certain other articles as proclaimed by the President.

B. CURRENT BASES

The statutory provisions that now govern valuation are those of the Tariff Act of 1930[2] as amended, which, except for minor changes, have been carried forward from the Tariff Act of 1922.[3] Both these Acts were passed in periods when protectionist sentiment was strong in the United States—as it was in most other countries.

Section 402 of the 1930 Act sets forth the conditions that determine which of the various statutory bases for valuation is to be used for each particular kind of merchandise:

(a) *Basis*: For the purposes of this Act the value of imported merchandise shall be—

(1) The foreign or the export value, whichever is higher;

(2) If the appraiser determines that neither the foreign nor the export value can be satisfactorily ascertained, then the United States value;

(3) If the appraiser determines that neither the foreign value, the export value nor the United States value can be satisfactorily ascertained, then the cost of production;

(4) In the case of an article with respect to which there is in effect under section 366 a rate of duty based on the American selling price of a domestic article, then the American selling price of such article.

Initially the importer may not know which of these bases will be used. Prior to 1953, if he finally entered the goods at a value estimated on a basis different from that finally selected by the appraiser, or the courts, the effects of his mistake might be very serious indeed. Section 503 of the Act provided that the duty was payable on the entered value or on the final appraised value, whichever was higher (except an entered value declared by the importer to be higher than the dutiable value). And in the second place, in order to discourage undervaluation, section 489 imposed an additional duty, popularly referred to as a penalty duty (though not strictly a penalty in the technical legal sense) "of 1 per centum of the total final appraised value . . . for each 1 per centum that such final appraised value exceeds the value de-

[2]U.S., 46 Stat. 590.   [3]U.S., 42 Stat. 858.

clared in the entry. . . ."[4] The additional duty could not exceed 75 per cent of the final appraised value, but if the appraised value exceeded the entered value by more than 100 per cent fraud was presumed and the goods were subject to seizure. However, under circumstances prescribed by the Treasury, the importer might be allowed to change the entered value "at any time before the merchandise has come under the observation of the appraiser for the purpose of appraisement."[5] The phrase "under the observation of the appraiser" was interpreted to mean before the appraiser has made final appraisement and stamped the appraisal form.

This clause was used to encourage the importer to furnish the appraiser with all the relevant information in his possession. Specifically, between the receipt of invoice by the importer and the arrival of the merchandise, or perhaps at the time of initial entry, the importer might submit to the appraiser a form giving full information concerning the goods and asking to be advised as to the latest information before the appraiser as to the value of the merchandise. If the appraiser was satisfied with the co-operation of the importer he entered the information before him, and, if the goods had been entered, withheld final appraisal for a few days to allow the importer to amend his entry.[6] It was specifically stated on the submission form, however, that the value suggested by the appraiser in his advisory capacity was not an appraisal nor binding on the appraiser.

Once the appraisal was completed, the penalty duty could not be remitted except in cases where the undervaluation resulted from a clerical error or on successful appeal to the United States Customs Court,[7] where the importer was required to show that in undervaluing the goods he was acting in entire good faith, that he knew of no circumstances that would cause a prudent and reasonable person to

[4]The provisions that imposed a penalty duty and required duties to be assessed on the higher of entered or appraised value were deleted by the Customs Simplification Act of 1953. Duty is now assessed on the appraised value. The United States Tariff Commission had recommended the abolition of the penalty duty as early as 1918: U.S. Tariff Commission, *Report upon the Revision of the Customs Administration Laws*, pp. 18–19. Quoted in memorandum submitted by Alfred F. Beiter, U.S. House, *On H.R. 5106* (1953), p. 88.

[5]U.S. Tariff Act, s. 487.

[6]An amendment of customs regulations, s. 8. 29(c), provides that the importer shall be notified if the examiner believes the entered value or rate of duty to be too low and that he be given reasonable opportunity to present objections to proposed advances in rate of value prior to completion of appraisal. *Federal Register*, Jan. 12, 1954.

[7]See testimony of John Graham, U.S. House, *On H.R. 1535*, p. 42.

question the values he supplied, and that in making entry he had disclosed fully all the material facts in his possession.

The importer or prospective importer, as we have seen, may not know which of the possible valuation bases will be applied to his merchandise. Even if he knows which one of the bases actually does apply, however, he still may not know what value will be determined when this basis is used. In what follows the statutory definitions are stated and illustrations are given of the difficulty of interpreting them.

(1) Foreign Value and Export Value

If both the foreign and the export value can be ascertained the higher must be used; if only one of these it becomes the basis for valuation. It appears that these bases account for some 95 per cent of all appraisements.[8] Subsections c and d of section 402 define these two bases.

(c) *Foreign Value*: The foreign value of imported merchandise shall be the market value or the price at the time of exportation of such merchandise to the United States at which such or similar merchandise is freely offered for sale for home consumption to all purchasers in the principal markets of the country from which exported, in the usual wholesale quantities in the ordinary course of trade, including the cost of all containers and coverings of whatever nature, and all other costs, charges and expenses incident to placing the merchandise in condition, packed ready for shipment to the United States.

(d) Export Value: The export value of imported merchandise shall be the market value or the price, at the time of exportation of such merchandise to the United States, at which such or similar merchandise is freely offered for sale to all purchasers in the principal markets of the country from which exported, in the usual wholesale quantities and in the ordinary course of trade, for exportation to the United States, plus, when not included in such price, the cost of all containers and coverings of whatever nature, and all other costs, charges and expenses incident to placing the merchandise in condition, packed ready for shipment to the United States.

The interpretation of these definitions depends on Treasury decisions and many of these ultimately on decisions of the customs courts, some recent, and, as has been suggested, some very old. So many legal niceties and subtle interpretations have been introduced that the application of the definitions is seldom the one that would appear self-evident to the unaided common sense of the importer or exporter. In fact, of course, the entry is typically made by an experienced customs broker; even so, disputes as to valuation are sufficiently numerous to provide a substantial part of the occupation of the con-

[8]Smith, p. 152.

siderable number of lawyers who specialize in customs cases. The complexities of the law in this respect can only be illustrated in what follows, but the number of appeals for reappraisal during the last few years is shown in Table 10.

TABLE 10

UNITED STATES APPEALS FOR REAPPRAISEMENT
(fiscal years, 1937, 1939, and 1949–53)[a]

Year	Pending beginning of year	Filed during fiscal year	Disposed of during fiscal year	Pending end of year
1937	6,186	6,193	1,099	11,280
1939	13,899	5,502	2,250	17,151[b]
1949	15,302	9,936	2,708	22,530
1950	22,530	16,424	1,698	37,256
1951	37,256	14,966	3,291	48,931
1952	48,931	14,977	961	62,947
1953	62,947	9,321	7,603	64,665

[a]1937 and 1939 from U.S. Attorney General *Annual Reports,* report of the Assistant Attorney General in charge of Customs; 1949 to 1953, Administrative Office of U.S. Courts, *Annual Reports of the Director,* reports of the U.S. Customs Court; not including appeals on remand and on rehearing.

[b]Prewar appeals in cases pending.

This judicial precising has produced results surprising to the un-initiated who attempt to enter the United States market. In addition, because of it, more and more cases are being found in which a foreign value cannot be ascertained; in these cases, export value must be used or failing that United States value, either of which may be lower than foreign value.

Since the interpretable phrases of the two definitions are similar they may be treated together. The marketing arrangements apparently envisaged by the legislators and the courts and the ones to which the wording of the statute could be most easily applied are approximately these: manufacturers sell in relatively large quantities but at prices which may vary with the quantity; the goods may be purchased at these prices in these quantities by anyone, but in fact are usually or wholly (in the ordinary course of trade) purchased by wholesalers; wholesalers are those who sell to retailers, in smaller quantities, but who sell or offer to sell to any buyer on these same terms; and retailers are those who sell to the consumers in unit quantities. Purchases by wholesalers take place in one or a few principal markets, either where the plants of the manufacturers or producers are located or at central points to which the producers send their produce to be sold. Under these circumstances, the foreign value would be the price at which the commodity was freely sold for cash or offered for cash, by the manufacturer, in the quantity most frequently sold at wholesale. However, the actual market structures, for many commodities and in many countries, diverges from this simple idealized model in many different ways. To each commodity imported the definitions must be applied and a foreign value found; or a decision must be reached that no foreign value or export value can be ascertained. The courts have held that at any one time and place there can be only one foreign value or export value; the principal problem then is to decide which, if any, of the many prices at which a commodity is sold in the foreign country is to be selected as *the* foreign (or export) value of the merchandise.

The primary meaning given to some of the phrases used in defining these values will be outlined below but the various phrases and circumstances are closely interrelated and an exhaustive analysis is not attempted here.

(a) *Usual wholesale quantities.* The usual wholesale quantity has been interpreted to mean the quantity involved in the greatest number of transactions at wholesale;[9] and not the quantity in which the largest total volume of the merchandise is sold. Prior to 1922 it had been held that a retail price could not be selected as the foreign value even though no other basis for foreign value existed.[10] However, in 1922 the wording of the Act was changed, though it is not clear that a change in meaning was intended, from "actual market value or wholesale price" to "market value or the price . . . in the usual wholesale quantities" and since that change a trend has appeared in the direction of abandoning the wholesale price in favour of retail price when both prices exist for the quantity selected as the usual wholesale quantity.[11] Even if the market structure is such that the usual wholesale quantities selected as the basis of foreign value do fairly represent the bulk of wholesale trade in the domestic market, this quantity is very likely to be smaller (and the price correspondingly higher) than is typical of the export trade. This discrepancy is likely to be even greater when goods are exported from a country with a small domestic market to

[9]G. W. *Pleissman* v. *United States*, (1929) 16 C.C.A. 507; cited Smith, p. 172.

[10]*Keve and Young* v. *United States*, (1921) 11 C.C.A. 94.

[11]Stemming from *United States* v. *A. W. Faber Inc.*, (1933) 21 C.C.P.A. 290; cited Smith, p. 173.

a much larger foreign market. Accordingly, even if manufacturer's price is accepted as foreign value, it is likely to be higher than the actual selling price of exports.

This circumstance sometimes bears heavily on Canadian exports to the United States. Ferro-chromium, for example, is sold at a lower price in car lots than in less than car lots; in Canada the most frequent sales are less than a car lot. Therefore, when exported to the United States it has been appraised at l.c.l. prices even though usually sold for export in car lots and at correspondingly lower prices. Similarly, pharmaceuticals are appraised by the United States customs at a value consistent with trade-size packages. This is said to hinder the development of a Canadian export trade in pharmaceuticals. Recently, the Court of Customs and Patent Appeals decided a case concerning the valuation of a shipment of Canadian plywood imported in 1947. Most of the Canadian manufacturer's output, some 95 per cent of it, was sold in quantities of 5,000 square feet or more at a substantial quantity discount. The remaining 5 per cent was sold in small lots and accounted for more transactions than the other 95 per cent. Accordingly, the usual wholesale quantity was held to be the small lot and the price in the usual wholesale quantities the price without quantity discount.[12]

To avoid the anomalies, and the heavy and erratic protection, concealed in this interpretation, the Treasury proposed that the term be defined in the Act. Even as late as 1953 the Customs Simplification Bill proposed that usual wholesale quantities be defined as "the quantities usually sold in the class of transactions in which the *greater aggregate quantity* of the 'such or similar' merchandise, in respect of which value is being ascertained or estimated, is sold in the market under consideration."[13] This section of the Bill was not passed by Congress.

(*b*) *Freely offered*. The importance of the trend in interpreting the phrase "usual wholesale quantities" has been increased by the emphasis placed on the last part of the phrase "freely offered for sale . . . to all purchasers" at the expense of the phrase "in the usual course of

---

[12]*Bell Report*, p. 49. See also testimony of W. R. Johnson, Assistant Commissioner of Customs, concerning another case. "A particular example of that occurred recently in the case of certain timber products. Eighty per cent of the product was sold in carload lots; but odd sizes were frequently ordered to fill in the stock on hand, so that about 60 per cent of the sales accounted for 20 per cent of the volume. That 20 per cent of the volume incidentally, was 20 per cent higher in price. It just made an unrealistic basis of valuation." U.S. House, *On H.R. 1535*, p. 55.

[13]U.S. House, H.R. 5106, s. 15(h) (5). Italics mine.

trade." For example, in several cases where the merchandise was frequently sold to wholesalers in small quantities; and where the manufacturers sold in these quantities to wholesalers at a wholesale price and also to ultimate users but at a higher price, it has been held that the price charged wholesalers was not a price at which the commodity was freely offered, and that the price at which the usual wholesale quantities were freely offered was the price charged consumers or ultimate users in the domestic market since this was the price at which the merchandise was "freely offered to all purchasers."[14]

However refusal to accept as "foreign value" manufacturers' prices to jobbers, dealers, and wholesalers, when the goods are not freely offered to all who are willing to buy in similar quantities, sometimes works to the advantage of the United States importer and the foreign exporter by preventing entirely the ascertainment of a foreign value.

When a manufacturer sells to different classes of buyers, sales of relatively small quantities at correspondingly higher prices are likely to be more numerous than large sales at low prices, even though the bulk of the merchandise is sold at these lower prices. If so, and if it is decided that a foreign value can be found, it is likely to correspond with the highest prices charged by the producer for these smaller quantities, and not, of course, with the specific export price of the shipment being appraised, nor with the price charged domestic buyers for the quantity typically sold for export. Dutiable value is not influenced by the status of the buyer. It is the price at which the merchandise is freely offered to all purchasers in the quantity most frequently sold at wholesale.[15]

The duty-raising effect of this interpretation of "freely offered for sale . . . to all purchasers . . . in the usual wholesale quantities" is well attested by the experience and complaints of Canadian manufacturers attempting to enter the United States market. A few illustrations may suffice. One case, decided by the Court of Customs Appeal, involved a shipment of rubber tires from Canada in the early twenties. The Canadian company apportioned the domestic market by districts among a relatively small number of automobile manufacturers, jobbers, and dealers and established prices for sale to each of these classes in

[14]See e.g. *American Shipping Co., General Electric X-Ray Corp.* v. *United States,* (1942) 29 C.C.P.A. 250, cited Smith, p. 177.

[15]T.D. 42216 stated in part: ". . . Section 402(b) does not provide that the wholesale price shall be the price in the usual wholesale quantities. The law is not concerned with the persons who buy but with the manner in which they buy."

the domestic market. In addition it sold tires at prices lower than any of these to any person who would agree to export them. In this case, the Court gave a judgment favourable to the importer who contended that no foreign price could be established and the export value should therefore apply.[16]

Such cases as this have led United States producers to accuse experienced foreign exporters of arranging methods of distributing their products for the purpose of preventing the foreign value from being ascertained.[17] Whatever may be true of experienced exporters, the inexperienced and the unwary are frequently caught. Exports of cream separators from Canada to the United States were excluded in the early thirties because United States Customs began to collect duty on a higher valuation. A certain Canadian manufacturer sells his product to distributors at a 50 per cent discount, and to dealers at a 25 per cent discount from list price. The value for duty when exported to the United States has been taken as the list price, even though the product was being imported by a distributor in the United States who was entitled to and had received the 50 per cent discount. The use of list price rather than invoice price, therefore, at least doubled the duties payable. If the goods had been finally entered at the invoice price they would have been subject not only to duty on the higher price but to a penalty duty as well, equal to 75 per cent of the invoice price; indeed in this case the goods might have been subject to seizure.

Certain rubber products, including hockey pucks exported to the United States from Canada, were valued at prices charged by dealers, not at the manufacturers' prices at which they were purchased. This procedure increased the duty by 35 per cent and prevented further exports. Bicycles and motor cycles, for example, and plastic sheetings have been similarly valued, as indeed the United States statutes may require. Power chain saws exported from British Columbia to the United States were also appraised at list price. On appeal, however, the Customs Court, after a delay of about a year, decided that the saws should be valued at their wholsesale price.[18] On new articles such as this, the belief that the higher duty is chargeable, or a year of uncertainty, may result in the loss of the market.

[16]*Goodyear Tire and Rubber Co.* v. *United States*, (1922) 11 C.C.A. 351.

[17]Statement of W. R. Johnson, U.S. House, *On H.R. 1535*, p. 55, also statement of Robert E. Canfield, American Paper and Pulp Association, U.S. Senate, *On H.R. 5505* (1952), pp. 66–7.

[18]U.S.C.C., R.D. 6061, affirmed by R.D. 6289.

The duty on auto parts imported into the United States was reduced at Geneva from 25 per cent to 12½ per cent but Canadian car manufacturers charge that these parts were valued for duty not on the manufacturer's price but at the service parts price less 40 per cent which still left the duty prohibitive.

The Customs Simplification Bill, even in 1953, proposed that "freely offered for sale" be defined in the statute as "sold or offered to all purchasers at wholesale, or to one or more selected purchasers at wholesale at a price not less than that at which it would be sold to all purchasers at wholesale, without restrictions as to the disposition or use of the merchandise by the purchaser except restrictions . . . which (A) are imposed or required by law, or (B) limit the price at which or the territory in which the merchandise may be resold, or (C) do not substantially affect the value of the merchandise to usual purchasers at wholesale." "Purchasers at wholesale" was to be defined as "purchasers who buy in the usual wholesale quantities for industrial use or for resale otherwise than at retail; or if there are no such purchasers, then all other purchasers for resale who buy in the usual wholesale quantities; or if there are no purchasers in either of the foregoing categories, then all other purchasers who buy in the usual wholesale quantities."[19] These definitions would have brought the meaning of "freely offered" more nearly into conformity with actual market structures but it was deleted along with the other provisions concerning valuation.

(c) *Principal market.* The term "principal market" has been less frequently the subject to dispute than "freely offered" or "the usual wholesale quantities." For a number of reasons, especially in small countries, geographical price differences are less important than other price differences; in addition, the chief markets are frequently found by the appraisers to be at the place of manufacture or, in the case of raw produce, at some obvious and generally recognized marketing centre. However, if prices are usually quoted f.o.b. a stockyard or distribution warehouse or other recognized centre, or if sales are usually made there, then that centre may be judged to be the principal market; and prices f.o.b. that centre may be selected as the foreign value, even though all exports are sold f.o.b. the manufacturer's plant and are not shipped to the principal market at all. However, if the goods are invoiced f.o.b. port of exit, the charges for transporting the goods from the principal market to the port are not part of dutiable value, if these charges are shown separately and in detail on the

[19]U.S. House, *On H.R. 5106,* ss. 15 (h)(2) and 15 (h)(3).

invoice; but if the goods are typically sold at a uniform c.i.f. price, whether delivered to the principal market or the port of exit, no deduction for inland transport charges is allowed because the price in the principal market includes these charges.

The duty-raising effect of the interpretation of "principal market," when combined with other valuation provisions, is seen in the valuation of Canadian fireclay wares discussed below.

(d) *Country from which exported and time of export.* The "country from which exported" is usually interpreted to mean the country from which the merchandise is immediately imported, rather than the country of origin, unless it can be shown that it was consigned unconditionally to the United States at the time of its original shipment.[20] In one early case, the Supreme Court held that tea shipped from India to Halifax and reshipped to the United States should be valued at the prices prevailing in London, England, since Nova Scotia was an English colony and London was the principal English market for tea.[21] As late as 1891 the United States Board of General Appraisers considered that they were governed by this decision but in 1921 the Court of Customs Appeals ruled that Canada was a separate nation and that a large shipment of textiles whose appraisal had been appealed must be valued at the price in Canada, which included the Canadian duty, rather than at the price in England whence they had been originally exported to Canada.[22]

It is clear that the strict interpretation of country of export militates against the development of entrepot trade outside the United States, or of processing or packaging in any third country that imposes a duty on the commodity in question, even though the duty is remitted or is not collected on re-exports. Canadian regulations have a similar effect. Canadian regulations under section 46 of the Customs Act permit the goods to be valued as if imported direct provided that the bill of lading shows the ultimate destination to be a specified port in Canada without any contingency of diversion; that the goods were not entered for consumption or for warehouse nor remained for any purpose other than transshipment in any intermediate country.

The goods are valued at the *time of export*, which, in the case of

---

[20]U.S.C.R., 14.3(d).

[21]*Stairs* v. *Peaslee*, (1855) 18 Howard 521; cited in Smith, pp. 186–7.

[22]Smith, 187. In this case the Canadian duty would have amounted to almost $8,000 on a shipment otherwise valued at about $38,000. In addition to paying the regular duty on the higher valuation, the importer had to pay penalty duties amounting to nearly $8,000. *Marer* v. *United States*, (1921) 11 C.C.A. 115.

goods shipped by boat, is interpreted as meaning the date of sailing from the last port of the country of export. Nominally, valuation at date of export instead of date of purchase favours the importer in periods of falling prices and injures him in periods of rising prices. However, since delivery tends to be prompt in periods of falling prices and slow in periods of rising prices and scarcities, the net effect of this procedure is to increase the total duties paid.[23] It increases the uncertainty of the importer with respect to his laid-down cost and the danger that he may be subjected to penalty duty if he is not aware that prices in the foreign market have risen between the time of purchase and the time of export.[24] However, time of export is probably much easier to establish than time of sale, and makes for easier administration.

(e) *Such or similar.* The difficulty of defining a commodity has been treated already in discussing classification; the meaning of the term is likely to depend on the purpose for which it is being used. Even for the purpose of valuing imported merchandise, success of the search for a foreign (or export) value may turn on the phrase "such or similar merchandfise." "Such" is interpreted to mean "identical"; to be "similar," goods must be similar in material, in construction, in potential and actual use, and in commercial value (since 1930), and, perhaps, also commercially exchangeable.[25] Goods produced especially for a foreign market are likely to be slightly different from those produced for the domestic market, and the prospect of having exports valued at the (usually lower) export value is a further incentive to differentiate the products. Much litigation has failed to develop criteria that can be readily applied. In recommending the definition of "such or similar" contained in the Customs Simplification Bill of 1951, the Tariff Commission described current uncertainty with respect to the meaning of this term. "The definition of such or similar merchandise in clause (4) will for the first time provide a specific and practical definition of this commonly used term, the lack of which has greatly impeded the smooth operation of the valuation law. Even now, after many years of litigation and judicial construction, there is no definite definition of the term 'such' and 'similar' available as a practical guide to the Customs appraisers."[26] The suggested definition,

[23]Smith, pp. 188–9.
[24]E.g., screenings purchased in Canada for $5.75 rose to $15.00 before actual exportation to U.S.: Reap. no. 431, Smith, pp. 188.
[25]Smith, p. 169.
[26]Statement of U.S. Tariff Commission, House, *On H.R. 1535*, p. 233.

which is too long to reproduce here, was included also in the Bill of 1953,[27] but was later deleted.

(f) *Foreign taxes, charges, and deductions.* Whether or not a tax, duty, commission, or other charge incurred abroad will form part of the dutiable value of imports to the United States does not depend upon whether the exported merchandise is or is not subjected to the charge. Nor does it depend entirely on the way in which the charge is levied and collected. Indeed, there are many charges which are included in the dutiable value of some commodities imported from a particular country which are excluded from the value of other goods imported from the same country or from the value of the same commodity when imported from a different country. And yet this apparent confusion is the result of the consistent application of certain principles developed in the process of applying the definitions of foreign and of export value. Whether or not a particular foreign charge is to be included in the dutiable value of a particular commodity when imported from a particular country is determined by the market structure in the country whence exported; for that determines whether the value for duty is to be the foreign value, the export value, or value estimated on some other basis. The foreign value, if it can be ascertained, is some particular price that prevails in the foreign market with respect to sales for home use. If the price selected includes any tax or charge, then that charge is part of the foreign value; for example, if the price selected as the foreign value of a particular sort of merchandise is the price at which the manufacturer (a dealer) sells to the ultimate user, then taxes imposed on the seller at that level are included in dutiable value.[28]

However, the market structure may be such that no foreign value can be determined, or, in rare cases, the export value may be higher than the foreign value. The export value does not include domestic taxes or charges that are not levied on exports or that are refunded prior to exportation; nor foreign duties if re-exports are exempt from them. Indeed, strangely enough, the export value seldom contains even an export tax actually paid on the goods, because usually an export tax is not included in the value of the goods "laid down ready

[27]See U.S. House, *H.R. 5106*, s. 15(h)(4).

[28]Ordinarily local, provincial, or municipal taxes are not included in foreign value; but see Smith, p. 163: ". . . an auction sale tax levied by the Province of Quebec on certain horses was held to be part of the value of horses exported to U.S. in absence of evidence as to whether the tax was levied in all Canadian provinces" (Reap. no. 4329).

for export"; it is paid only when they are actually exported. Drawbacks of duty on goods exported, of course, do not affect foreign value, but if export value is used, drawbacks serve to reduce the dutiable values.

The Pitcairn case,[29] in which it was decided after five years of litigation that the British purchase tax should not be included in dutiable value, illustrates the effect that a narrow interpretation of "freely offered . . . to all purchasers" may have upon the selection of a price as the dutiable value and, consequently, upon the inclusion or exclusion of a domestic tax. In 1941 a shipment of chinaware was entered at the export price. The appraiser purported to find a foreign price which included the British purchase tax, which on some of these articles amounted to $16\frac{2}{3}$ per cent and on others to $33\frac{1}{3}$ per cent, and added this tax to the entered value. The appraisal was appealed from court to court until in 1946 judgment was given by the Court of Customs and Patent Appeals. The British purchase tax is not collected if the goods are exported, and if they are consumed at home it is collected by the government only when the goods first pass into the hands of an unlicensed dealer for home consumption. Since all wholesalers and many large retailers are licensed, purchase tax is not included in the selling price until the retail level is reached. The tax, that is to say, is not part of the price received by the wholesaler on sales to the retailer since it is the government and not the wholesaler who receives the tax, even though the wholesaler may collect it.

The court held that the tax was not included in any price at which such or similar merchandise was freely offered for sale in the usual wholesale quantities for home consumption to all purchasers in the principal markets and in the usual course of trade and that the foreign value did not include the tax. The entered value was therefore confirmed. This decision, of course, applied to a great many importations from Britain that had accumulated by the time judgment was finally given. The court distinguished the British purchase tax from the German sales tax, which had been held dutiable in the Passavant case[30] (long the leading case on the inclusion of foreign internal taxes), by the fact that in the British case the tax was not collected and did not enter into price paid to the manufacturer; while in the Passavant case the tax was collected from the manufacturer and, therefore, formed part of the price in all subsequent transactions.

[29]United States v. Wm. S. Pitcairn Corp., (1946) 33 C.C.P.A., 183; C.A.D. 334, affirming C.D. 5976 and C.D. 6121.

[30]United States v. Passavant, (1898) 169 U.S. 16; cited Smith, p. 155.

Two years later (presumably after official Canadian enquiries and representations) the Canadian sales tax, which like the British tax, is not collected until the product is sold to an unlicensed buyer, was eventually excluded from foreign value by action of the United States Treasury. However, the special excise tax of 25 per cent, collected (at that time) from manufacturers on the sale of certain luxury products, continued to be included in the foreign value of goods exported to the United States.[31]

The status of foreign taxes in the valuation procedures of the United States is highly unsatisfactory in two principal respects. It may simply prevent foreign governments from collecting their taxes in the most convenient, economical, or equitable way; and it is confusing not only to domestic importers and foreign exporters, but even to the United States customs officials as well.

The first effect is illustrated by the action of the Canadian Government in removing the special excise tax from certain commodities in 1948, after the United States authorities reported that they could not exclude it from foreign value by administrative action.[32] The second defect arises not from faulty logic but from the difficulty of applying to actual market conditions the judicial construction of the definitions of foreign value and export value; and to the fact that when so applied, the results appear paradoxical. Dr. R. Elberton Smith described the results as follows: "Under the law an importer is compelled to pay duty on Chinese taxes on someone else's goods that never leave China and is exempt from duty on Chinese taxes on his own goods which he must pay before they can leave the country for exportation to the United States."[33] That the treatment of foreign taxes and charges has embarrassed the United States Customs Administration is clearly stated in the following extract from a memorandum of the United States Tariff Commission:

One of the most prolific sources of litigation in customs appraisement is the question as to whether a particular internal tax imposed in the country of exportation with respect to sales for domestic consumption is to be included . . . the situation has become so complex that the determination . . . depends upon the fortuitous circumstances of the time when and the manner in which the tax accrues. At the present time the customs authorities are not at all certain under what circumstances a tax is or is not to be included in dutiable value.[34]

[31]T.D. 51966, July 15, 1948. See also H. R. Kemp, as quoted in *Industrial Canada*, July, 1948, p. 261.
[32]Can., Commons, *Debates*, 1948, p. 2131; reply of Finance Minister Abbott.
[33]Smith, p. 163.
[34]Memorandum of U.S. Tariff Commission, House, *On H.R. 1535*, p. 232.

(g) *Conversion of foreign currencies.* The foreign value (and usually the export value) is a sum stated in terms of a foreign currency; if used for appraisal, it must be converted to United States dollars. Conversion of foreign currencies, accordingly, plays an important role in valuation though it is regulated by a different section of the Tariff Act. Since 1905,[35] prevailing foreign exchange rates have been used for the conversion of foreign currency if they differed from the Mint ratios proclaimed by the Secretary of the Treasury by more than the percentage permitted by statute. Since 1921[36] the Federal Reserve Bank of New York has been required to certify daily rates to the Secretary of the Treasury, which are used if the certified rate for any currency differs by more than 5 per cent from the proclaimed par, or if no par has been proclaimed. When multiple exchange rates were certified, the Treasury began to require conversion at the certified rate which in most cases would produce the highest value. However, a decision of the Supreme Court in 1945[37] (concerning merchandise imported from the United Kingdom in 1940) upset this practice. Currently, when multiple exchange rates exist and are certified, appraisal must be made in accordance with the certified rate which reflects the value of the currency for the type of transaction in question.[38] The section of the Customs Simplification Bill relating to currency conversion was not passed by Congress. It would have substituted proclaimed par of exchange for Mint par and it prescribed a method of treating multiple rates which was considered to be consistent with the decision in the Barr case and with current customs practices.[39]

(2) *United States Value and Cost of Production*

When no foreign value and no export value can be satisfactorily ascertained either because the goods are not sold at all in the foreign market or are not freely offered there in the usual wholesale quantities,

[35]*United States v. Whitridge,* (1905) 197 U.S. 135; cited, Smith, 267.

[36]U.S. Emergency Tariff Act of 1921, s. 403; carried forward in the Tariff Act of 1930, s. 522.

[37]*Barr v. United States,* (1945) 324 U.S. 83. reversing *United States v. John Barr,* (1944) 32 C.C.P.A. 16.

[38]For a protectionist criticism of this practice see testimony of John Breckenridge, U.S. Senate, *On H.R. 5106,* pp. 191–2.

[39]H.R. 5106, s. 22. See statement of H. Chapman Rose, Assistant Secretary of the Treasury, U.S. Senate, *On H.R. 5106,* pp. 31–2. For the view that importers have been hampered by failure of the Secretary of the Treasury to publish all certified rates, and the contention that the proposed amendment would further increase administrative discretion, see statement of Hadley S. King, U.S. House, *On H.R. 1535,* pp. 447–8.

either for domestic use or for export[40] to the United States, the appraiser is instructed to apply United States value or, if no such value can be ascertained, then cost of production. These values are defined as follows:

(e) *United States Value*: The United States value of imported merchandise shall be the price at which such or similar imported merchandise is freely offered for sale, packed ready for delivery, in the principal market of the United States to all purchasers, at the time of exportation of the important merchandise, in the usual wholesale quantities and in the ordinary course of trade, with allowance made for duty, cost of transportation and insurance, and other necessary expenses from the place of shipment to the place of delivery, a commission not exceeding 6 per centum, if any has been paid or contracted to be paid on goods secured otherwise than by purchase, or profits not to exceed 8 per centum and a reasonable allowance for expenses, not to exceed 8 per centum on purchased goods.

(f) *Cost of Production*: For the purposes of this title, the cost of production shall be the sum of—

(1) Cost of materials of, and of fabrication, manipulation or other process employed in manufacturing or producing such or similar merchandise at a time preceding the date of exportation of the particular merchandise under consideration, which would ordinarily permit the manufacturing or production of the particular merchandise under consideration in the usual course of business;

(2) The usual general expenses (not less than 10 per cent of such cost) in the case of such or similar merchandise;

(3) The cost of all the coverings and containers of whatever nature and all other costs, charges and expenses incident to placing the particular merchandise under consideration in condition, packed ready for shipment to the United States; and

(4) An addition for profit (not less than 8 per cent of the sum of the amounts found under paragraphs 1 and 2 of this subdivision) equal to the profit which ordinarily is added in the case of merchandise of the same general character as the particular merchandise under consideration, by manufactures or producers in the country of manufacturing who are engaged in the manufacture of merchandise of the same class or kind.

United States value may be applied, for example, to goods consigned or sold to agents, sole distributors, or a parent firm in the United States, when the goods are subsequently freely offered for sale in the United States in wholesale quantities. Save for the limitation

[40]"Transactions which ordinarily might be considered as evidence of export value may be disregarded by the examiner because the importer has the exclusive sales agency in the United States for the manufacturer's product; or because all the negotiations leading up to the sales, and the sales themselves, were made in the United States." A.G. Com., Mon. 27, p. 107.

on rates of commission if consigned, or expense and profits if sold, it is to reach approximately the export price of the commodity. It cannot be applied, however, unless the commodity has been sold in the United States. It is to be noted that, when it can be found, the United States price from which deductions are made is frequently the highest wholesale price in the principal market of the United States (usually New York), since it is the price of the commodity in the quantity most frequently sold in that market. Generally speaking, no United States value is established until at least one shipment of the merchandise has been imported and sold; frequently the first shipment must be valued at cost of production while later shipments are appraised at United States value. This circumstance together with the obligation to re-appraise in case of faulty appraisals makes it unwise for an importer to assume that the dutiable value of subsequent shipments of any article will correspond closely with that of a trial or sample shipment.

If an article is not sold or freely offered for sale in the United States, no United States value can be ascertained and value must be assigned on the basis of cost of production. It has been estimated that less than 5 per cent of the imports to the United States are valued at cost of production.[41] As was mentioned above, cost of production may be used in valuing the initial shipments of goods which, when sold, establish a United States value that will be used for subsequent shipments. Cost of production is also used to value merchandise imported from a branch plant abroad to be further processed in the United States without being offered for sale in its imported form; or goods which are distributed both abroad and in the United States under exclusive arrangements. Establishing or verifying costs of production is often very difficult; frequently, if an article must be valued in this way, appraisal is very much delayed. The goods may be cleared, but if they are, the importer is not permitted to avoid paying the duty, if it proves to be too high, by re-exporting them.

In addition, Treasury agents abroad have frequently demanded access to the foreign plant and to information that was not made publicly available. The Act of 1922[42] provided that if a foreign producer refused a Treasury agent access to his records, his exports to the United States would be held in Customs until access was given or, if not given, sold at auction at the end of a year. Foreign producers

[41]W. R. Johnson, Assistant Commissioner of Customs, U.S. House, *On H.R. 1535*, p. 83.
[42]U.S. Tariff Act of 1922, s. 502.

and governments, notably France, objected to this provision; it was dropped from the Tariff Act of 1930.[43]

The tendency, since the revenue is affected, is to apply the law strictly and to include in costs items which might not ordinarily be included. If sales of the commodity for home consumption exist, for example, profit on these sales is to be added to cost even though they are less in number and in aggregate value than sales for exportation to the United States.[44] The value of parts or materials (or even plans) made in the United States or expenses incurred in research done in the United States are not excluded from cost of production when the article made with them is imported.[45] The Detroit Board of Commerce has repeatedly called attention to the effect of including in value for duty the value of American materials exported for processing and then reimported. This valuing procedure has tended to diminish international division of manufacturing processes along the Canadian border. "Typical cases were exportations of ingots to be made into slabs preparatory to them being rolled into sheets still in American steel mills; exportation of lever arms for adding machines for having angles bent in them; automobile truck and tank wheels and parts for flanging, stamping, drilling, etc.; piston rings for grinding." The Chamber supported a bill, introduced in 1953, to enlarge paragraph 1615 (g) of the Tariff Act to permit American goods processed abroad to be reimported on payment of duty on the added value.[46] Similarly, when engraving is done in Canada from a painting produced in the

[43]The unfortunate effects of valuation procedures and foreign investigations on the foreign relations of the United States are evidenced by incidents extending back to the Civil War. Protectionists have argued that the ill-will was attributable to the penalty for refusing access to records and not to the requirement to disclose secret or confidential information; see e.g., statement of Edwin G. Martin, Attorney for the American Knit Handwear Association, U.S. House, *On H.R. 1535*, p. 483.

[44]T.D. 52453.

[45]See Smith, pp. 215–16, who gives instances to show that valuation on the basis of cost of production has imposed insuperable barriers against certain sorts of collaboration between university presses in the United States and the presses in other countries. See also *Oxford University Press, N.Y., Inc. (M. Farris & Co., Inc.) v. United States*, (1949) 36 C.C.P.A. 102. In this last case, the cost of production of unbound books was raised by the decision that overhead cost could be apportioned only over the 20,000 copies actually printed rather than the 65,000 said to be projected over a series of years.

[46]U.S. House, *On H.R. 1535*, statement of John C. Ray, p. 282, and U.S. House, *On H.R. 5106*, letter in support of H.R. 4034, p. 199. See also *Bell Report*, p. 54. An amendment to make duty chargeable only on the value added abroad, proposed by Victor A. Knox, was accepted by the House (July 1953) but failed to pass the Senate.

United States for the sole purpose of making the engraving, the value for duty on export to the United States includes the value of the painting.

One cost of production case of little commercial importance illustrates the amount of time, trouble, and expense that may be occasioned when a new or unusual item is appraised at cost of production. A firm in Ontario was accustomed to destroy the scrap ends of the silk cord used in the manufacture of parachutes. However, in April 1940 it shipped a hundred pounds of these scrap ends to its parent company in Buffalo, for use of the Boy Scouts of that city. Though the shipment had no commercial value, it was entered at a nominal value of $5.00. In June 1941 the shipment was appraised, on the basis of cost of production, at $475, which required payment of $427.50 more in ordinary duties and a penalty duty of $325.25. On appeal, this appraisal was upheld in June 1943; on appeal for review the case was remanded to the original judge for further evidence in January 1944. On May 9, 1946, the entered value of $5.00 was at length confirmed (six years, and three hearings after entry).[47]

(3) American Selling Price

American selling price was prescribed in the Tariff Acts of 1922 and 1930 as a special basis of valuation, with the avowed intention of imposing protective duties in excess of 100 per cent of the foreign value without including such high rate explicitly in the Act.[48] It is defined in paragraph 402 as follows:

(g) *American Selling Price*: The American selling price of any article manufactured or produced in the United States shall be the price, including the cost of all containers and coverings of whatever nature and all other costs, charges, and expenses incident to placing the merchandise in condition packed ready for delivery, at which such article is freely offered for sale to all purchasers in the principal market of the United States, in the ordinary course of trade and in the usual wholesale quantities in such market, or the price that the manufacturer, producer, or owner would have received or was willing to receive for such merchandise when sold in the ordinary course of trade and in the usual wholesale quantities, at the time of exportation of the imported article.

The Tariff Act prescribes American selling price as the basis for valuing certain coal-tar derivatives; and may be applied by proclamation of the President to any merchandise if, after investigation by

[47]*Carey and Skinner, Inc.* v. *United States.* See U.S. *Treasury Decisions:* July 8, 1944, Reap. no. 5896; Jan. 27, 1944, Reap. no. 5975; June 13, 1946, Reap. no. 6279. Cited in Chamber of Commerce, *Customs Administration and Procedure between Canada and the United States.*

the Tariff Commission, it appears that his power to increase a duty by 50 per cent is insufficient to equalize domestic and foreign costs of production. However, this power has not been frequently used; proclamations have been issued with respect to some eight items including at present canned clams, rubber footwear, and wool knit gloves.[49]

American selling price was avowedly introduced to allow greater protection to be given to certain commodities by selecting a high value as the basis of computing *ad valorem* duties; but the rigid interpretation of "freely offered" has given the producers of coal-tar intermediates even more power than was intended of determining the value for duty and hence the amount of protection. If they are careful to restrict their discounts from list price so that they are not offered to all who purchase, they may sell the bulk of their output at whatever prices they wish while establishing list prices (which are accepted as the dutiable value of competing imports) as high as they wish.[50] They must, however, arrange matters so that there is a market in the United States in which the competitive domestic product is freely offered in the usual wholesale quantities; otherwise the imports are appraised at their United States value.[51] However, importers of products hitherto considered not to be competitive, or for which no American selling price could be established, are subject to surprise if a decision is reached that the American selling price of a competing product can now be determined.[52]

The continuing application of American selling price, to even a small range of imports, demonstrates the power of the protectionist proponents of some form of American value to get this basis introduced into the Act and to keep it there. Its results in the small range to which it applies show how seriously such a method of valuation would affect imports into the United States if it were made to apply to more classes of commodities.

[48]Statement of W. R. Johnson, U.S. House, *On H.R. 1535*, p. 150.

[49]*Ibid.*, p. 149.

[50]See Smith, p. 232.

[51]For an unconvincing argument that such manipulation is impossible since it could be only accomplished by a monopoly and a monopoly cannot exist under the anti-trust laws of the United States, see statement of Edwin G. Martin on behalf of the American Knit Handwear Association, *Ibid.*, p. 484.

[52]For a recommendation that such a decision should not be enforced except after sixty days' notice see statement of Eugene R. Pickersgill, U.S. House, *On H.R. 1535*, p. 455.

(4) The Five Bases

Of the five bases of valuation American selling price applies to less than one per cent of imports to the United States. It is a special basis of appraisal selected because it is much higher than any of the others. Legally, however, the other four are generally applicable, subject only to market conditions. Of these the foreign value is normally higher than export value.[53] United States value too is likely to be higher than export value because the maximum deduction allowed for commission or expenses and profits is usually smaller than those actually paid, and also because the "usual wholesale quantity" sold in the United States will often be smaller (and the price higher) than the usual wholesale quantity sold for export to the United States. There is no uniform or necessary relationship between foreign value and the United States value; either may be the higher. No valid generalization can be made, either, concerning the relation of cost of production to the other types of value, because of the difficulties involved in deciding which items, or what part of which items, are to be included in value on any basis, as well as the uncertainties and difficulties involved in ascertaining the "profit which is ordinarily added . . . in the country of manufacture" by producers of the same class of merchandise. Innovators who venture to ship across the border an article that they have not shipped before and expect that it will be valued at something approaching its invoice price are likely to be surprised that their export is found to be so valuable, especially if a foreign value can be established.

Almost as important as the increase in duties arising from appraisal at a high value is the delay that often occurs between entry and appraisal. Excepting articles subject to duty on their American selling price, the customs officials of the United States are required to attempt to ascertain *both* the foreign value *and* the export value of each imported commodity in the country from which it is exported to the United States: foreign value in particular, as has been shown, cannot be ascertained without detailed knowledge of the current marketing and tax structures of the country whence exported. Should no foreign, export, or United States value be found, an even more difficult investigation would be required to ascertain the cost of pro-

---

[53]However, the alternative bases were introduced apparently to prevent the establishment of an artificially low foreign price in a small foreign market; see the example of Canadian ferro-silicon, before 1922, of which only 10 per cent was sold in Canada, reported by Viner, *Dumping*, pp. 7–8.

duction. The delays in liquidation which may beset the importing of a new commodity when the Bureau of Customs requests an investigation by its agents stationed abroad concerning the value of an article is vividly described by Benjamin A. Levett:

The Bureau of Customs may investigate the situation abroad through one or more of its Treasury attachés or Treasury representatives, which numbered, at the beginning of 1954, less than a dozen, though once 35 or 40. "When that happens the importer may as well resign himself to the situation, take his medicine, pay or give a bond for any extra duties that might finally be assessed and perhaps in the course of one, two or more years *possibly* find the appraiser ready to accept his figure, but usually learn that in the opinion of the appraiser the price he paid is too low." Then he must either accept the appraiser's figure or file an appeal to the courts. "And when he comes into the court and his case is called several months later. . . . But suppose the special agent reports in his favor, cannot he depend upon that? Oh yes, provided he can prevail upon the United States Attorney to produce the report, which so far as the importer is concerned, is more secret than the atomic bomb."[54]

Of the hundred thousand invoices which had been in the offices of appraisers more than ninety days on June 30, 1952, approximately a third were awaiting report on foreign inquiries; a tenth were awaiting reply from the Customs Information Exchange; and another tenth were awaiting court action on related cases.

The uncertainties and delays introduced by difficulties in choosing between alternative bases of valuation is illustrated by recent litigation concerning shipments of fireclay products from British Columbia.[55] Between December 29, 1939, and April 21, 1941, M. V. Jenkins and others imported into the United States from British Columbia twelve shipments of firebrick squares and other firebrick products. It is convenient in what follows to confine attention to the appraisal of the squares; the values of the other shapes in all the decisions is closely related to this basic value. In some of these shipments, the squares were entered and appraised at $57.50 (Can.) per thousand; in others at $50.00 (U.S.) per thousand.

The collector at the Port of Seattle appealed, claiming that the foreign value of the squares was $66.00 (U.S.) and that the value of

[54]Levett, "Reduction of Trade Barriers."

[55]M. V. Jenkins et al. v. United States, 13 U.S.C.C. 345; 14 U.S.C.C. 393; 34 C.C.P.A. 33; C.A.D. 341; 21 U.S.C.C. 288; 23 U.S.C.C. 266; 23 U.S.C.C. 286; 24 U.S.C.C. 517. United States v. M. V. Jenkins et al., 26 U.S.C.C. 467.

the other products was similarly higher. The trial judge of the Customs Court held (July 10, 1944) that the squares were not freely offered for sale by the manufacturer, f.o.b. factory, even at his list price, from which discounts to dealers was allowed; and that the foreign value was the price charged by dealers in Vancouver. He, therefore, fixed the dutiable value at $66.00 (Can.) per thousand as the collector had claimed. On appeal for review, a division of three judges upheld this decision (April 20, 1945). However, on further appeal, the Court of Customs and Patent Appeals held (June 27, 1946) that the customs courts had nowhere determined "the usual wholesale quantities in which each of the various articles here involved was freely offered for sale to all purchasers in the principal markets." It, therefore, reversed the judgment and instructed that the case be returned to the trial division of the Customs Court.[56] The trial judge reviewed the evidence, found that no foreign value could be determined on the evidence, and ordered the case to be restored to the calendar (August 18, 1948). Subsequently, counsel for the importer and for the Assistant Attorney-General submitted to the Court a schedule showing the cost of production of each article for different relevant periods and stipulated that no foreign value, export value, or United States value existed. In the schedule the cost of firebrick squares was stated as follows:

Feb. 1, 1939, to Jan. 31, 1940	$52.70
Feb. 1, 1940, to Jan. 31, 1941	$52.79
Feb. 1, 1941, to Jan. 31, 1942	$59.16

On August 12, 1949, the trial judge accepted the agreed statement and schedule and decided that the costs of production contained in the schedule were the legal dutiable values. At this stage, it appeared that, after almost ten years, the case might at last be finally decided in favour of the importer; though, presumably, on the earlier shipments duty would be computed on the higher entered values. An additional or "penalty" duty might also have been payable on the last shipments.

However, in fact, the case was not yet finally determined. On October 3, 1949, the Government's Counsel stated that it was through inadvertence that he had stipulated that no foreign value existed; and a motion was granted, setting aside the judgment and providing for a retrial. Though the Attorney General's department withdrew its admission that a foreign value did not exist, the trial judge decided that

[56]The Customs Court had held that, where an article was sold in different wholesale amounts at different prices, the highest wholesale price was the value for duty.

the dutiable value was the cost of production as previously determined (January 18, 1950). The case, now become *United States* v. *M. V. Jenkins et al.*, was appealed for decision by a division of three judges which affirmed the decision of the trial judge on December 26, 1950, ten years after the products were entered; one of the judges, however, set forth his (different) reasons in a concurring opinion. To complete the picture it should be mentioned that in 1941 the appraiser began to attach higher dutiable values to the imports of fireclay products. Between January 13, 1941, and September 8, 1941, three shipments were appraised at $70.00 (Can.) per thousand plus (after April 29) the Canadian tax of 8 per cent calculated on the appraisal value. The $70.00 was supposedly the foreign value ascertained from prices charged by dealers in Vancouver. On appeal by the importer, the trial judge sustained the appraisal (January 31, 1945).[57] A motion for a rehearing, filed on March 2, was denied on April 18, 1945, but an amended decision provided that the Canadian sales tax should be computed on the manufacturer's price, as was required by Canadian law, rather than upon the appraised value. The duty, subsequently reduced to 6¼ per cent, is currently charged on dealer's prices in Vancouver, and amounts to approximately 10 per cent of the price charged by the manufacturer, f.o.b. factory. A statement of the legal work involved in the "case" is given in an appendix to this chapter; it does not include, of course, the additional hours of work required of the exporter in preparing facts and figures.[58] It is not suggested, of course, that the firebrick case is representative of the treatment of all imports into the United States, or even of all disputed entries; but it is not unique.[59]

Most of those who have been most interested in simplifying customs procedure in the United States, in diminishing the number of surprises for importers and exporters, and in lessening the delay in appraisal, have recommended that export value (amended to conform with

[57]*M. V. Jenkins* v. *United States*, 14 U.S.C.C. 304.

[58]It has been extraordinarily difficult to refrain from entitling the account of this case "Jenkins says thumbs up!"

[59]The pertinacity of the Government in this case may or may not be related to an attempt to resist the trend of court decisions toward defining foreign value out of existence. *United States* v. *Minkus*, 721 C.C.P.A. 382, T.D. 46912, was quoted to the effect that the phrase "usual wholesale quantities" might relate to a number of different quantities. The plaintiff argued that this decision might be extended so that a foreign value might be found even though "the usual wholesale quantities" were sold at many different prices. The Court rejected this argument.

"actual" value as described in the General Agreement) be adopted as the fundamental basis for appraisal in the United States, and that if export value cannot be ascertained then United States value appropriately modified. Generally speaking, they have advocated the deletion of both cost of production and American selling price.[60]

The Customs Simplification Bill originally contained important proposals of this kind for modifying and re-defining the bases for determining dutiable values. These proposals were retained, with little change, in section 15 of the Simplification Bill as it was presented to Congress in 1953 but were deleted from it.[61] The proposed amendments eliminated foreign value and made export value the preferred basis of appraisal. If export value could not be "determined satisfactorily," then the United States value was to be used; if United States value could not be ascertained then the "comparative" value; if none of these could be satisfactorily determined, then the "constructed" value based on cost of production. The bill presented in 1951 proposed to delete American selling price; but the 1953 bill proposed that it be used as at present for valuing a limited number of articles.[62]

In the determination of United States value, the actual commissions and margins for profits and general expenses were to be deducted; the current maximum limits were to be removed. For determining the United States value of new imports, the earliest actual sales in the United States might be considered, provided they were made within ninety days after importation.

Comparative value, a new basis, was defined as "the equivalent of the export values as nearly as such equivalent may be ascertained or estimated by the appraiser or the appropriate court" on the basis of "the export or United States value of other merchandise exported from the same country" and "comparable in construction and use, . . . with appropriate adjustments for differences in size, material, construction, texture, or other differences." Constructed value was to be based on

[60]See, e.g., Smith, chap. xi; National Council of American Importers Inc., *Customs Administrative Law*; and Harry S. Radcliffe, Executive Secretary of the National Council of American Importers, "The Tariff Act as *not* Amended"; International Chamber of Commerce, United States Associates, *Simplifying U.S. Customs Procedure.*

[61]See U.S. Senate, H.R. 5505, s. 13; H.R. 5106; and the Customs Simplification Act of 1935, H.R. 5877.

[62]The original Customs Simplification Bill provided, in conformity with the General Agreement, for the determination and proclamation of equivalent rates of duty on one of the other bases, for any item now appraised according to its American value.

cost of production including the allowance for general expenses and profits usually added by producers "of the same general class or kind" of merchandise in the country whence exported; the prescribed minimum mark-up of 10 per cent and 8 per cent were to be removed. Foreign internal taxes refundable on exportation, or from which the imports were exempt, were to be excluded from value. As we have seen, the new section also defined a number of terms to correspond more closely with actual market conditions. "Freely sold or offered for sale" was defined so that it did not exclude transactions in which goods were sold subject to restrictions on resale as to price or territory, restrictions required by law, or trivial restrictions. "Usual wholesale quantities" was to mean the usual quantities in the class of transactions in which the greater aggregate quantity of such or similar merchandise is sold. The phrases "ordinary course of trade," "purchasers at wholesale," and "such or similar merchandise" were also defined to correspond more closely with actual market structures and commercial usage.

These proposed amendments to the definition of value, regarded by the administration as the most important of those brought forward, would have eliminated the need to try to determine a foreign value with its concomitant foreign investigations and surprises for importers; and it would have reduced very considerably the need to use constructed value which requires knowledge of foreign costs.

By and large the valuation proposals of the Customs Simplification Bill represent an able and honest attempt to remove the greatest of the administrative difficulties involved in valuation and to conform with the articles of the General Agreement. Whether, had it been enacted, the ensuing process of judicial interpretation of the various phrases of the new definitions would have been as lengthy as some of its opponents contended may never be known.[63]

It is far from reassuring to importers and exporters that the valuation amendments have not been enacted. They have been described by the United States Administration and many others as the most important provisions of the Act;[64] and they were an attempt to remedy

[63]See e.g., letter of John G. Lerch published in U.S. House, *On H.R. 5106*, p. 69. This view was partly confirmed, partly countered, by W. R. Johnson, House, *On H.R. 1535*, p. 140.

[64]In a prepared statement, John S. Graham, Assistant Secretary of the Treasury, described the section on valuation section as "undoubtedly the most important single provision of this bill." U.S. Senate, *On H.R. 5505*, p. 28. Similarly, H. Chapman Rose, Assistant Secretary of the Treasury, "it is perhaps the most important section of the . . . bill." U.S. House, *On H.R. 5106*, p. 28.

a valuation system under which "delay and confusion are so common that the law must be regarded as unworkable."[65]

Though the amendment of the basis of valuation was rejected, the Customs Simplification Act of 1953 did make important amendments closely related to valuation. It removed the undervaluation (penalty) duty and the provision that imports were subject to seizure and forfeiture if the appraised value exceeded the entered value by more than 100 per cent. It provides also that duty is to be calculated and collected on the final appraised value; and not, as formerly, on the higher of appraised value or entered value.[66] A related amendment removed the provision which formerly allowed the importer to amend entries prior to appraisement, now no longer necessary; and another extends the conditions under which the importer will receive written notice of appraisement. These amendments will relieve the importer of a very difficult "heads I win, tails you lose" guessing competition; they will relieve the customs of the burden of dealing with an immense number of amending entries; and they will relieve the Customs Court as well of the duty of ruling on a multitude of petitions for refund of undervaluation duties to which they were required to give priority.

C. ANTI-DUMPING AND COUNTERVAILING DUTIES

As popularly used, the term dumping has the vague and broad meaning of sale at a low price. Technically, however, it means price discrimination as between different national markets: the sale of a commodity for export at a price different from (usually lower than) that charged domestic consumers, at the same time and under similar conditions of sale, for the same commodity.

The United States' Antidumping Act of 1921 is carefully drawn so that it will apply only to such price discrimination between international markets, and then only when a United States industry is actually injured, or is, or is likely to be, prevented from developing.[67] The special dumping duty is defined as the difference between the "foreign-market value" (or, in its absence, cost of production) and the purchase price (or, in its absence, "exporters' sale price") at date of purchase of the goods; "foreign-market value" and "cost of production" are very similar in meaning to "foreign value" and "cost of production," respectively, as defined for ordinary *ad valorem* duties, though if necessary the foreign-market value may be found from

[65]*Bell Report*, p. 49.
[66]Customs Simplification Act, 1953, s. 18(b) and (d).
[67]Viner, *Dumping*, pp. 262 ff.

exports to countries other than the United States. "Purchase price" and "exporters' sales price" are defined carefully to make them appropriately comparable with dutiable value. The two prices are compared as of the date of purchase; non-dutiable charges and commissions are subtracted from the actual price paid; foreign taxes, customs duties, and quantity discounts not included in the actual selling price but included in foreign value or cost of production are added back into the purchase price. Similarly, foreign bounties on export or production are added to the actual price since these practices are not offset, as in Canada, by dumping duties, but by countervailing duties.

When an appraiser suspects dumping, he is required to make a preliminary investigation including a request for additional information from the importers, if he is not satisfied, he refers the matter to the Bureau of Customs. In addition, many of the complaints of dumping are received from domestic interests.[68] If informal investigation reveals no evidence of dumping the complaint is dropped; but if symptoms of dumping are found the Treasury gives notice of suspected dumping and undertakes a formal twofold inquiry: as to the existence of dumping, on the one hand, and as to injury or danger to domestic producers on the other. If both these conditions exist, he makes a public finding of dumping with respect to the particular class or kind of merchandise and its country of origin.

Appraisement is suspended on all entries of the affected merchandise made after notice of the dumping inquiry has been given, and importers are required to file a special bond to secure to the government any additional duties found to be payable. When the investigation is concluded, appraisement is resumed and, if found applicable, the special duty is collected. The administration of the Antidumping Act is subject to review by the Customs Court and the Court of Customs and Patent Appeals.[69]

From 1921 until 1935, some 125 investigations were made,[70] and there were 56 findings of dumping,[71] chiefly during periods of falling prices. From January 1, 1935 to January 1, 1951, there were 31 inquiries but only 6 findings of dumping.[72]

[68]Between one-half and two-thirds of dumping inquiries are initiated by complaints of domestic interests. Statement of W. R. Johnson, U.S. House, On H.R. 1535, p. 74.

[69]Smith, p. 252, says except for the Secretary's actual findings of fact. Bidwell says that the Customs Court is not authorized to review the Treasury's findings as to injury sustained by American producers (Invisible Tariff, p. 105).

[70]Smith, p. 259.   [71]Bidwell, Invisible Tariff, p. 100.

[72]Hawkins, Commercial Treaties, p. 234; also statement of W. R. Johnson, U.S. House, On H.R. 1535, p. 75.

Bidwell notes[73] that, when applied, dumping duties apparently exclude the dumped article entirely or almost entirely. There has been some complaint[74] that the Treasury has at times issued findings of dumping without sufficiently careful investigation, but by and large the Antidumping Act does not appear to have been used actually to impose duties more widely than was intended. The principal hidden or unintended effect has come from withholding of appraisal until the Treasury has completed its investigation; the fear that additional duties might be assessed has impeded importation even in those investigations which showed that no dumping duty was applicable. Importers complain of the uncertainty created by the investigations, and of delays in completing them.[75] Although the investigation may take a considerable time to complete, the effects of the announcement are speedy. "Wherever there is possibility of dumping the mere initiation of an investigation is nearly always sufficient either to stop the dumping or stop the imports."[76]

The Report of McKinsey and Company recommended deferring action under the anti-dumping provisions until evidence of injury had been established in order "to prevent the harassment of importers by dumping investigations when injury to domestic industry was not . . . proved." This recommendation, however, was not incorporated in the Customs Simplification Bill.[77] One section of the original bill did propose an amendment that would have made dumping duties applicable only on proof that domestic industry was being *materially* injured, or prevented, or *materially* retarded. This section was omitted from the later bills.

Few findings of dumping have been made with respect to merchandise imported from Canada. In 1927 a finding with respect to rugs[78] imported from Canada and in 1934 a finding concerning a shipment of wheat[79] were each voided on the basis of technical defects in

[73]Bidwell, *Invisible Tariff*, p. 101.

[74]E.g. Larkin, *The President's Control of the Tariff*, p. 166.

[75]See, e.g., statement of Fred Bennett, Commerce and Industry Association of New York, U.S. House, *On H.R. 1535*, pp. 286–7. It is stated also, by those who should know, that when appraisers suspect that a dumping investigation may be in prospect, they tend to keep putting entries of the suspected imports at the bottom of the box.

[76]Statement of Philip Nichols, Jr., Assistant General Counsel, Treasury Dept., U.S. House, *On H.R. 1535*, p. 70.

[77]U.S. House, *On H.R. 1535*, p. 80.

[78]*United States* v. *Tower and Sons*, (1927) 14 C.C.A. 421, cited Smith, p. 252.

[79]*C. J. Tower and Sons* v. *United States*, (1934) 21 C.C.P.A. 417, cited Smith, p. 252.

procedure. A finding of dumping covering veneer chair seats from Canada was published in 1922. It was declared to be no longer in effect in 1938, though not revoked for record purposes until 1949.[80]

The Secretary of the Treasury is required to impose a countervailing duty on any dutiable import on the production or export of which a foreign bounty has been paid; no finding of injury is required. By way of dictum the courts have interpreted "bounty or grant" broadly to include drawback of import duties or refund of excise taxes, but in practice countervailing duties have not been applied by reason of true drawback of import or refund of excise taxes.[81] Between 1930 and January 1, 1948, countervailing duties were applied only in some 30 instances; the most important being the applications to German goods in the thirties to offset the effects of multiple exchange rates.[82] However, countervailing duties have been imposed on some imports from Canada: on dried salt fish from Nova Scotia, imposed in 1937;[83] on Canadian cheese, imposed in 1940;[84] and on blue-vein cheese of the Roquefort type produced in Canada, in 1953.[85]

The provision of the United States Tariff Act with respect to countervailing duties are inconsistent with complete acceptance of the General Agreement in two respects; it may be (though it has not been) applied to refunds of foreign import duties and excise taxes; and it must be applied even though the foreign bounty has not injured, or delayed development of, a domestic industry. The earlier versions of the Customs Simplification Bill contained amendments which would have removed these discrepancies;[86] they were not contained in the Bill introduced in 1953.

APPENDIX

Work done by lawyers in fireclay products dispute, summarized in the text, included the following:

1. Extensive investigation and consultations in Vancouver and Seattle prior to trial.

2. Trial in the United States Customs Court of the initial case.

---

[80]Published, T.D. 39027, March 3, 1922; declared no longer in effect, Circular Letter no. 1855, June 4, 1938; revoked for record purposes, T.D. 52370, Dec. 15, 1949.

[81]Viner, *Dumping*, pp. 173–8; Bidwell, *Invisible Tariff*, pp. 87–8, who cites *Downs* v. *United States*, 187 U.S. 502, 515; and *Nicholas and Company* v. *United States*, 249 U.S. 34.

[82]Hawkins, *Commercial Treaties*, pp. 133–4; for the difficulty of deciding whether a particular export is being subsidised or taxed when a country maintains many exchange rates, see statement of Frank Southard, U.S. Senate, *On H.R. 5505*, pp. 18–25.

[83]T.D. 49196, Oct. 12, 1937. [84]T.D. 50093, Feb. 9, 1940.

[85]*Industrial Canada*, Feb. 1953, p. 26. [86]H.R. 5505, s. 2.

3. Trial in the United States Customs Court of the second case.

4. Writing of briefs in both cases.

5. Application for review of an adverse decision in the first case, briefing and oral argument before the Customs Court in New York.

6. Appeal to the Customs Court, briefing and oral argument in Washington, D.C.

7. Briefing before the Customs Court upon remand by the Court of Customs and Patent Appeals.

8. Second hearing in Seattle of the initial case upon remand by the Court of Customs and Patent Appeals.

9. Briefing before the Customs Court.

10. Application by the government to review, briefing and oral argument before the Customs Court in New York.

11. Briefing and oral argument before the Court of Customs and Patent Appeals in Washington.

This does not include the time spent in preparation of facts and figures.

(Courtesy of R. M. Hungerford)

VII

VALUATION AND ANTI-DUMPING DUTIES
CANADA

It is protection. There is no getting away from that fact. But it is protection in a different manner from that of raising the Tariff.

Canada, Commons, *Debates*, vol. 96, Dec. 15, 1953, p. 920.

A. General Comparison

IN CANADA, the responsibility of the Cabinet to Parliament and the less rigorous insistence on the principle of separation of powers have favoured greater flexibility in the controlling statutes and greater delegation of powers to the Government and to the Department. Customs matters have been regarded primarily as political and economic rather than legal; historically the Customs Act and the Customs Tariff Act have provided rather limited opportunities for judicial appeal; and little use has been made of the courts even when appeal to them was possible. Customs procedure has changed more rapidly in Canada than in the United States, where revision of the statute is difficult and where judicial interpretation is more important and, though presumably rigorous, often slow.

Since World War I there have been two waves of administrative protectionism in Canada. The first, relatively mild and short, was associated with postwar depression and the Emergency Tariff in the United States. It began in 1922 when a coalition Government amended the Customs Act and the Customs Tariff. However, most of the provisions then introduced were repealed or amended in 1922 by a new Liberal Government. The second, beginning in 1930, was larger and its recession more gradual. Its crest was associated with the great depression, the Hawley Smoot Tariff in the United States, and the victory of the Conservative party in 1930. It receded gradually under the influence of the Ottawa Agreements, the trade agreements with the United States, the exigencies of war and price control, and finally the General Agreement on Tariffs and Trade.

B. DEVELOPMENT PRIOR TO 1921

The principal provisions for the valuation of imports into Canada were developed before or shortly after Confederation; and even the protective devices used in the thirties were based on a considerable amount of prior experience and experimentation.[1]

As in the United States, dutiable value in Canada is the value of the imported commodity in the country from which it is exported to Canada; carrying charges from the country of export, accordingly, have been excluded from dutiable value. From Confederation (and even before, in the provinces of old Canada)[2] until the revision of the valuations clauses after the Geneva Agreement, the wording of the leading paragraph in the valuation sections of the Customs Act has remained almost unchanged: "Where any duty, ad valorem, is imposed on any goods imported into Canada, the value for duty shall be the fair market value thereof, when sold for home consumption in the principal markets of the country whence and at the time when the same were exported directly to Canada."[3] In wording, this provision resembles closely the United States definition of foreign value but, as will appear later, it is interpreted differently.

The definition of fair market value prohibited the deduction of discounts for cash.

Such market value shall be the fair market value of such goods in the usual and ordinary commercial acceptance of the term at the usual and ordinary credit, and not the cash value of such goods, except in cases in which the article imported is by universal usage considered and known to be a cash article and so *bona fide* paid for in all transactions in relation to such article, and all invoices representing cash values except in the special cases hereinbefore referred to, shall be subject to such additions as to the collectors or appraisers of the port at which they are presented may appear just and reasonable to bring the amount up to the true and fair market value as required by this section.[4]

The amending Act of 1907 made little change in the wording of earlier acts except with respect to the allowance for cash discounts. "Such market value shall be the fair market value of such goods, in the usual and ordinary commercial acceptation of the term, and *as sold*

[1]On Canadian valuation in this period see McDiarmid, *Commercial Policy,* chap. XIII.

[2]In the Galt Tariff of 1859, the rates were all *ad valorem,* based on the value in the country of origin. To a protest from the United States that this method discriminated against them, Galt replied that he was merely adopting the American method of valuation. I am indebted to Gordon Blake for this reference.

[3]R.S.C., 1927, c. 42, s. 35. Cf. R.S.C., 1952, c. 58, s. 35(1).

[4]S.C., 1883, c. 12, s. 69.

in the ordinary course of trade, provided that *the discount for cash for duty purposes shall not exceed two and one half per cent*, and shall not be allowed unless it has been actually allowed and deducted by the exporter on the invoice to the importer."[5] Another section of the 1907 amendment provided that "duty shall not be assessed on less than the invoice value of the goods in any case, except on account of reduction in the fair market value of such goods between the time of their purchase by the Canadian importer and their exportation to Canada."

Two matters may be noted at this point. In the first place, United States appraisers, in determining "foreign value" or "export value," are required to deduct any discount for cash customarily offered from the market price selected, whether taken or not. The Canadian practice, on the other hand, has been to disallow it or limit it to a relatively small percentage; it has never been allowed unless actually taken and shown as deducted in the invoice. Ordinarily it is not shown as deducted unless the seller has received payment for the goods before shipping them; and many Canadian importers remit only on receipt of the merchandise.[6] In the second place, the Canadian provisions relate to the "ordinary commercial acceptance" of the term market value and not to "the usual wholesale quantity" nor to the condition of being "freely offered for sale." Accordingly, it has been the usual Canadian practice to consider the actual selling price fair if it is the usual price at which the merchandise is sold, by the person from whom it is purchased, in similar quantities and to a buyer with similar market status, wholesaler, dealer, jobber or retailer, as the case may be. In the Canadian procedure, then, the specific quantity included in a particular transaction may be important in determining dutiable value and also the status of the buyer; whereas, in the United States procedure, neither is taken into account.

The provision that the dutiable value may not be less than the invoice value (except to the extent that prices have fallen between the date of sale and the date of exportation) has the effect of establishing a minimum dutiable value which may be above the invoice price in periods of rising prices, and below the invoice price during periods of falling prices. It has the effect of valuing goods, imported in small amounts and at a high price, at a correspondingly high value and

[5]S.C., 1907, c. 10, s. 3.

[6]For evidence that, at some periods in the past, cash discounts were now and then fraudulently represented as trade discounts, see Royal Commission on Customs and Excise, *Interim Report*, no. 10, p. 42.

serves, accordingly, to protect Canadian wholesalers and retailers. This Canadian provision is by no means the same as the United States provision that the duty shall be levied on the basis of entered value or appraised value whichever is the larger, because, in the United States' practice, the entered value need not be the price paid by the importer. This difference in procedure is further evidence of a difference in general principle or point of view. In the Canadian practice, the status of the buyer is taken into account in determining which foreign price is to be taken as dutiable value; whereas, in the United States, dutiable value is independent of the status of the importer or the specific quantity or the specific price actually paid by him. In this respect, Canadian value for duty approaches more closely than that of the United States to a specific purchase price. In another respect, however, United States and Canadian practices are similar: in computing *ad valorem* duties, both use the value at the time of export and not at the time of purchase.

The development of complicated marketing structures, and the use of branded lines of merchandise and of special agents and distributors, have posed valuation problems for Canada as they have for the United States. By 1906 there had appeared in the Canadian Customs Act a section empowering the Governor in Council to fix maximum discounts from list prices.

> If any difficulty arises in determining the fair market value for duty of goods imported into Canada, which are the manufacture or production of foreign countries or of Great Britain, such as musical instruments, sewing machines, agricultural machines or implements, medical preparations, commonly called patent medicines, and other goods, the prices of which are published by the manufacturers or producers, or persons acting on their behalf, the Governor-in-Council may from time to time fix and determine a certain rate of discount which may be applied to such published prices . . . and such published prices, subject to deduction of the amount of the discount according to such rate, shall be deemed and taken to be the fair market values of any such goods.[7]

This section and its successors allowed the Government to value, expeditiously, a great many of the items which, in the United States, give rise to difficulty with respect to the meaning of "freely offered" and "usual wholesale quantities"; however, no appeal could be taken from the decision of the Government. As later amended it was to be a cause of complaint in the period following 1930.

Prior to 1921, in Canada (as in the United States) the current rate of exchange at the date of export was used to convert into dollars dutiable values and prices expressed in foreign currencies. Later,

[7]S.C., 1906, c. 48, s. 12.

arbitrary currency valuation was to be used to protect Canadian industries against the effects of depreciating foreign currencies.

As early as 1859 the Canadian Tariff provided for an undervaluation duty, equal to 50 per cent of the ordinary duty, when the appraised value exceeded by as much as 20 per cent the value declared on entering the merchandise. The penalty duty was removed in 1904 when the dumping duty was first introduced.

The dumping duty has played such an important part in the history of indirect protection in Canada that it must be treated in some detail. In 1904 a new clause was introduced into the Customs Tariff[8] which imposed a special duty on goods that were dumped in the technical sense of the term. Its two principal provisions were as follows:

1. Whenever it appears to the satisfaction of the Minister of Customs, or to any officer of Customs authorized to collect customs duties, that the export price or the actual selling price to the importer in Canada of any imported dutiable article of a class or kind made in Canada, is less than the fair market value thereof as determined according to the basis of value for duty provided in the Customs Act in respect of imported goods subject to an ad valorem duty, such article shall, in addition to the duty otherwise established, be subject to a special duty of customs equal to the difference between such fair market value and such selling price. Provided however that this special customs duty on any article shall not exceed one half the customs duty otherwise established in respect of the article, except in regard to . . . [certain primary iron or steel items], the special duty of customs on which shall not exceed fifteen per cent ad valorem, nor the difference between the selling price and the fair market value of the article.

2. The expression "export price" or "selling price" in this section should be held to mean and include the exporter's price for the goods *exclusive of all charges thereon after their shipment from the place whence exported directly to Canada*.[9]

Additional subsections authorized the Governor in Council to order such action as was needed to prevent evasion by shipping goods on consignment. They excluded from the special duty goods subject to Canadian excise duties and empowered the Minister to provide by regulation for the exemption of any article subject to a duty of 50 per cent *ad valorem* (or its equivalent), or when the difference between the fair market value and the selling price was small; or temporarily when an article was not made in Canada in substantial quantities or not offered for sale to all purchasers on equal terms. By section 6 of the Tariff of 1907, introduced in 1906, the special duty was made applicable to free as well as to dutiable imports and was limited to

[8]S.C., 1904, c. 11, s. 19. For a concise and authoritative history of the dumping provisions, see statement of Dr. McCann, Can., Commons, *Debates*, vol. 96, pp. 857–9, Dec. 12, 1953.
[9]S.C., 1904, c. 11, s. 19.

15 per cent *ad valorem*. The section provided that, for purpose of the special duty, foreign internal taxes were to be disregarded on goods entitled to enter under the British Preferential Tariff (extended to all goods in 1919); and it exempted from special duty goods subject to excise duty, sugar refined in the United Kingdom, and certain binder twine. By regulation a margin of 5 per cent on iron and steel, and of 7½ per cent on other products, was also exempted: an exemption that was varied from time to time and finally removed in 1921.

The Canadian dumping duty was introduced to counter protectionist demands for higher ordinary duties. It was opposed by those who favoured high protection and supported by their opponents.[10] Prior to 1921 (except perhaps with respect to internal taxes of non-British countries refunded on export) it was applicable only when technical dumping occurred, and seems to have been successful in stopping it. Later, after being used more widely to give high protection even in the absence of price discrimination, it was to gain the support of protectionists.

Prior to 1921, then, broadly speaking, the Customs Act provided that goods be valued at their fair market value in commercial acceptation of the term, when sold for home consumption in the country whence exported to Canada at like terms of sale, in similar amounts and to buyers whose status corresponded to that of the importer; provided that cash discounts could not exceed 2½ per cent. In difficult cases, however, a maximum discount from list price might be established by order in council. Dumping duty was applicable, equal to the difference between the fair market value at the time of export and the actual purchase price (but not to exceed 15 per cent of the fair market value of the goods) except that, for computing dumping duty, foreign internal taxes and excise duties were not to be included in the fair market price. Foreign currencies were to be converted at current exchange rates.

C. DEVELOPMENT, 1921–1939[11]

(1) 1921–1930

The change in the dumping duty provisions in 1919 had been in the direction of liberalizing customs administration and removing dis-

[10]See Can., Commons, *Debates*, Aug. 8, 1904 and July 17, 1905. Also *Industrial Canada*, Nov. 1903, p. 201. Contrast, *Industrial Canada*, May 1, 1950, p. 78.

[11]On Canadian valuation in this period, see McDiarmid, *Commercial Policy*, especially chap. XIII; Parkinson, *Commercial Policy*, chap. VI; and Taylor, "The Results of the Imperial Economic Conference," and "Tariff Administration and Non-Tariff Methods of Trade Control."

crimination. However, in 1921 this policy was sharply reversed; two significant changes were made in the valuation provisions.

To the fundamental section defining fair market value (section 40 in the Revised Statutes of 1907) an additional subsection was added: "(2) Provided that the value for duty of new or unused goods shall in no case be less than the actual cost of production of similar goods at the date of shipment to Canada, plus a reasonable profit thereon; and the Minister of Customs and Excise shall be the sole judge of what shall constitute a reasonable profit in the circumstances." This amendment for all practical purpose gave the Minister the power to establish an arbitrary value for duty; in conjunction with the dumping provisions it also gave him the power to apply the special anti-dumping duty up to the limit, at this time, of 15 per cent of the dutiable value of the goods. With the return of prosperity and the advent of a new Liberal Government in 1922, this amendment was repealed, though it was to appear again when the Conservatives were returned in 1930.

After World War I the pound sterling as well as many other currencies fell to a substantial discount in terms of the Canadian dollar. To guard against the effects of very rapidly depreciating currencies a second important amendment introduced in 1921, to section 59 of the Customs Act, limited to 50 per cent on the par value the reduction in the value of a foreign currency that might be recognized in converting dutiable value from foreign currencies to Canadian dollars.

59.6 Notwithstanding any of the provisions of this section, in computing the value for duty of the currency of an invoice, no reduction shall be allowed in excess of fifty per cent of the value of the standard or proclaimed currency of the country from whence the goods are invoiced to Canada, irrespective of the rate exchange existing between such country and Canada on the date of the shipment of the goods; and in respect of goods shipped to Canada from a country where the rate of exchange is adverse to Canada, the value for duty of the currency of the invoice shall be computed at the rate of exchange existing between such country and Canada at the date of shipment of the goods.[12]

This amendment had the effect, not only of providing that when depreciation of the foreign currency exceeded 50 per cent the *ad valorem* duties would be levied on a dollar value higher than the importer had to pay, but also, apparently, that in these circumstances the special dumping duty would be collected on imports "of a class or kind made in Canada."

Strictly speaking, of course, dumping in the technical sense is not occasioned by a depreciated currency. Indeed the existence of depreci-

[12]S.C., 1921, c. 26, s. 8.

ation is not even evidence that the competitive position of the foreign producer is more favourable than it was when the currency was at par; foreign exporters have a market advantage only if, and so long as, the external depreciation exceeds the rise in their own costs.

A new parliament was elected in 1921 and a Liberal Government took office. In the new House the Progressives, opposed to protection, came to hold what amounted to the balance of power between Liberals and Conservatives. In this peculiar political situation the Government avoided the extremes of protectionism that characterized the post-war tariff policies of many other countries. The cost-of-production clause was repealed and the section on currency valuation was replaced by a complicated set of provisions designed, it would appear, to prescribe some approach to a reasonable value for duty purposes when rapidly fluctuating exchanges interfered with ordinary valuation procedures. Such a provision tends, however, to protect not only domestic producers but also exporters in countries which have not devalued their currencies, or allowed them to depreciate. It tends, therefore, to diminish substantially the favourable effects of depreciation on the balance of payments of the depreciating country.

2. In the case of importations of goods the manufacture or produce of a foreign country, the currency of which is substantially depreciated, the value for duty shall not be less than the value that would be placed on similar goods manufactured or produced in Great Britain and imported from that country if such similar goods are made or produced there.

3. If similar goods are not made or produced in Great Britain, the value for duty shall not be less than the value of similar goods made or produced in any European country the currency of which is not substantially depreciated.

4. The minister may determine the value of such goods and the value so determined shall, until otherwise provided, be the value upon which the duty on such goods shall be computed and levied under regulations prescribed by the minister.[13]

This provision remained in the Act until, after Geneva, section 35 was entirely rewritten. Apparently, however, subsections 2 and 3 were seldom used.

In 1922, too, provision was made for a restricted use of arbitrary valuation in combination with the anti-dumping duties to give seasonal (and geographically flexible) protection to the producers of certain fresh fruits and vegetables by adding the following subsection to section 47 of the Tariff Act:

If at any time it appears to the satisfaction of the Governor in Council on a report of the Minister of Customs and Excise that natural products of a class or

[13]S.C., 1922, c. 18, s. 2.

kind produced in Canada are being imported into Canada, either on sale or consignment, under such conditions as prejudicially or injuriously to affect the interests of Canadian producers, the Governor in Council may in any case or cases authorize the Minister to value such goods for duty, notwithstanding any other provisions of the Act, and the value so determined shall be held to be the fair market value thereof.[14]

A related provision authorized the Minister to suspend the application of an official value to imports into a particular area of the country.

The provision relating to official valuation, of course, placed a great deal of discretionary power in the hands of the Government and of the Minister. In practice during the twenties, this power was used to prevent so-called seasonal dumping into Canada of such fresh fruits and vegetables as asparagus, cucumbers, mushrooms, rhubarb, lettuce, beets, cabbage, cauliflower, strawberries, carrots, green peas, cherries, raspberries, loganberries, onions, celery, apricots, apples, cantaloupes, muskmelons, peaches, pears, plums, and spinach. Typically these begin to come on the market from Canadian sources when production in the neighbouring part of the United States is at its peak and prices are correspondingly lower than they were at the beginning of the American season. Official values were fixed to give substantial protection in each region in Canada from the time the local crop came on the market until storage supplies were consumed. The dates at which the higher value was imposed and withdrawn varied for any item and region, from year to year, to correspond to annual differences in the season. Usually no advance notice of the date was given, but the official value was not applied to goods purchased and in transit to the Canadian purchaser prior to the date at which the higher value was imposed. Five to ten days' notice of the suspension of the valuation and cancellation of the general order was usually given. Seasonal specific rates of duty were already provided for in the Customs Tariff itself but these new provisions gave the Government even more flexible duty-making powers.

Owing to the narrow range of items affected by these provisions as applied in the twenties, and to the manner in which they were actually used, trade was less seriously disturbed than might have been expected. They were very important, however, as precedents for the great extension of arbitrary valuation in the early thirties. In both the twenties and thirties agricultural interests were, perhaps, the most powerful opponents of duties on manufactures; but the use of arbitrary valuation to give protection to agriculture in prosperous times increased the difficulty of opposing its extension to other products during a serious depression.

[14]S.C., 1922, c. 18, s. 3.

By 1922, then, the administration had been granted considerable discretionary power in determining value for duty purpose with respect to (a) imports from countries with seriously depreciated currencies, (b) the discount permitted from manufacturers or sellers list prices, and finally (c) imports of agricultural produce, but it pursued a tariff policy which in liberality was uncommon in this period.

From 1922 to 1930 few changes were made in valuation provisions. However, in the Revised Statutes of 1927 the clauses were rearranged and renumbered. The fundamental definition of dutiable value as fair market value became subsection 1 of section 35 and was followed in subsections 2, 3, and 4 by the currency provisions. Section 36 amplified the meaning of fair market value. The provision concerning discounts from a list price appears as section 37 and the power to value agricultural products as section 43. In addition the provision which gave the Minister power to determine the dutiable values in certain difficult cases became section 46 of the Customs Act. The dumping clause continued to be section 6 of the Customs Tariff Act.

(2) 1930–1939

In September 1930 the Conservatives, newly elected, summoned a special session of Parliament to consider proposals for unemployment relief and customs revision. Great and growing unemployment and the Hawley Smoot Tariff, just adopted by the United States, had fostered not only protectionist sentiment but the desire to retaliate. In addition to increases in rates of duty, a number of changes were made in the Customs Act, some of major and some of minor importance, but all tending in the direction of giving the administration power to impose heavy protective charges beyond the rates explicitly listed in the Customs Tariff. Cash discounts, formerly deductible up to 2½ per cent if actually credited to the importer on the invoices, now became part of dutiable value. The cost-of-production clause of the 1921 Act, which had been repealed in 1922, was reintroduced (with an additional provision concerning jobber prices) by repealing section 36, which had amplified the definition of fair market value, and replacing it as follows:

36(1) Such market value shall be the fair market value of such goods in the usual and ordinary commercial acceptance of the term, and as sold in the ordinary course of trade, *such value in no case to be lower than the selling price to jobbers or wholesalers generally at the time and place of shipment direct to Canada.*

(2) Provided that the value for duty of new unused goods *shall in no case be less than the actual cost of production* of similar goods at date of shipment direct to Canada *plus a reasonable advance for selling cost and profit,* and the

Minister *shall be the sole judge* of what shall constitute a reasonable advance in the circumstances *and his decision thereon shall be final.*[15]

The first of these subsections was supplemented by revision of section 37 which permitted the Governor in Council to fix the discount that was to be applied to listed prices, and made the value so determined the fair market value of the goods.[16] In addition, by amendments in 1930 and 1931, subsection 6 of section 38 was made to provide that no discount could be allowed in estimating value for duty unless it was shown, allowed, and deducted on invoices covering sales for home consumption in the country of export in the usual and ordinary course of trade.[17] This last provision was later interpreted to disallow the deduction of discounts, given, for example, to national distributors in Canada, larger than the discount allowable to ordinary or regional dealers in the United States. These discount provisions, as administered, affected unfavourably United States firms which sold on the basis of discounts from a list price and which had no branch plants in Canada.

Subsection 2 of section 36, quoted above, seems at first glance to give the Minister power to fix the dutiable value of any article at any amount he may choose, provided it is sufficiently high; and makes him the sole and final judge of the matter. However, some attempt presumably had to be made to ascertain foreign costs of production before this section could be used; and checking foreign costs was difficult and time-consuming. Accordingly, still another basis of appraisement was provided which could be used quickly to apply any desired degree of protection without fuss, expense, or delay. Formerly, section 43 had given the Governor in Council power to fix the dutiable value for any agricultural product when it appeared that imports from abroad were injuring the Canadian producers; in 1930 this provision was extended to apply to imports of any kind which the Minister deemed were injuriously affecting Canadian producers or manufacturers.

These changes were made fully effective by complementary changes in the anti-dumping section of the Customs Tariff. The maximum level of the dumping duty was raised from 15 per cent to 50 per cent of the dutiable value, except for certain articles on which the dumping duty was bound at 15 per cent by an agreement with Australia. Dumping duty, it was provided, was to be applied to any imported article of a

[15]S.C., 1921, c. 2; italics mine.
[16]S.C., 1930, c. 2.
[17]S.C., 1931, c. 29; R.S.C., 1952, c. 58, s. 36 (5).

class or kind made in Canada, when the export selling price was lower than the value for duty as ascertained under whichever of the methods of appraisal was used: the fair market value in the ordinary commercial acceptance of the term, but not less than the price to jobbers or wholesalers; the cost of production plus an advance for selling cost and profit determined solely and finally by the Minister; the list or published price less the discount fixed by order in council, which might not be greater than the discount given to domestic buyers; or the value fixed by the Minister if he considered that imports of the merchandise were injuring domestic producers. However, for computing dumping duty freight allowances were disregarded when similarly allowed in the country of export; as were excise duties, excise taxes, and United Kingdom duties on wines when the import was entitled to entry under terms more favourable than the General Tariff. Authority was transferred from the Governor in Council to the Minister, to impose the special duty when he considered that payment of dumping duties was being evaded by shipping on consignment, or by selling at unreasonably low prices goods purchased from a foreign firm by a Canadian business not completely independent of it. Finally, from time to time rates of exchange for depreciated currencies were fixed by order in council; and dumping duty was applied if the amount of Canadian funds paid by the importer was less than the dutiable value converted at the ordered rate.[18]

This set of administrative provisions was Canada's distinctive contribution to the trade barriers of the great depression. It was adopted, partly as a flexible method of increasing protection; partly as a method of retaliating against countries that had raised their tariffs; and partly to facilitate the negotiation of trade agreements, not only by encouraging other countries to make concessions but also, it may be supposed, by assuring home producers that the negotiations were being undertaken by a Government which had their interests at heart. And it was adopted at a time when all countries were increasingly obstructing trade; some by ordinary customs duties, more by prohibitions, quotas, and other direct controls. That Canada's methods were effective in obstructing trade is attested by the complaints of British and foreign exporters and of Canadian importers; by the reports of a Canadian Royal Commission and of the United States Tariff

[18]Explicit authority for this practice was given in 1933, and made retroactive to 1931, by adding subsection 9 to section 6 of the Tariff Act. Paragraph (c) of subsection 9 reads: ". . . this subsection shall be deemed to have had effect from and after the first day of September 1931." S.C., 1933, c. 37, s. 1.

Commission; by the pains taken to obtain concessions for Empire goods at the Ottawa Conference and by the fact that the Government was able to pacify Canadian manufacturers while making concessions;[19] by the United States' threat to exclude Canada from the

TABLE II

DUMPING DUTIES AND TOTAL DUTIES, CANADA, 1925–1952[a]

Year	Duty on articles lower than home trade price	Total duty
1952	$1,373,929	$393,804,690
1951	1,547,287	375,955,841
1950	1,735,543	276,531,599
1949	1,673,925	251,009,818
1948	1,343,550	242,804,007
1947	758,132[b]	325,654,359
1946	392	229,155,887
1945	622	168,277,533
1944	3,082	177,852,885
1943	100,385	173,504,597
1942	318,413	154,046,069
1941	1,547,427[c]	160,164,225
1940	2,747,581	139,194,135
1939[d]	1,445,315	103,366,037
1938[d]	885,574	89,362,465
1937	1,335,925	92,282,059
1936	1,200,890	82,784,317
1935	1,264,660	84,627,473
1934	1,764,762	73,154,472
1933	4,101,257	77,271,965
1932	1,976,625	113,997,851
1931	1,339,695	149,250,992
1930	793,722	199,011,628
1929	472,427	200,479,505
1928	579,801	171,872,768
1927	530,131	158,966,367
1926	226,499	143,933,110
1925	286,213	120,222,454

[a]*Trade of Canada*; see also Can., Commons, *Debates*, vol. 95, p. 983.

[b]Suspension of dumping duties rescinded April 1, 1947.

[c]Dumping duties suspended, except in respect of importations of fresh fruits and vegetables, effective Dec. 19, 1941 (W.M. 55; P.C. 9888).

[d]Before 1939, year ends March 31; after 1938, year ends Dec. 31.

[19]For a brief description of the consideration given to customs administration at the Ottawa Conference, see Taylor, "The Results of the Imperial Economic Conference," pp. 21–2.

benefits of the earlier treaties under the Trade Agreements Act; and finally by the provisions of Canada's trade agreements with the United States in 1935 and 1938.

The provisions of 1930, strengthened by two later amendments made to apply retroactively,[20] represent the peak of administrative protection in Canada;[21] except for the application of a 33⅓ per cent surtax during a brief trade war with Japan, the subsequent changes in Canadian customs administration have been liberalizing. This development is reflected, though inadequately, in the relationship between dumping duties collected over this period and the total duties collected. It appears from Table II that dumping duties increased from a small fraction of 1 per cent of total duties in the twenties to as much as 5 per cent of total duties in some years during the thirties. The amount of dumping duties collected, however, is a poor measure of their protective effects; it is reported that, when official valuations were imposed on a commodity, imports often ceased entirely.[22]

The relative importance of the different sections changed from time to time. Accordingly, it is convenient to examine separately their protective effects and their gradual liberalization.

(a) *Official valuation under section 43 (now 38)*. In the early thirties official valuations were proclaimed under section 43 on over 100 commodities. In addition to the fresh fruits and vegetables these included:[23] automobiles; peas (dried); beans (dried); meats (fresh and preserved); live stock; market poultry; baby chicks; eggs (in shell); eggs (frozen, powdered, or desiccated); nursery stock; bituminous coal; hats, hoods, shapes, bodies, and capelines; slack cooperage stock; ferromanganese; lime; hardwood doors; women's and children's clothing; metal name plates; brass and copper products; jute twines; cotton and artificial silk fabrics; electric lighting fixtures;

[20]In addition to adding subs. 9 to s. 6 of the Customs Tariff Act in 1933, it was deemed necessary in 1936 to add s. 43A to the Customs Act (S.C., 1936, c. 24, s. 3; repealed 1950). It provided that "all values fixed by the Minister, the Deputy Minister of National Revenue for Customs and Excise or the Assistant Commissioner pursuant to the provisions of . . . section forty-three . . . [which empowered the government by order in council to fix arbitrary values] . . . shall, notwithstanding any alleged defect or omission or want of authority . . . be deemed to have been lawfully fixed."

[21]For a criticism of these measures and examples of their effects, see speech of Mr. Ralston, Can., Commons, *Debates*, April 11, 1932.

[22]Can., Dept. of Trade and Commerce, D.B.S., *Canada's Balance of Payments*, p. 56.

[23]This list was provided through the courtesy of the Department of National Revenue.

lamps and shades; knitting machine needles; refined granulated sugar; wire rope; fringes, tassels, gimps, etc.; cotton wiping rags; umbrellas; thumb tacks and furniture nails; sheet rubber goods; berets; wood lead pencils; dried loganberries; canned salmon; casein; roses (cut); timothy seed; canned asparagus; dried egg albumen; rubber foot-wear; packaged raisins; and many textile items. The effects of these valuations are illustrated by exhibits presented to the Royal Commission on Textiles[24] and by examples in a report of the United States Tariff Commission.[25]

TABLE 12

ILLUSTRATIONS OF CANADIAN SYSTEM OF ARBITRARY VALUATIONS OF FRESH FRUITS AND VEGETABLES UNDER SECTION 43, 1936.[a]

(figures, except rates, are in cents per pound)

	Aspara-gus[b]	Toma-toes[b]	Rad-ishes[b]	Straw-berries[b]	Apples[c]
1. Invoice value (assumed)[d]	7.0	3.0	7.0	7.0	3.0
2. Arbitrary advance over invoice charged as dumping duty	5.5	3.0	5.0	2.0	1.0
3. Total value for duty	12.5	6.0	12.0	9.0	4.0
4. Rate of duty proper, percentage	30	30	30	20	20
5. Amount of duty proper	3.75	1.8	3.6	1.8	.8
6. Total duty (2+5)	9.25	4.8	8.6	3.8	1.8
7. Minimum specific duty	(3.0)	(2.0)		(3.0)	(0.6)
8. Total *ad valorem* duty had it been computed on invoice value	2.1	.9	2.1	1.4	.6
9. Excess of actual duties over (8)	7.15	3.9	6.5	2.4	1.2
10. (9) as percentage of invoice value (1)	102.	130.	93.	34.	140.
11. (9) as percentage of (8)	340.	444.	310.	171.	200.

[a]Lines 1–7 taken from U.S.T.C., *Report 111*, p. 98; lines 8–11 computed from above data.

[b]Arbitrary value imposed only during competitive season.

[c]Arbitrary value imposed all year.

[d]Assumed, but correspond closely to recent (1936) average invoice values of imports from U.S. into Canada during the relevant season; U.S.T.C., *Report 111*, p. 97.

[24]Can., Royal Commission on the Textile Industry, *Report*, especially pp. 12–16 and chap. IV.

[25]U.S. Tariff Commission, *The [First] Trade Agreement with Canada (Report 111).*

TABLE 13

EFFECTS OF OFFICIAL VALUATION ON DUTIES ON BABY CHICKS,[a] EGGS IN SHELL,[a] AND BROCADED RAYON TAFFETA,[b] 1935.

	Baby chicks	Eggs in shell	Rayon taffeta
1. Invoice value (assumed)[c]	12.0 cts. ea.	25.0 cts. doz.	$ 43.60 per M yds.
2. Minimum value for duty	30.0	35.0	136.75
3. Excess over invoice value	18.0	10.0	93.15
4. Amount charged as dumping duty	15.0[d]	10.0	68.37
5. *Ad valorem* duty proper	20%		40% less 10%
6. Amount of *ad valorem* duty	6.0 cts. ea.		$ 49.26 per M yds.
7. Packing 4.5 yen— 20 per cent less 10 per cent			40
8. Specific duty		10.0 cts. doz.	43.76
9. Excise 3 per cent			6.90
10. Total duty and excise (4+6+7+8+9)	21.0 cts. ea.	20.0	168.66
11. Total duty if computed at invoice value	2.4	10.0	59.46
12. Excess of 10 over 11	18.6	10.	109.20
13. Excess as per cent of invoice value	11.55%	40%	250%
14. Excess as per cent of 11	875%	100%	184%

[a]Data in lines 1–10 from U.S.T.C. *Report 111*; 11–14 computed.

[b]Data in lines 1–10 from *Textile Report*, p. 13, illustrates how a piece of 27-inch brocaded rayon taffeta of 1,000 yards weighing 109.4 lbs. imported from Japan and invoiced at 144.3 yen would have been dutiable at the rates prevailing in 1935. Actually it was imported in 1936 and subjected to an additional surtax of $33\frac{1}{3}$ per cent. For additional examples of the valuation of textiles see *Textile Report*, chap. IV.

[c]For eggs the value given represents approximately the average at which good fresh eggs have been sold at wholesale in northern United States markets during the season of large production in normal years shortly preceding 1936.

[d]May not exceed 50 per cent of dutiable value.

Valuations under section 43 sometimes provided for a specified advance over the invoice value, as with the items in Table 12; in other cases a minimum value for duty was proclaimed, as with the items in Table 13. It will be observed that the additional duty attributable to the advance in value ranged from 100 per cent to 875 per cent of the duty had it been calculated at invoice value and represented an increase in duty of from 34 to 250 per cent of the invoice values.[26]

On the occasion of the Ottawa Agreements, as a concession to Great Britain, Canada undertook to remove British imports from the provisions of section 43. Accordingly, in November 1932 the section was amended to exclude from its provisions goods entitled to entry under the British Preferential Tariff or any lower tariff.[27] However, relief was not immediate; the Department of National Revenue interpreted the amendment to mean that, while no further official valuations of British goods might be proclaimed, the valuations already in effect might remain. Importers appealed to the Tariff Board, which expressed the opinion that the amendment had the effect of annulling the orders of the Minister made under the old section 43. From this decision a Canadian manufacturer appealed to the Governor in Council; and in 1934 the Government referred the matter of the Tariff Board's jurisdiction to the Supreme Court of Canada. The Supreme Court gave its opinion that the Tariff Board was not competent to pass on what was purely a question of law; that it had no power, therefore, to determine that the value-fixing orders of the Minister prior to the amendment were annulled with respect to goods entering under the preferential tariff and that the Exchequer Court was the competent authority.[28] The Exchequer Court held that the orders in council in question were inconsistent with the new section and were therefore voided by amendment; and it ordered that the additional duties collected after November 1932 should be refunded to the importer.[29]

In the trade agreement that ended the tariff war with Japan, Canada agreed to suspend the official valuations that had been proclaimed on certain products imported from Japan, especially textiles; and on the occasion of the trade agreement with the United States, Canada agreed to remove fixed values from still other products including minor fruits and vegetables. With respect to some twenty major fruits and vege-

[26]This statement takes no account of the fact that, in the absence of overvaluation specific minimum duties indicated in brackets on Table 12 would have lessened the reduction of duties that would have been produced by accepting the invoice value for duty purposes. The "excise" referred to in Table 13 was a tax applied to imports but not to domestically produced goods.

[27]S.C., 1932, c. 7.

[28][1934] S.C.R. 538.

[29]*Blakey and Co. Ltd.* v. *The King*, [1935] Ex. C.R. 223.

tables, moreover, she agreed that advances in value should not exceed 80 per cent of the lowest advance over invoice price that had been effective in any of the years 1933, 1934, and 1935. By 1936, in addition to the fruits and vegetables, arbitrary values remained on the following items only:[30] pot cleaners, knitting machine needles, refined granulated sugar, wire rope, thumb tacks and furniture nails, casein, and rubber footwear.

In 1936, too, subsection 3 was added to section 43 to provide that any interested person might appeal to the Tariff Board from a valuation fixed by the Minister under this section. A finding of the board that no official valuation was needed, or only a lower one, became effective at once.

(b) *Discounts.* Section 37 (now repealed), which gave the Government power to determine the maximum discount that might be deducted from listed or published prices when computing value for duty, was used to give additional protection to domestic firms. Discounts fixed under this section affected especially importation of automobiles from firms which had no branch plants in Canada; it was widely applied also to many kinds of electrical equipment. The following example shows its application to automobiles for which the permissible discount was fixed at 20 per cent instead of the 25 per cent actually allowed.

TABLE 14
AUTOMOBILES, 1935[a]

1. American list price (assumed)	$ 1,000
2. Discount regularly allowed to dealers	25%
3. Net price to dealers	$ 750
4. Discount permitted by Canada for duty purposes	20%
5. Net value for duty purposes	$ 800
6. Dumping duty (5−3)	$ 50
7. Rate of *ad valorem* duty	20%
8. Amount of *ad valorem* duty	$ 160
9. Duty paid value basis for excise	$ 960
10. Rate of excise tax	5%
11. Amount of excise tax	$ 48
12. Total duties and tax	$ 258
13. Total cost	$ 1,008

[a]U.S.T.C., *Report 111*, p. 101.

On the occasion of the first trade agreement with the United States, Canada stated that in future no rate of discount established under

[30]U.S.T.C., *Report 111*, p. 99.

section 37 would operate to increase the value for duty of any imported good beyond the price at which it is freely offered for sale in the country of export.[31] In fact, in 1936, section 37 was repealed, and trade discounts were made deductible if given in the home market in exactly the same way in the ordinary course of trade with similar buyers, though retroactive or conditional discounts were not allowed unless conditions were fulfilled. The agents of foreign firms, however, were not recognized as independent buyers, and their imports were valued under the provisions for difficult appraisals. Deduction of cash discounts was not allowed during the thirties, but in March 1934 the Commissioner of Customs ruled that a cash discount extended generally to customers in the home market might be taken when earned without subjecting the goods to dumping duty.[32]

(c) *Cost of production.* Section 36(2), reinserted in the Customs Act in 1930, required that the dutiable value of new or unused goods should not be less than the cost of production including a reasonable advance for selling cost and profit, and it made the Minister sole judge of what constituted a reasonable profit. Goods entitled to enter under the British Preferential or more favourable tariff were excluded from its provisions in 1932. This section, used only on complaint, was intended as a defence against unusual sales of job lots, for example, or bankrupt's stocks at slaughter prices,[33] but it could be used much more widely in a serious depression, even without fixing unreasonably high profit margins. Among the commodities affected by this section were certain textiles, radio parts, dry batteries and electrical wiring devices, various other electrical apparatus, oak flooring, fir panels, packaged raisins, and coated and other textile fabrics.[34]

In fact, in Canada as in the United States, cost of production has proved an awkward basis. The *Textile Report* mentions two defects of cost of production as a basis for dutiable value:

(1) the difficulty of application of the 'actual cost of production' formula . . . and (2) the suggestion supported by exhibits 827, 828 and 829 that the machinery for arriving at the foreign cost of production may be used on occasion unduly to

[31]*Ibid.*, p. 100.

[32]U.S., Dept. of Commerce, *Preparing Shipments to Canada*, p. 19. The term "cash discount" is not unambiguous; certain imports from England are sold at 2½ per cent, sixty days. This discount is said to have been excluded if called trade discount; included if called a cash discount.

[33]Taylor, "Tariff Administration," p. 33.

[34]U.S.T.C., *Report 111*, p. 101, and *Textile Report*, p. 78. The latter gives a summary of the way in which the Canadian valuations of textile fabrics imported from the United States were based on New York spot raw cotton prices.

enhance the value of imported goods for duty purposes, for instance, by using one rule of costs for goods produced in a given country regardless of where they might be produced in that country or by whom they might be produced. However [the Commissioner continues], I was assured at the time of the argument that the policy of fixing general valuations of too broad a character has since been discontinued.[35]

Exporters from the United States complained not only that value for duty was raised but that the cost established by any method employed was so arbitrary as to create great uncertainty. They did not complain of "general valuations of too broad a character" but rather of the variation in methods of applying the valuations. "In the case of some articles, the increased valuations applied only to certain products of certain individual manufacturers. In the case of others, they applied to the products of all manufacturers shipping into Canada. The uncertainty of application of arbitrary values under this section was the subject of complaint by many exporters."[36] The United States Tariff Commission illustrates the effect of applying a cost-of-production value by the duties applied to oak flooring.

TABLE 15

CANADIAN SYSTEM OF VALUATION AS APPLIED TO OAK FLOORING, 1936.[a]
(per 1000 board feet)

1. Invoice value (assumed)	$ 57.50	
2. Advance made by Canadian customs for selling cost and profit (also charged as a dumping duty)	21.00	(customs)
3. Total value for duty purposes	78.50	
4. Ad valorem rate of duty	25%	
5. Amount of ad valorem duty	19.62	
6. Total charge (2+5)	40.62	
7. Total cost (1+6)	98.12	

[a]U.S.T.C., Report 111, p. 102.

The Canadian statement appended to the trade agreement with the United States promises in part that the value for duty established under authority of section 36(2) shall not include an advance for selling cost or profit greater than that wnich is added in the ordinary course of business under normal conditions by producers in the country of export. In 1936, accordingly, the clause was amended to provide that the advance for selling cost and profit should not "be greater than that which in the ordinary course of business under normal conditions

[35]Textile Report, p. 71.   [36]U.S.T.C., Report 111, p. 101.

of trade, is added, in the case of goods similar to the particular goods under consideration, by manufacturers or producers of goods of the same class or kind in the country of export when sold for home consumption."

No general cancellation of the valuations already established under section 36 occurred at the time of the Agreement though several of them were revised shortly afterward. In fact, with the power to value under sections 43 and 37 reduced or abolished, cost of production came, for a time after 1935, to be used more frequently than before[37] as the basis of valuation.

(d) *Difficult appraisals.* The powers of the Minister (under section 41, now repealed) to determine the value of imports under certain difficult conditions, and to decide whether these conditions existed, changed very little during the period. Though the severity of the decisions may have diminished, the section probably came to be applied more widely. Difficult cases include those in which there is no foreign selling price for the imported article; for example, when a parent concern ships to a Canadian branch a semi-finished product or a component which it does not sell for domestic consumption in the foreign market, or perhaps does not sell at all. In the later thirties at any rate, Canadian customs officials determined dutiable value by obtaining a statement from the exporter of the cost of producing the goods in condition as exported. This amount was increased by a percentage which was related to the mark-up for marketing and profits included in the price of the finished product when sold for home consumption in the foreign market. The whole of this mark-up was applied to the cost of the semi-finished product if it was small (say 15 per cent) or if little cost was incurred in finishing or manufacturing the goods in Canada. When the mark-up was larger it was reduced to an extent which depended also on the extent of the manufacturing process to which the import was subjected within Canada. Fifteen per cent, however, seems to have been regarded as the minimum advance on the cost of the merchandise in condition as imported. Other methods were used when the difficulty of valuing the import was occasioned by other circumstances. Goods imported subject to lease or royalty, for example, were commonly valued at the cost of production, plus 50 per cent, plus one year's average rental.

The comprehensiveness of the Minister's power was judicially established in a case which arose from the importation of canned corned beef from Argentine, Uruguay, and Brazil in 1940, 1941, and 1942.[38]

[37]Parkinson, *Commercial Policy*, p. 113.
[38]*King v. Weddell Limited*, [1945] Ex. C.R. 97.

On these shipments duty had been paid at the entered value; but in December 1942 the importer was notified by the Commissioner of Customs that he proposed to call for amending entries on all shipments entered after January 1, 1940. The amended valuation was considerably higher than the entered value and the importer appealed to the Minister on June 29, 1943. The Minister made an appointment to hear the importer before deciding under the power given by section 41, and in August 1943 determined the value at an amount higher than the entered value though lower than the appraiser's amended valuation.

On appeal, the Exchequer Court held that the Minister has sole power to determine that one of the circumstances mentioned in section 41 exists; "that his findings thereon, even if erroneous, are not subject to review by the Court; that having made such findings the Minister may determine the value of duty of such goods; that such determination is an administrative act; that it is conclusive of the value upon which duty on such goods is to be computed, and levied, and that it is not subject to review by the Court."

In giving judgment, the court commented on the respective roles of the Minister, the Courts, and Parliament:

The powers of the Minister under section 41 of the Act are very wide and might conceivably be abused without any power on the part of the court to intervene. While the exercise of the powers in the present case seem to bear harshly upon the defendant, it must be borne in mind that the court is not aware of all the facts that may have caused the Minister to make his determination. In any event, the Court cannot concern itself with the wisdom of the policy or the harshness of its effects in any given case, for those are matters for Parliament to determine.[39]

Many problems of appraisal were solved without resort to section 41, by applying, or purporting to apply, the fundamental criteria: fair market value but not less than cost of production. If, on an import of a class or kind made in Canada, the value so established exceeded the specific export selling price, dumping duty was commonly applied, and some importers who were ignorant of the law in this respect, or did not foresee its particular application, have been very disappointed. One such ruling related to the value of certain lithographed material. A firm with branches in Canada and the United States was accustomed to make large bulk purchases of stationery for the use of all its plants and sell or consign it to them at the low bulk purchase price. In 1932, however, it was ruled that this low price was not acceptable as value for duty. It was raised by 30 per cent if the stationery was entirely

[39]*Ibid.,* 110.

of one colour and by 35 per cent if of two or more; dumping duty was applied as well.[40]

It is probably not purely by accident that defective goods, seconds or goods of poorer quality, remnants, job lots, and closed-out or obsolete lines have often been assigned a value higher than the invoice value and have given rise to other problems as well. Indeed, the establishment of cost of production as a minimum value was defended on the grounds that it might be used to discourage imports of this kind which might seriously affect the small Canadian market. Such goods were to be valued at fair market value or cost of production; dutiable value not to be more than 20 per cent below the price of first quality or regular or current goods.[41] In the home market (and for export) goods of this kind are frequently sold at a price much lower than 20 per cent below the price on the standard lines. Additional complications are involved if the foreign purchasing agent neglects to specify that the goods in question are seconds or discontinued lines. This provision seems to be meticulously observed; in one shipment only 20 per cent discount was allowed on third-quality goods but dumping duty was not charged because it was decided that third quality of the article was not made in Canada; by exception this decision was not received until several months had elapsed after entry of the shipment.

(e) *Foreign taxes, excise, and duty.* No allowance was made for drawbacks of duty except United Kingdom duties on certain wines. In 1931 the Governor in Council was empowered to disregard excise taxes and duties levied by British countries and in 1934, as a concession to the United States, this provision was extended to all countries. From time to time particular taxes were excluded. In 1934 and 1935, for example, United States processing or compensatory taxes were excluded: on hog products, cotton products, gasoline and lubricating oils (July 1934); on wheat products, corn products, and vegetable oils (November 1934); and on rice (November 1935).[42] Taxes were excluded from goods entitled to the Preferential Tariff in the same piece-meal way; British excise taxes were excluded from the value of imported whiskey after April 1935.[43] For purposes of dumping duty, internal taxes were excluded from the value of goods entitled to enter under the Preferential and Intermediate Tariffs, and when, on

[40]Letter from Commissioner of Customs to the Collector, Port of Toronto, July 26, 1932.

[41]Can., D.N.R., *Appraisers' Bulletin*, no. 11, June 10, 1939.

[42]U.S., Dept. of Commerce, *Preparing Shipments to Canada*, p. 20.

[43]*Canada Year Book*, 1948–9, p. 907.

January 1, 1936, all imports from the United States became entitled to the Intermediate rates this treatment was extended to all her products.

(f) *Conversion of currencies.* In the earlier part of the thirties, the currency provision was used to impose heavy charges on the goods of countries whose currencies were substantially depreciated. When, in 1931, Britain left the gold standard, and the pound sterling and many other currencies became depreciated, Canada fixed the official conversion rate of sterling for duty purposes at $4.86 to the pound. This practice, of course, raised the value to which ordinary *ad valorem* rates of duties were applied; it was interpreted as making the goods subject to dumping duty as well,[44] if they were of a kind made in Canada. Depreciated foreign currencies were treated similarly, but the currencies of certain other British countries could not be thus overvalued for duty purposes without breach of trade agreements with them.[45]

Although the official conversion rate of sterling was gradually lowered toward the current sterling-dollar (Canadian) exchange rate,[46] complaints were numerous against the added burden of the duties and against the increased uncertainty introduced into international trade by the possibility that the official rate might be changed between the time of purchase and the date of entry of the goods into Canada.

In the agreement with the United Kingdom in 1932, Canada agreed to remove all existing surcharges on imports from the United Kingdom as soon as finances permitted and to "give sympathetic consideration to the possibility of reducing and ultimately abolishing the exchange dumping duty insofar as it applied to imports from the United Kingdom." After sterling rose to a premium in 1933 it was mainly imports

[44]This practice received specific statutory sanction in 1933, when an additional subsection, 9, was inserted in the anti-dumping section of the Customs Tariff Act and its provisions made retroactive to September 1931. S.C., 1933, c. 37, s. 1.

[45]It is said that for a time after 1931 importers were permitted to use the official conversion rate in stating the invoice value of the goods but this practice was discontinued; Parkinson, *Commercial Policy*, 129.

[46]On Sept. 29, 1931, the rate of exchange between the pound and the Canadian dollar was frozen at the old par. On Sept. 30 a dumping duty was imposed on British goods (P.C. 2428). On Oct. 23, the pound was revalued at $4.40 and thereafter the average current exchange rate was announced by the Minister on the first and sixteenth of each month. On March 22, 1932, it was reduced to $4.25. However, unless goods qualified as to Empire content, the pound remained at $4.86. The gold parity of the yen was maintained from Dec. 1931 to Aug. 1935. See McDiarmid, *Commercial Policy*, pp. 313 ff.

from Japan that were affected. Against Japanese goods arbitrary valuations, as well as relatively high currency conversion rates, were established, and the higher values obtained by these methods was used as the dutiable value in determining both the ordinary and the special duty. In retaliation, Japan imposed a 50 per cent surtax on imports from Canada. Canada replied by imposing a 33⅓ per cent surtax on Japanese goods;[47] however, the surtax was not applied to goods shown to be contracted for before the date of the order imposing the surtax if imported before November 5.[48] This brief trade war was terminated by a trade agreement that involved cancelling a number of arbitrary valuations and fixing the conversion value of the yen at its average value over the years 1930–4. Subsequently, the Canadian authorities began to value imports from most countries at current rates of exchange.[49] In two respects at least, the protection given by overvaluing dutiable imports and collecting the overvaluation as a dumping duty was even greater that it appears at first glance. The domestic sales tax was calculated on the duty-paid value of the imports; accordingly, the value base for this tax was raised not by the official overvaluation but by the additional normal and dumping duty that the overvaluation occasioned. In the second place, domestic manufacturers who imported their raw materials free from the country whose currency was depreciating had the costs of the raw materials reduced by any excess of external over internal depreciation as well as benefiting from the additional duty occasioned by official overvaluation; the value added in Canada might be only a small part of the total value of an article, yet the overvaluation and the dumping duty was applied to the whole value of imports of the finished article.

D. War and Post-War

By 1939 Canada had modified considerably her protective valuation practices. The use of arbitrary valuation was limited by treaty obligations, and appeal to the Tariff Board was permitted; the blanket power of fixing the rate of discount from list prices had disappeared entirely. The provision with respect to cost of production, however,

---

[47]P.C. 2108, July 22, 1930. Effective Aug. 3.

[48]P.C. 2317, Aug. 3, 1935.

[49]See, e.g., Can., D.N.R., Series D, no. 83, April 27, 1937, current rate proclaimed for German mark to apply to all goods imported after April 23, 1937; D, 85, July 22, 1937, P.C. 29/1703, July 16, 1937 (suspends P.C. 137/1588, Aug. 13, 1928), current rate of exchange on date of shipment now to be taken as value for duty for French franc. See also D, 59, Dec. 27, 1940, and D, 101, rev. Nov. 15, 1939.

might still be used in certain cases consistently with the general policy announced in the statements appended to trade agreements, in particular to protect against special slaughter prices; the Minister had retained the power to determine value in difficult cases; and dumping duties were still important. Examples given by importers from their experience between 1938 and 1942 show that increases in duty of from 5 to 25 per cent in the laid-down cost of imports from the United States were attributable to an increase in the invoice price, attested by the exporter to be the fair market price in the United States. During the war and the years immediately following, a number of steps were taken that reduced the difficulties of customs officials and importers, and assisted also in maintaining the price ceiling; some of these affected valuation procedures. Excise duties and taxes imposed by any country were excluded from the value for duty of goods imported into Canada.[50] Dumping duties were suspended except with respect to fresh fruits and vegetables.[51] Provision was made to permit the Minister of National Revenue to accept the actual invoice value for duty purposes, and this provision was applied to a considerable number of important commodities.[52]

After 1945, the wartime controls were gradually dismantled and the discretionary powers of the Government gradually reduced. In the process the special orders concerning customs were rescinded. Dumping duties became applicable after April 1, 1947, though a substantial list of imports was exempted from their operation primarily to relieve certain British exports which might otherwise have been subject to them.[53]

[50]P.C. 62/450, Jan. 20, 1942.

[51]P.C. 9888, Dec. 19, 1941.

[52]P.C. 9889, Dec. 19, 1941; extended to other countries in Feb. 1942; also Can., Wartime Prices and Trade Board, *Report*, pp. 85–6. For wartime import controls see R. W. James, *Wartime Economic Co-operation*, pp. 215–19.

[53]Exemptions were permitted by s. 6(2) (ii) introduced into the Tariff Act in 1948. P.C. 3550, Aug. 9, 1948, effective May 19, 1948, exempted motor vehicles, linoleum and oilcloth, confectionery, sanitary earthenware, and sporting equipment of various kinds. Other items were exempted from time to time, including soda ash, lawn mowers, gramophone records, cocoa butter, certain preparations of cocoa and chocolate, glass and white potter cement. Domestic manufacturers objected to many of these exemptions (see *Industrial Canada*, Feb. 1951, p. 47; July 1951, p. 67). During 1950 and 1951 they were removed piece-meal. See D.N.R., Series D, no. 51, M.C.R. 8, 7, Sup. no. 6, dated Nov. 15, 1950. For report and critical comment, see U.S.T.C., *Operation of the Trade Agreements Program*, p. 131. On the post-war use of dumping duties see article by K. R. Wilson in *Financial Post*, March 12, 1949, p. 1.

Throughout the post-war years customs regulations in Canada continued to be administered liberally; the loss of foreign exchange was countered by other measures. However, the statutes still conferred on the administration many broad discretionary powers with respect to valuation, relics of depression and not currently in use, which showed clearly their protective origin and intent; these powers could not have been used consistently with the General Agreement except with respect to goods entering under the General Tariff. In 1947, the Customs Act provided that imported goods should be valued at their fair market value, at the time of exportation, when sold for home consumption in the principal markets of the country whence exported directly to Canada (s. 35); but this principal basis was buttressed and qualified. The value was not to be less than the invoice value unless the foreign price had fallen between the date of purchase and the date of exportation (s. 38 subs. 6; now included in s. 35(1)); for new or unused goods, not less than the cost of production of similar goods at the date of shipment plus a reasonable advance for selling cost and profit not in excess of the usual advance for similar goods in the country of origin (s. 36, now repealed). The Minister had power to determine the value for duty in certain difficult cases (s. 41, now repealed) as well as the value of materials imported to be used in the production of medicinal or toilet preparations (s. 42, now repealed), and from ministerial rulings in these cases no appeal was provided. The Government was empowered to order that foreign internal taxes, excise and other duties be excluded from the dutiable value of goods imported from any specified country (s. 36A, now repealed); but drawbacks "allowed by a foreign country and the value of special arrangements between exporter and importer, with respect to such matters as royalty, rent of machines, and territorial rights, were to be included in value for duty"; as were discounts not given on similar sales for home consumption in the ordinary course of trade, and the value of packing and of packages unless the charges for them were shown separately on the invoice.

A number of lengthy and complicated sections prescribed methods of converting foreign currencies to dollars. Section 35 (2), (3), and (4), now repealed, empowered the Minister to value goods imported from a country whose currency was substantially depreciated and to require that their value for duty should not be less than the value of similar goods produced in Great Britain or in some other European country whose currency was not substantially depreciated; some of these powers had seldom been used and all had fallen into disuse.

Again, a foreign currency might be converted at a rate proclaimed by the Governor in Council based on the standard coins or currency of the country; but for many countries this section, too, was obsolete. Most widely used were the provisions which permitted conversion of a depreciated currency at a rate certified as the true value of the currency at time of exportation by a Canadian consular or trade official resident in the country, or at the current exchange rate as certified by the bank through which payment was drawn or by some other bank (section 55); but the practice, becoming increasingly common abroad, of prescribing different exchange rates for different classes of exports (and imports) presented serious problems for Canada as it had for the United States.

Finally, in addition to the power of the Minister to fix value in difficult cases and on importations from a country with greatly depreciated currency, the Government was empowered by section 43 (now s. 38), subject to appeal to the Tariff Board (now abolished for this section), to determine the value for duty (or the method of valuation) for goods not entitled to the British Preferential or lower tariff, when imported into Canada under such conditions as prejudicially or injuriously to affect the interest of Canadian producers or manufacturers.

An appraisal by a local customs official might be overruled by any Dominion appraiser, subject to appeal by the importer to the Tariff Board (s. 48 and s. 36 (4)). Obsolete sections provided for appeal by a dissatisfied importer to a board of review consisting of three experienced persons selected respectively by the importer, the collector, and the Minister. Additional provisions required an appraiser to adopt as the average value the highest quality article in a package containing similar goods of different qualities invoiced at an average price (s. 38 (3));[54] and empowered the Governor in Council to permit goods passing in transit through a third country to be valued as if they had been shipped direct to Canada.

The valuation provisions were in need of substantial and systematic revision for other reasons. They were scattered over a number of sections of the Customs Act, just as they had been developed by piecemeal amendments, and there was considerable overlapping and repetition. In addition, while they did not (with minor exceptions) *require* practices contrary to either the spirit or the letter of the Geneva

---

[54]In practice, however, and when practicable, permission was given the importer to separate goods of different qualities and values under customs supervision.

Agreements, they did permit such practices, and they were open to misinterpretation abroad. Accordingly, in 1948 (and 1950) the Government took steps to amend these provisions; to reduce them to order and to make it perfectly clear that Canada was, in fact following the G.A.T.T. prescriptions on valuation. At the same time complementary amendments were made in the Customs Tariff Act.

As did the United States administration when arguing for the Customs Simplification Bill, the Canadian Government supported the customs amendments, on the ground that they were administratively desirable even apart from their conformity with the General Agreement. In advancing this argument, Mr. St. Laurent also explained the reasons for speeding the amendment.

Quite independently of the changes in the tariff rates agreed to at the Geneva conference it would be beneficial to trade to have those customs practices in the form provided by the amending legislation . . . that creates a greater certainty and enables a prospective exporter or importer to get in advance a more definite idea of what he is going to have to pay than if the practices remained as they were. Probably my Honourable friend has had representations from Canadian exporters as to the difficulties they have run into because of the manner the United States tariff was being applied in practice by the customs officials. *So it was felt desirable to take out of our statute anything they might look upon as a pretext for maintaining those practices in their administration.*

With respect to certain practices, including some relating to appraisal, he remarked: "These practices could be dealt with here by the governor in council and by administrative action in the United States. It was part of the protocol that they would be provisionally applied as from January 1, 1948, and they are being applied provisionally as from January 1, 1948." But he added: "Our information is that there was much less complaint about our customs practices than about the customs practices of some of the countries to which we were exporting."[55] Some of his phrases suggest that Mr. St. Laurent may have had a somewhat exaggerated opinion of the reforms that could be and had been made in the United States by administrative action.

E. CURRENT, 1948–1953

In 1948 the provisions of the Customs Act relating to valuation were almost completely repealed and revised, and minor changes were made in 1949 and 1950. The numerous changes thus introduced were

[55]Can., Commons, *Debates*, 1948, pp. 4744, 4742; italics mine. Mr. St. Laurent also said: "My information is that Canadian exporters to the United States have been much more concerned about the practices of appraisal than about the rates of duty" (p. 4743).

not required primarily to bring contemporary practice into harmony with the provisions of the General Agreement. Rather they represent the adoption of the wording, often the exact phrasing, of the General Agreement, and the deletion of certain clauses which had conferred on the Minister powers that if used in certain ways would have been contrary to the General Agreement but which for many years had not been so used. Primarily, then, these statutory changes had the effect of assuring the signatories that Canada was conforming with the letter and spirit of the Agreement in the field of valuation. Canadian officials explained the position clearly, and repeatedly. In bringing the measure before the Senate in 1948, for example, Senator Robertson explained: "The wording of the Act has been changed to eliminate any conflict with these undertakings [G.A.T.T.], *but the changes so made are not of a substantial character*."[56] Mr. G. B. Urquhart, speaking to the Canadian Manufacturers' Association in 1948, remarked: "With minor exceptions, the Agreement will require very little change in our administration," and again, "We will be able to maintain our principles of valuation which have been in effect for over half a century";[57] he repeated the last statement almost verbatim in a similar address in 1950.[58] Similarly, Mr. J. J. Deutsch, addressing the same body, explained other provisions of the General Agreement and concluded that no great changes were required in Canadian procedures.[59]

Though the statutory changes had little effect at the time on contemporary practice they do appear to have had implications for the future. Certain trends seem to be discernible already. It is desirable then to consider the more important of them in some detail. The section that prescribed the fundamental basis of value was reworded; that which gave the Minister power to determine the value when appraisal was difficult was repealed, as was the provision that value must not be less than cost of production. The new provisions were consolidated in the new section 35:

35 (1) Whenever any duty *ad valorem* is imposed on any goods imported into Canada, the value for duty shall be the fair market value of *such or the like goods* when sold for home consumption *in the ordinary course of trade under fully competitive conditions, in like quantities* and *under comparable conditions of sale* at the time when and *place whence such goods were exported* by the vendor abroad to the purchaser in Canada; or, except as otherwise provided in this Act, the *price at which the goods were sold* by the vendor abroad to the purchaser in Canada, exclusive of all charges thereon after their shipment from the place whence exported direct to Canada, whichever may be greater.

[56]Senate, *Debates*, June 24, 1948, p. 646; italics mine.
[57]*Industrial Canada*, July 1948, p. 262.
[58]*Ibid*., July 1950, p. 226.   [59]*Ibid*., July 1948, p. 255.

(2) When the fair market value of any goods is not ascertainable under subsection one, the value for duty of such goods shall be the nearest ascertainable equivalent of such value.

(3) When neither the fair market value nor the equivalent of such value can be ascertained, the value for duty shall be the actual cost of production of similar goods at date of shipment to Canada, plus a reasonable addition for administration, selling cost and profit.

(4) The value for duty shall not include the amount of any internal tax applicable within the country of origin or export from which the imported goods have been exempted or have been or will be relieved of by means of refund or drawback.[60]

Another subsection was added in 1949, to replace the former section 36A.

35 (5) The governor in council may order that import duties of a country of export shall be disregarded in whole or in part in estimating the value for duty of goods of any kind imported in Canada from a country specified in the order.[61]

(1) Fair Market Value

The fair market value when sold for home consumption is still the fundamental and the preferred basis of dutiable value;[62] but its definition has been changed in a number of ways. In subsection 1 the phrases, "in the ordinary course of trade," "under fully competitive conditions," and "like quantities," were taken directly, or with trifling changes, from the General Agreement.[63] Two other changes prescribed, by statute, procedures which had already been adopted administratively, in ordinary cases, under the broader terms of the former definition:

In the first place the phrase "at the time when and place whence such goods were exported by the vendor abroad to the purchaser in Canada" was substituted for "in the principal markets whence and at the time when the same were exported directly to Canada."[64] That

[60]S.C., 1948, c. 41.   [61]S.C., 1949, c. 41, s. 2.
[62]Or specific selling price if higher. See also s. 38(5), (R.S.C., 1952, s. 35(1)) which makes invoice value a minimum, subject to reduction in fair market value between purchase and exportation.

[63]Especially arts. VI and VII.

[64]This change was in conformity with administrative usage prior to 1948, confirmed repeatedly by order in council; for example, P.C. 850, April 19, 1937, which prescribed among other things, the form of the invoice certificate of value. In this certificate the exporter was required to declare that the "invoice . . . exhibits the fair market value of the said goods at the time and place of their exportation to Canada and as when sold at the same time and place in like quantities and condition for home consumption in the principal markets of the country whence exported directly to Canada. . . ." This wording had been in use since 1904 at least.

this may tend toward making dutiable value differ from invoice value when point of export is different from point of sale is suggested by a recent declaration of the Tariff Board. A Canadian company imported gilsonite mined in Colorado and delivered to the railhead by the mining company. It was valued by Canadian Customs as though sold at railhead. The Tariff Board held that it was exported from the mine but that no fair market value at minehead could be established. The nearest ascertainable equivalent was declared to be the value at railhead less the common carrier rate for trucking gilsonite from the mine to railhead (ten months).[65]

A second change was the insertion of the phrase "under comparable conditions of sale." This describes the administrative practice which formerly had been found satisfactory in most ordinary cases. However, since this condition has been prescribed rigidly as part of a statutory definition, its application has become more difficult. Certain exporters, for example, by maintaining differences in the conditions of sale for export and in the domestic market have been able to contend successfully that no fair market value exists; indeed, in some cases, it has been suspected that a few sales have been made in the domestic market at specially low prices under conditions of sale similar to those of the export sales and used as evidence in attempting to establish a low fair market value. Accordingly, Canadian customs officials have sometimes had to reject what was proposed as a fair market value because it was supported by only a few sales for domestic consumption in the foreign market. The tendency to increase in the number of cases for which no fair market value can be found has some superficial resemblance to the similar tendency in the United States, with respect to foreign value. However, the analogy is by no means exact: the United States tendency has been attributable, in part, to judicial precising and the United States statutes envisage a single foreign value for all shipments of any commodity exported from the same country at the same time; while the Canadian law and practice recognizes different values depending on quantity, the status of the purchaser, and other conditions which affect the price charged in the principal market of the individual foreign seller in ordinary sales for consumption in his domestic market. It would appear that the new statutory definition of fair market value affords more potential grounds for appeal to judicial review of valuation, though the meaning of several of the new phrases has not actually been tested. However, an opinion has been elicited from the Department of Justice as to the

[65] A–251, T.B.C. 260, Dec. 29, 1952.

relation of cost of production to fair market value: "Fair market value may bear no necessary relationship to production cost. A market value which is consistent and not the result of temporary panic selling under extraordinary circumstances, may be a fair market value, within the meaning of s. 35(1) and 6(1) although such value may be less than cost."[66]

(a) *Foreign internal taxes and duties.* In conformity with the provisions of the General Agreement, the Customs Act now provides (s. 35 (4)) that "the value for duty shall not include the amount of any internal tax applicable within the country of origin or export from which the imported goods have been exempted or have been or will be relieved by means of refund or drawback." Formerly such foreign excise taxes *might* be excluded. The terms of this Canadian clause are very broad, and export refunds by some foreign countries not only of excise and sales taxes but of turn-over taxes, taxes on wages, and certain other domestic imposts have given rise to difficult problems. The import duties of any country may be excluded as before, by order of the Governor in Council. This authority has been used to exclude from value for duty import duties on wines, liquors, tobacco, and stout,[67] entitled to entry under the British Preferential and the Most-Favoured-Nation Tariffs.[68]

(b) *Direct shipment.* After a lengthy (and rather confused) debate, section 46 (now section 41) was amended to require (instead of permit) that goods *bona fide* exported to Canada through another country be valued (subject to regulations to be prescribed by order in council) as though they were imported direct. The regulations, since proclaimed, provide: (1) that the bill of lading shall show the ultimate destination of the goods from the place of original shipment to be a specified port in Canada; (2) that the goods shall not be entered for consumption or for warehouse, or remain for any purpose other than transhipment, in any intermediate country; and (3) that the original bill of lading and certified copies of it be filed with the customs entry by penalty.[69]

(c) *Currency conversion.* For converting foreign currencies, the amendments of 1948 repealed the cumbrous and obsolete provisions described above. Instead section 55 (now s. 47), as revised, provides

[66]Opinion of Department of Justice; see statement by Minister of National Revenue, Can., Commons, *Debates*, March 12, 1952.

[67]G. B. Urquhart, in *Industrial Canada*, July 1950, p. 226.

[68]See e.g. *Can. Gaz.*, Dec. 10, 1942, p. 1008, S.O.R. 52–507, P.C. 4522.

[69]Can., D.N.R., Series D, no. 144, July 15, 1948.

that the rate of exchange used shall be that declared by the Bank of Canada. However, "where the rate of exchange of the currency of any country has not been so declared, or where multiple rates of exchange exist, a conversion rate which *shall reflect effectively the current value of such currency in commercial transactions* may be determined and ordered by the Minister." The italicized words are taken directly from article VII of the General Agreement. This amendment removes the power formerly possessed by the Minister of fixing arbitrarily the values to be used in converting appreciated or depreciated currencies. It would appear, however, that where no rate is declared or where multiple rates exist, a considerable range of discretionary power may still exist.

In practice the Bank of Canada furnishes exchange rates but does not declare them. At one time Canada converted foreign currency into Canadian dollars at the par proclaimed by the country whence the goods were shipped to Canada even when the foreign exporters were paid at a different rate. Currently the rate selected as reflecting effectively the current value of currency in commercial transactions is typically the rate at which the payment is made. New York quotations of this rate are converted into Canadian dollars.

When the Canadian dollar was freed the rates fluctuated from day to day. Initially noon rates were wired to port collectors, effective the next day. Subsequently daily bulletins were issued which reached different ports at different times and became applicable the following day. Where practicable, under these arrangements currencies are converted at the noon rates on the day of exportation. At ports on the United States border, however, the latest effective rate is the quotation received on the preceding day. For the convenience of brokers and others the conversion rate is changed only when it has increased or decreased by a full one-half of one per cent. To this small extent importers are benefited when the United States dollar is rising and penalized when it is falling.

(2) Nearest Ascertainable Equivalent

If no "fair market value" can be ascertained, an imported article is to be valued at the nearest equivalent of such value. This provision appears to allow very considerable administrative discretion; but it has not yet been established that the discretionary power is as absolute as that formerly given the Minister in difficult cases. It would appear, for example, that a value determined under this subsection is determined by appraisal and not by an administrative act of the Minister;

and an appraisal is subject to appeal and judicial review whereas the decision of the Minister was not. Similarly, the decision that fair market value cannot be determined is now subject to review. The terms of the definition of equivalent value seem very broad, but its scope has not as yet been rigorously tested. It may prove to be very difficult to defend (or to challenge) a valuation which is proposed as the "nearest ascertainable equivalent" of fair market value, for example, when it is found that "fair market value" itself is not ascertainable.

In certain difficult cases, the Tariff Board has not shown an inclination to find other methods more suitable than those in present use. One declaration of the Tariff Board, for example, dismissed an appeal from a decision of the Deputy Minister concerning the value of blueprints imported into Canada. In accordance with usual practice, the blueprints had been appraised at the "nearest ascertainable equivalent" of fair market value estimated by including in their value 40 per cent of the architect's fee which in turn was usually a percentage of the value of the building. The Board dismissed the contention that the fee should be entirely excluded on the ground that the value would then be "a quite unsubstantial and indeed inconsequential item" though its argument on this point is, at the very least, elliptical. It supported the practice followed by the architectural profession in Canada in estimating the fee, on the grounds that the profession in the United States follows much the same practice; and it justified the use of the Canadian value of the Canadian building on the grounds that (standard plans excepted) in many instances no similar building would be built in the United States. The Board concluded that, while the method followed by the Department might not be the right one, the appellant had failed to indicate "what in its stead, would be a just and proper method and, more precisely a just and proper value" (eleven months).[70]

The Board heard and decided this appeal while, in its other capacity as a fact-finding and advisory agency of the Government, it was considering a reference from the Minister of Finance which included the valuation of architects' plans. In its report on the reference, the Board was unable to suggest a more appropriate general method though it recommended two minor changes in the procedure.[71]

(3) Cost of Production

Cost of production of similar goods, plus a reasonable markup for administration selling cost and profit, has been removed as a general

[70]A-215, T.B.C. 250, Dec. 7, 1951.   [71]T.B.C., Ref. 111, April 2, 1952.

minimum value for duty; but it remains (s. 35 (3)) as a method to be used in valuing those imports for which neither a fair market value nor its equivalent can be ascertained. It continues to be used, as it formerly was, under authority of the section relating to difficult appraisals, for example in valuing semi-finished products shipped between branch plant or subsidiary and parent company, products which are not sold abroad either for domestic use or for export, and for which no prices exist. Although the current provision allows the Department to continue former practices in these and certain other appraisals it is not a suitable method in all cases of difficult decisions formerly decided by the Minister. Should "nearest ascertainable equivalent" be interpreted narrowly, a suitable valuing basis would be lacking for used goods, for example, and perhaps for substandard products and certain other imports.

Formerly cost of production was also a general minimum value applied, after investigation, on complaints from the business community; it was invoked to increase the normal dutiable value and to secure the application of dumping duties on imports purchased at low end-of-season or end-of-run prices which prevailed at times in the United States; the amendment removed this possibility.

(4) Average Value

Since wartime scarcities began to disappear this change, though required by the General Agreement, has been strongly criticized by representatives of certain domestic industries; and the Canadian Manufacturers' Association, too, has complained that the Act has been unduly weakened and has urged the Government to reinstate cost of production plus a reasonable advance as a minimum value for duty purposes.[72] The Government has been under pressure, inside as well as outside Parliament, to interpret fair market value as being related to cost of production; or to reinstate cost of production as a minimum; or to provide some substitute for it, to give protection against temporarily or seasonally low prices, especially in the United States.

In December 1953 a sixth subsection was added to section 35[73] of the Customs Act to permit the Minister to value imports of manufactures at an average of prices during a reasonable period prior to shipment when he considered the price was abnormally low as the result of the advance of the season or the marketing period.

(6) Notwithstanding anything in this Act, where the market price of any manufactured goods in the country of export has, as the result of the advance of

[72]*Industrial Canada,* July 1952, p. 58.
[73]2–3 Eliz. II, c. 3.

the season or the marketing period, declined to levels that do not reflect in the opinion of the Minister their normal price, the value for duty shall be the amount determined and declared by the Minister to be the average price, weighted as to quantity, at which the like or similar goods were sold for consumption in the country of export during a reasonable period, not exceeding six months, immediately preceding the date of shipment of the goods to Canada.

In Parliament the bill was given a mixed reception, some sections of the Opposition contending that it might be used to grant too much protection; some that it granted too little.[74] It was presented as being in conformity with the General Agreement; it is based on actual prices at (or rather during) a time determined by the country in question. But it will admittedly involve administrative difficulties. It is proposed that decisions as to its use will be by Ottawa officials though the local collectors may advise the importer at the time of entry that any invoice may be held to be abnormally low. It was proposed to increase by eighteen the number of investigating officers; at the time the bill was passed only two investigating officers, stationed at Ottawa, were being employed to make investigations in the United States.[75] It is still too early to evaluate the results of this innovation. It seems probable that its intimidating effects will be substantial in deterring the importation of end-of-season or end-of-line goods purchased at bargain prices. Unquestionably it will increase the uncertainty of importers and discourage attempts to secure bargains.

(5) Official Valuation

As originally introduced the bill to amend the Customs Act in 1948 contained a proposal to amend section 43[76] (now s. 38), which granted power to the Government to fix the value for duty of imports (except those eligible to enter under preferential or lower rates) deemed injurious to Canadian producers. Though giving up or narrowing its other powers of restricting imports by valuation practices the Government did not propose to give up the powers it already enjoyed under this section.[77] Rather, the proposed amendment sought to eliminate the appearance or possibility of discrimination by extending the provisions to include British goods as well as others. The proposed

---

[74]See e.g., Can., Commons, *Debates*, Dec. 10, 1953, vol. 96, pp. 799–812; and Dec. 11, pp. 836–59.

[75]*Ibid.*, Dec. 16, 1953, vol. 96, pp. 986–7.

[76]Bill 226, 1948, s. 4.

[77]That is, the Government did not propose that its powers be confined by the wording of the Customs Act as narrowly as they are limited by article xix with respect to imports from member countries. Canada's obligations in this respect,

amendment, however, was withdrawn under heavy pressure from the Opposition.[78]

In the revisions of 1948, section 43 had been continued in part to allow a seasonal duty to be levied on imported fresh fruits and vegetables, not contrary to the General Agreement with respect to their amounts but inconsistent with it in being imposed by varying the value rather than the rate of duty; and incidentally confusing to foreign exporters.[79] In 1950 the Customs Tariff was amended to empower the Minister to apply seasonal specific duties in place of the seasonal changes in valuation formerly made;[80] and since that time official values have not been applied to fresh fruits and vegetables. Between December 31, 1947, and July 10, 1953, official values had been fixed under section 43 only on knitted wool gloves and mitts[81] and on muskrat skins not dressed in any manner,[82] when entered under the General Tariff. It appears that several other Canadian manufacturers have complained to the Minister of Finance that their businesses had suffered from foreign competition but no other official values were proclaimed.[83]

On appeal, the official values for knitted woolen gloves and mitts were reduced in 1949;[84] in a subsequent appeal, by the Canadian Woollen and Knit Goods Manufacturers Association, the Board declined to hear evidence purporting to show that the values fixed by

however, have been explicitly recognized both by Ministers and senior civil servants. Mr. G. B. Urquhart pointed out that the clause could not be used under article XIX unless Canadian producers were "very seriously damaged." (*Industrial Canada*, July 1948, p. 263.) And Dr. McCann stated, in the House, that the permissive authority for fixation of values "is intended to provide authority, for use if necessary, if as the result of unforeseen developments a product is being imported in such increased quantities and under such conditions as to cause or threaten serious injury to domestic producers of like and directly competitive products" and might be so used consistently with the General Agreement. Can., Commons, *Debates*, 1948, p. 4745.

[78]McCann, Commons, *Debates*, 1948, pp. 4745, 5634. No discrimination, consistent with obligations, is in fact possible as between British countries or countries with which Canada has a general Most-Favoured-Nation agreement.

[79]See U.S.T.C., *Operation of the Trade Agreements Program.*

[80]Customs Tariff, s. 14 and items 84, 85, 87, 92, 94, and 95; D.N.R., Series D, no. 47, T.C. 302, revised.

[81]Effective March 21, 1949 (P.C. 436, March 15, 1949); revised by Tariff Board ruling on June 21, 1949; became inoperative after Dec. 31, 1950.

[82]Published May 22, 1952 (P.C. 2931, May 20, 1952); not to apply to shipments *bona fide* purchased and in transit on or before May 23, 1952.

[83]*Industrial Canada*, Dec. 1952, p. 52.

[84]A–135, T.B.C. 186, June 21, 1949.

the Minister were too low, and, finding that the evidence advanced to support reductions was not conclusive, it confirmed the official values.[85]

In 1950, section 43 (now s. 38) was in fact amended, but in another way. This time the spokesmen of the Government stated clearly that the section was intended for use only against goods entering under the General Tariff.[86] The amendment removed the right of appeal to the Tariff Board formerly granted to importers and other interested parties. In justification of the change it was stated that the trade agreements which originally caused the provision to be written into the Act were no longer operative;[87] that the decision to declare an arbitrary value was a Government decision as to policy; and that to appeal to the Tariff Board from a policy decision of the Government would put the Board in an "impossible position."[88] Though this conclusion was not allowed to pass unchallenged,[89] the amendment was passed. Formerly, section 43 (now s. 38) was the only section which explicitly provided for appeal to the Tariff Board by parties other than the importer—by British exporters, for example; and the 1950 amendments which removed this right under section 43 extended the right of making such an appeal with respect to values established under other sections of the Customs Act to "any person who deems himself aggrieved by a decision of the Deputy Minister," and provided that any interested person might enter an appearance and be heard on any appeal to the Tariff Board,[90] and might appeal from its decision. Thus, paradoxically, in this matter of appeal, an amending act of a government committed to a liberal tariff policy removed all rights of

[85]A–158, T.B.C. 202, March 27, 1950.

[86]Sinclair, Commons, *Debates*, May 29, 1950, p. 2954; McKeen, Senate, *Debates*, May 18, 1950, pp. 335, 343; Urquhart: "This Section 43 was retained for use as an emergency measure against General Tariff Countries where the ordinary provisions of the Customs Act and Tariff would not be effective." *Industrial Canada*, July 1950, p. 227.

[87]Senate, *Bill K7*, explanatory notes; McKeen, Senate, *Debates*, 1948, p. 335.

[88]Sinclair, Commons, *Debates*, p. 2954.

[89]Fleming, *ibid.*

[90]Customs Tariff Act. Now R.S.C., 1952, c. 58, ss. 44 and 45. The new s. 49(2), (now s. 44(2)) provided: "Notice of the hearing of an appeal under subsection one shall be published in the Canada Gazette at least twenty-one days prior to the day of the hearing, and any person who, on or before that day, enters an appearance with the secretary of the Tariff Board may be heard on the appeal." See remarks of Senator McKeen, Senate, *Debates*, 1950, pp. 344, 394, and of G. B. Urquhart to the Canadian Manufacturers' Association: *Industrial Canada*, July 1950, p. 227.

appeal from official valuation, although the right had originally been granted to allow foreign exporters and domestic importers to challenge a value as too high; but it extended to domestic producers the right of becoming a party to an appeal to the Tariff Board and appearing at its hearing. The restraints to international trade are clearly multi-dimensional and interrelated.

(6) Dumping Duties

In 1948 the section of the Customs Tariff that imposed dumping duties was revised to conform more closely with the provisions of the General Agreement and with the revised valuation provisions of the Customs Act. Dumping duty equal to the difference between "the export or actual selling price to a Canadian importer," and "the fair market value or value for duty as determined under the Customs Act" is still to be applied up to 50 per cent *ad valorem*; and the authority of the Minister is continued, to apply dumping duty on goods imported on consignment or on sale between related businesses. The provision that duties and taxes imposed in any country of export are to be disregarded in estimating value for dumping duty superseded the former permissive and discriminating provisions concerning certain duties and taxes. Exemption of goods subject to Canadian excise duties in Canada was continued and in addition a new provision was introduced exempting goods declared exempt by the Governor in Council; the authority of the Governor in Council to fix a rate of exchange for appreciated or depreciated currencies was deleted to conform with the changes in the Customs Act. Most other provisions of the old section are continued. Under order in council goods may not be treated as of a class or kind made in Canada unless production within Canada equals at least 10 per cent of the national consumption. In recent practice the Department has required that this provision be generously fulfilled and, after decision, has given three weeks' notice before a commodity is treated as being of a class or kind made in Canada.

Under the general regulations of the Department, *bona fide* samples are admitted without special duty; advance in market price subsequent to purchase by the importer is disregarded, as may also be increases in the rate of exchange; under specified conditions, cash discounts and freight and deferred quantity allowances do not subject imports to special duty if they are allowed on similar dates in the country of export; and job lots and second-hand or defective goods are not subject to dumping duty unless the export price is less than the selling price in the home market.

The provisions with respect to dumping in the Canadian Customs Tariff now appear to conform with the provisions of the General Agreement except, perhaps, in one respect: except for escape clauses the General Agreement forbids the imposition of dumping duties on a product from another contracting party "unless it determines that the effect of the dumping . . . is such as to cause or threaten material injury to an established domestic industry, or is such as to prevent or materially retard the establishment of a domestic industry."[91] The Customs Tariff requires collection of special duty on all dumped goods of a class or kind made in Canada, unless specially exempted. Conceivably the authority of the Government might have been used to grant special exemptions[92] but it has not been so used. In June 1954 the only such exemption in effect was Belgian window glass, a concession granted under threat that Belgium might impose obstacles to the importation of Canadian wheat.

The substitution of seasonal duties on fruits and vegetables for official valuation and special duties has made it more difficult to enlist agricultural support for the granting of broad protection under the name of dumping; and the removal of cost of production as a minimum value removed the power to grant special duties except where technical dumping actually occurred.

It is too early to judge the effects of the new powers of the Government to appraise at an average of actual prices but it seems probable that the new method is not in conflict with the provisions of the General Agreement; in any event, a strong government is likely to be able to resist demands that it be used unless serious injury is threatened. Under conditions of widespread unemployment, however, a weak government might be induced to use it to give broad increases in protection. The provisions of the General Agreement preclude the fixing of an arbitrary value as the basis for duty or dumping duty on goods imported from a contracting party; except, perhaps, under procedure governing the use of the emergency escape provisions of article xix of the Agreement. However, dumping duty may be, and has

[91]G.A.T.T., art. v, s. S. See G. B. Urquhart in *Industrial Canada*, July 3, 1948, pp. 262–3. A question was asked in the House of Commons as to the method of determining whether an industry was being actually injured but it was interpreted to mean something else (*Debates*, vol. 96, Dec. 8, 1953, p. 693):
M. J. Coldwell: ". . . What steps will the Government take to investigate an industry to see if there is actual injury to that industry from competition abroad." *Mr. McCann*: ". . . We have special investigators who are trained in particular lines of industry and who make these investigations in the country of export."
[92]See Can. Customs Tariff, s. 6 (2) (ii).

been, applied by declaring a minimum value for goods entering under the General Tariff.[93]

Protectionists in Canada have complained that, since 1948, dumping duties have too seldom been applied.[94] In the United States, however, protectionists have advocated the adoption of the Canadian provisions, which do not restrict the application of duties, as does the United States Antidumping Act, to dumping which causes or threatens to cause material injury to a domestic industry, or which prevents or materially retards its development.[95]

(7) Summary

In summary, in 1947 Canadian practice with respect to valuation was for the most part consistent with the spirit, if not the exact letter, of the General Agreement; and in some respects it was more liberal. By 1950 practice and statutory provisions had been brought into close correspondence with the letter of the Agreement. Administrative powers whose exercise might have contravened the terms of the Agreement had been removed except for the power to fix official values and to apply dumping duties even though domestic industries were not being materially injured. Greater provision had been made for appeal to an independent tribunal except from official valuations, though in the process the rights of domestic interests to appeal had also been broadened.

It may be true with respect to customs procedure that there is a tendency for a minimum standard to become a maximum standard as well; but it is a tendency which, in Canada at any rate, has had little effect so far.

The recent introduction of another basis of valuation applicable at the discretion of the Minister is an indication, however, of the speed with which Canadian laws and practices could be changed in response to changes in business conditions, or to illiberal policies abroad.

[93]For example, S.O.R. 52–216 subjects muskrat skins to special duty whether sold prior to shipment or shipped on consignment.

[94]The Tariff Committee of the Canadian Manufacturers' Association, for example, recommended in 1950 that members be made aware of the need for reporting all cases of suspected dumping, that they may be followed up promptly with the Government in Ottawa, and that the executive council of the Association be made aware of the weaknesses of the new valuation sections of the Customs Act: *Industrial Canada*, May 1950, p. 78. See also the remarks of J. M. McDonnell, Commons, *Debates*, May 26, 1952, p. 2593.

[95]U.S. Senate, *On H.R. 5505*. Evidence of Howard Huston, Vice-president of American Cyanamid Co., p. 187, and of Richard H. Anthony, Secretary, The American Tariff League, p. 124.

VIII

OTHER RESTRICTIVE MEASURES

"How am I to get in?" asked Alice again, in a louder tone.
"*Are* you to get in at all?" said the footman. "That's the first
question, you know."

Alice in Wonderland

IN ADDITION to the procedures involved in assessing and collecting customs duties, articles crossing international boundaries (and
sometimes interstate or interprovincial boundaries as well) are subjected to inspection, and perhaps to marking or exclusion under many
other sets of regulations. Some of these regulations are issued under
the authority of acts specifically relating to customs matters; others
under special acts. In the United States, for example, there are in
force almost a hundred acts that affect importation. In Canada, too,
there are many acts affecting importation; and the Canadian Customs
administers regulations authorized by some fifteen of them. Often
they are long, detailed, and complicated. They include, for example,
regulations intended to inform consumers as to the country of origin
of the articles affected; to protect domestic owners of patents, copyrights, brand names, and marks; to protect the inhabitants of the
country against the spread of human, plant, or animal diseases, against
unwholesome or poisonous food, and against fraud with respect to
standards of weight or measure or degree of fineness; to exclude
obscene literature; and to conform with international agreements, for
the suppression of trade in narcotics, for example, or for the protection of wild birds and animals.

Some of these regulations are administered directly by customs
officials though formulated by other departments; some require that
the goods be held for inspection by officials of other branches of the
government. All involve at least some trouble and expense to importers (or exporters); some can be, and at certain times and places
have been, framed and administered so as to impose unnecessary
expense and delay and, accordingly, to give a greater amount of
incidental protection than is required by their ostensible purposes.

It would require a great deal of space to consider the procedures under each of these sets of regulations. In what follows, a few are described in order to suggest and illustrate the costs and obstacles to trade that may result from them. Prescriptions concerning the marking of imported goods to show the country of origin will be described first. Operation of other acts and regulations which may involve delay, expense and exclusion or destruction at port of entry will be illustrated from some of those governing foods and drugs, animals and animal products, and plants and plant products.

A. MARKS OF ORIGIN

Both Canada and the United States require that imports of certain classes of goods be marked clearly as permanently as possible with the name of their country of origin.[1] The direct and primary intention of the requirement is to inform the prospective buyer of the country of origin of the article so that, if he wishes, he may take this information into account when making his purchases. It might be supposed, therefore, that the regulations would be framed so as to allow this information to be conveyed in the least costly way. However, the marking requirement has sometimes been enforced, especially when protectionist sentiments were strong, by methods which, unintentionally or by design, imposed unnecessary costs, delays, inconvenience, and risk on the importer and exporter.

Indeed, quasi-judicial decisions in the United States concerning marking have at times been based explicitly on the assumption that the primary purpose of the marking requirements was to give protection to domestic producers. In 1925 Treasury officials and the Board of General Appraisers (later the United States Customs Court), in deciding that the domestic producers were entitled to the protection of the indirect effect of the marking requirements, used the following words: "The purpose of Congress in enacting this [marking] provision was to make competition with the domestic manufacturer more difficult and expensive, and, if compliance with its requirements should render articles less desirable to purchasers, or should be more expensive and difficult, such fact could not defeat the intention of Congress which was to reduce, if not prohibit, competition with American manufacturers."[2] The rank and file of customs employees in

[1]U.S. Tariff Act, s. 304; Can. Customs Tariff, s. 16.

[2]T.D. 40, 791, March 25, 1925, quoted in Viner, "Memoranda on Commercial Policy"; reprinted in Viner, *International Economics*, p. 172. Quoted also in Bidwell, *Invisible Tariff*, p. 69.

the United States may even believe still in the pervasiveness of such views. In 1951 a spokesman for the United States Customs Warehouse Officers' Association, emphasizing the importance of the provision that required unmarked imports to be marked under strict customs supervision at the expense of the exporter, remarked: "Congress further provided that the marking requirements be enforced whether or not the article is exempt from the payment of ordinary customs duties. The reason being that there is a higher interest involved; namely the adequate safeguarding of the interest of American producers."[3] No similar Canadian pronouncement has been discovered. Indeed, in the mid-thirties, a mildly contrary opinion was attributed to the Department of National Revenue in the monthly review then published by the Department: "The Department is inclined to the view that, while marking regulation possesses undoubted advantages, it should not be administered primarily as an additional tariff protective measure, nor so rigidly or strictly as to achieve the effect of prohibition of importation, in view of the fact that the definite object of the legislation is that of informing consumers of imported goods of the origin thereof."[4] However, Canadian marking requirements have not always been as easy as they are now.

The Canadian and United States marking requirements differ in scope. The United States statute requires that all imported articles be marked unless they are exempted by the Treasury; and the Treasury is permitted to exempt a class of merchandise only if it falls within one of the types of articles specified in the appropriate paragraph of the Tariff Act.

The scope of these exemptions was extended in 1938. In the liberalizing revision of that year the United States Treasury was empowered to issue regulations authorizing the exception of any article from marking if

(A) Such article is incapable of being marked;
(B) Such article cannot be marked prior to shipment to the United States without injury;
(C) Such article cannot be marked prior to shipment to the United States except at an expense economically prohibitive of its importation;
(D) The marking of a container of such article will reasonably indicate the origin of such article;
(E) Such article is a crude substance;

[3]Statement of Mr. McDonald on behalf of U.S. Customs Warehouse Officers' Association; U.S. House, *On H.R. 1535*, p. 431.

[4]*National Revenue Review*, Dec. 1936, quoted in Gordon Blake, "Customs Administration," p. 443.

(F)   Such article is imported for use by the importer and not intended for sale in its imported, or any other form;

(G)   Such article is to be processed in the United States by the importer or for his account otherwise than for the purpose of concealing the origin of such article and in such a manner that any mark contemplated by this section would necessarily be obliterated, destroyed or permanently concealed;

(H)   An ultimate purchaser, by reason of the character of such article or by reason of the circumstances of its importation, must necessarily know the country of origin of such article even though it is not marked to indicate its origin;

(I)   Such article was produced more than twenty years prior to its importation into the United States; or

(J)   Such article is of a class, or kind, with respect to which the Secretary of the Treasury has given notice by publication, in the Weekly Treasury Decisions within two years after July 1, 1937, that articles of such class or kind were imported in substantial quantities during the five-year period immediately preceding January 1, 1937, and were not required during such period to be marked to indicate their origin: *Provided*, that this sub-division (J) shall not apply after Sept. 1, 1938, to sawed lumber and timber, telephone, trolley, electric-light and telegraph poles of wood, and bundles of shingles; but the President is authorized to suspend the effectiveness of this proviso if he finds such action required to carry out any trade agreement entered into under authority of the Act of June 12, 1934.[5]

The proviso in subsection (J), inserted by Congress, illustrates the way in which special interests were able to restrict the liberalizing effects of a Treasury-sponsored amendment. It occasioned trouble and uncertainty for Canadian exporters. The Act of 1938 was approved on June 25; notification appeared in *Treasury Decisions*,[6] filed July 20, exempting from marking the permitted classes of articles in the exact words of the statute. Lists of articles, which had been admitted without marking as described in subdivision (J), were published.[7] One of these lists, filed August 8, 1938, contained the lumber items mentioned in the proviso and a statement that they had not been subject to marking but that they must be marked after September 1, 1938. The Canada–United States Trade Agreement, proclaimed November 25, 1938, contained an explicit provision that the lumber items enumerated in subdivision (J) should be excepted from the marking requirement. Accordingly, as from November 26, these items were excepted and a Treasury decision to this effect was filed on November 29.[8] It was

[5]U.S. Tariff Act, s. 304.   [6]T.D. 49658.
[7]T.D. 49690, Aug. 24, 1938; T.D. 49835, April 5, 1939; and T.D. 49896, June 26, 1939.
[8]T.D. 49750.

not decided until March 1941, however, that flooring not further advanced than tongued and grooved was to be included in "sawn lumber" and, accordingly, exempted from the marking requirement.[9]

That the United States lumber industry is politically powerful and sensitive to tariff considerations is illustrated once more, then, by the fact that, in a liberalizing revision of the marking clause, a proviso was inserted which subjected, at least temporarily to the marking requirements, lumber items previously excepted. Exporters of Canadian lumber claim that the expense, delay, and uncertainty introduced by such manœuvring is increased by the fact that some local customs officials seem to become aware more promptly of restrictive than of liberalizing changes in the regulations.

Prior to 1938, the United States Tariff required, not only that all non-exempted articles be individually marked, but that their immediate and outer containers be marked as well.[10] The 1938 amendments to the Tariff Act removed the double (or triple) marking requirement from the statute and permitted the Treasury to allow certain merchandise to be entered without marks on the individual article, provided the immediate containers were marked with the country of origin of the contents. However, when the Treasury has ordered that any article be admitted if marked only on the immediate container, it must be marked in this way, even though the article itself bears a mark of origin; otherwise the prospective buyer would not know the country of origin without removing the wrapper.

The application of the United States marking regulations to containers has occasioned many misunderstandings, losses, and delays. Many of the disputes arose out of the complaints of United States manufacturers. For example, in May 1935, after complaint by a United States glass manufacturer, the Treasury ruled that usual glass containers need be marked only with the country of origin of the contents; and that only unusual glass containers were to be marked to show as well their own countries of origin when imported full; but glass containers imported empty were to be individually and permanently marked with the country of their own origin.[11] The authority granted by the amendments of 1938 has been and continues to be used to liberalize the marking requirements; it was decided in 1950, for example, that fitted travelling bags[12] must be marked in a con-

---

[9]T.D. 50366, April 4, 1941. [10]Bidwell, *Invisible Tariff*, p. 74.

[11]T.D. 49771(6), May 24, 1935. For a description of the many difficulties see Smith, *Valuation*, p. 142–3.

[12]Such as are provided for in U.S. Tariff Act, par. 1531.

spicuous place on the bag itself, but that the individual articles comprising the fittings need not be marked if they originate in the same country as the bag, and if the bag and its contents are to be sold as a unit.[13]

Prior to 1938, especially, United States producers frequently offered complaints concerning entries which were not marked with precisely the name, and the spelling of the name, which for marking purposes was officially recognized as the English equivalent of the name of the country of origin. Though protests of this kind were often dismissed, importers were subjected to the trouble and expense of litigation.

Generally speaking, the United States has refused to accept marking with the names of territories, states, provinces, or large cities, and it is not always easy to know when an area with a distinctive name would be recognized as a "country" for this purpose and when it would not. Changes in political status and territorial boundaries, too, have required inconvenient marking changes. It was held, for example, that merchandise manufactured in Sudetenland before it was occupied by Germany and exported afterwards was not properly marked "Made in Czechoslovakia" but should have been marked "Made in Germany."[14]

More recently, the United States[15] has been moderately generous in accepting several variants of the names of certain countries and allowing a reasonable time for marks of origin to be adjusted to changed boundaries or political status.[16] When Newfoundland entered Confederation in 1949, for example, goods exported from Labrador or Newfoundland to the United States were accepted when marked as originating either in Newfoundland or in Canada for several months after the Confederation agreement became effective.[17]

Uncertainty also arises, from time to time, when an article is pro-

---

[13]T.D. 52453, April 12, 1950, which revoked T.D. 47489 (4).

[14]*United States* v. *Friedlaender & Co. Inc.*, C.A.D. 104; 75 T.D. 37, p. 39, Feb. 26, 1940 (Garret P. J. dissenting) cited in A.G. Com., Mon. 27, p. 115.

[15]Bidwell attributes the strictness of United States customs interpretation prior to 1938 to the trend of the decisions of the Customs Court and gives a number of examples (*Invisible Tariff*, pp. 74–6). The changes in administration since 1938 are expressly authorized by changes in the statute which, except the (J) proviso, were proposed by the Treasury Department.

[16]However, after the change in the status of India and the separation of India from Pakistan, some expense and delay were caused by marking difficulties.

[17]T.D. 47639 (5) of April 17, 1935, 67 T.D. 620, was revoked. See T.D. 52190, April 11, 1949, and T.D. 52275, July 22, 1949.

duced partly in one country and partly in another. When imported into the United States, ham and bacon from hogs killed and cured in Denmark but cut up, de-boned, and smoked in England were required to show England as the country of origin; and diamonds mined in South Africa, cut in Holland, and sold in France were considered the product of Holland.[18]

At one time in both Canada and the United States, if articles subject to the marking provision were imported unmarked, they were not only held until marked under customs supervision at the owner's expense, but in addition they were subjected to an extra duty of 10 per cent *ad valorem*. In Canada the marking duty was repealed in 1950 but the unmarked articles must be marked under customs custody. In the United States the Customs Administrative Act of 1938 provided for the remission of this duty if the goods were marked under customs supervision even after they had originally been released from customs custody. This amendment was even more important than it might appear. Before 1938 a domestic producer might protest the release of a shipment of goods if he could discover that the goods had not been marked strictly as required. However, even before 1938, if either the immediate container or the article itself was marked with the country of origin of the contents, the goods were released after the marking was completed, without payment of duty; and between 1938 and 1951 the Tariff Act did not permit a United States manufacturer to enter a protest against the correctness of a collector's findings unless the rate of duty depended on such finding. After 1938 no marking duty was collectible if the marking requirements were fulfilled even after importation; accordingly, it became questionable whether domestic competitors could any longer successfully protest against infringements[19] of the Marking Act which the administration considered insignificant.

Until 1953, many paragraphs of the United States Tariff prescribed in detail additional markings for certain items, for example, watches, clocks, and other time-measuring mechanisms.[20] Nominally these marks were intended to inform buyers as to the quality and origin of the article, but they were required most frequently (and copiously) on imports that compete with sensitive sections of the American economy.

[18]T.D. 48493, 1936, and T.D. 44370, 1930, cited by Hawkins, *Commercial Treaties and Agreements*, pp. 47–8.

[19]No such protest has been made. Even prior to 1938 a protest could not succeed under s. 516(b) unless it affected the rate of duty; see, e.g., *Latchford Glass Co.* v. *United States*, (1937) 22 C.C.P.A. 207.

[20]U.S. Tariff Act, pars. 367 and 368.

The marking on watches and similar articles, though it might be done under customs supervision after importation, had to conform exactly with the detailed statutory specifications.[21]

Until recently, other paragraphs of the United States Tariff Act required not only that certain items must be specially marked or labelled, precisely as required by statute, but that they must be so marked before being brought into the United States. Consistently with its special concern to protect domestic producers of certain coal tar products, the United States required that containers of coal tar dyes and dyestuffs be labelled to show chemical composition of the contents and certain details of the methods by which it was produced and was to be applied. The same information was required in the invoice. Similarly until recently the Tariff Act required that certain other articles, before reaching the United States, must be marked, in the manner prescribed, with the name of the maker,[22] *and under it* the name of the country of origin, in each of the places prescribed in the relevant tariff paragraph. Articles subject to these special marking requirements included knives, forks, shears, safety razors, surgical and scientific and laboratory instruments, pliers, pincers, and thermostatic containers.[23] If it was found after entry that any such articles were not properly marked, they were exported or destroyed. Thermostatic containers were required to bear the name of the maker or purchaser and beneath it the name of the country of origin etched with acid on the glass filler and die-stamped on the jacket or casing; and each label, wrapper, box, or carton, in which they were imported, was also to bear, when imported, the name of the maker or purchaser and beneath it the country of origin.[24] These special marking requirements were repealed in 1953, except those prescribed by paragraph 367 which relate to watches and clocks and watch or clock movements.

Canadian exporters to the United States have made many complaints concerning the scope of the general marking requirements; requirements which they consider unreasonable have imposed on them from time to time in the past heavy costs, or the uncertainty and delay

[21]U.S., Treasury Dept., Bureau of Customs, *Customs Information for Exporters to the United States*, p. 32.

[22]Some of these articles might be marked with the name of the purchaser, instead of the name of the maker.

[23]U.S. Tariff Act, pars. 354, 355, 357, 358, 359, 360, 361, 1553.

[24]The corresponding Canadian regulations require that the name of the country of origin be indelibly impressed on the container and etched on refills or inserts when imported separately; Can., D.N.R., Series D, no. 1 (revised, 1949), p. 7.

involved in obtaining reasonable treatment. A few actual cases, some of them drawn from the period before 1938, will illustrate the difficulties that have occasionally arisen. An exporter of miniature clothes pegs was faced with the requirement that each individual peg be marked. Since the cost of printing would have been a considerable proportion of the selling price of the merchandise, export was discontinued. A shipper of wrapped apples from Nova Scotia was once required to unpack and re-wrap his apples so as to show the country of origin on the wrapper of each apple. A Canadian exporter of agricultural implements and repair parts was given to understand that the implements need be marked with the country of origin on one exposed part only, and he complied with this requirement. However, he encountered repeatedly the request that the repair parts be stamped; eventually the United States authorities ruled that the repair parts need not be marked individually but that their containers must be.

Similarly, unfinished handles for brooms and mops in bundles of 100 had been shipped for some time when a carload was held and penalty duty imposed because each individual handle was not marked with the country of origin. Eventually, after 1938, a decision was secured that, if each bundle was marked, the shipment would be entered. This decision was based on the grounds that unfinished goods need not be marked, provided the manufacturer cannot fail to know the country of origin.

Another case illustrates the meticulous application of the marking regulations. A Canadian exporter of dice was met with the requirement that each individual piece bear an indelible mark of origin. This ruling was appealed on the grounds that such marking would introduce bias, or at least excite suspicion that the dice were biassed. After lengthy negotiation a ruling was secured that the marks of origin need appear only on the immediate containers of each pair of dice if they were intended for playing; but that each piece must be permanently marked if the dice were ornamental.

The Customs Simplification Act of 1953 extended the field within which exemptions from marking are permitted. It authorized the Secretary of the Treasury to exempt from the general marking provisions any article which cannot be marked after importation except at an expense which is economically prohibitive, when the failure to mark the article before importation was not due to any intent to avoid complying with the provision. It removed the special marking provisions from those tariff paragraphs which had forbidden rectification of marking after importation to the United States. Finally, it re-defined "supervision of customs officers" to include not only direct and continuous supervision but also supervision by occasional verifica-tion, a practice which had been previously instituted, and followed in spite of the statement by a customs judge that it was not in accordance with the law. If this power is liberally used it may relieve the importer who receives an unmarked shipment of part of the additional expenses he would otherwise have incurred.

Originally, Canada like the United States imposed a general require-ment that imported articles be marked to show the country of origin. A section inserted in the Canadian Customs Tariff in 1907 required that all goods capable of being "marked, stamped, branded, or labelled" were to show the country of origin in English or French words, in a conspicuous place not subsequently covered; marks were to be affixed in a way that made them as nearly indelible as possible.[25] In 1922 this sweeping provision was repealed. Instead the government was empowered by order in council to require that any description or class of goods specified be marked, in English or French, in the name of the country of origin;[26] all goods other than those specified are exempt from the requirement. The list of articles subjected to marking that was issued in 1922 was lengthened considerably during the protectionist thirties (at one stage it included building bricks) but was then shortened until in recent years it has contained only about fifteen items.[27]

[25]S.C., 1907, c. 19, s. 5.

[26]Now R.S.C., 1952, c. 60, s. 15. The country of origin of a manufactured article is defined as "the country in which the article has been finished by a substantial amount of labour amounting to not less than one-half the cost of pro-duction of such article in condition as imported to Canada." D.N.R., Series D, no. 43, p. 7.

[27]P.C. 4343. Aug. 31, 1949, orders the marking of fifteen classes of goods, and prescribes in some detail the content of the classes and the ways in which certain of these goods must be marked. The classes are: (1) "Printed or lithographed material of all kinds including books and pictures; except seals, tickets and labels, which are not capable of being marked legibly and each of which does not exceed one inch, in diameter, in which case the first package or covering shall be marked. . . ." Ordinarily printed or lithographed paper or other coverings or containers used merely to cover or contain goods consigned to Canada need not be marked. (2) Writing, marking, or drawing pencils of all kinds, penholders of wood, and fountain pens. (3) Empty paper or paperboard folding or set-up boxes or cartons and empty plain or corrugated or fibreboard boxes for use as containers. (4) Brushes of all kinds, including toothbrushes and toothbrush handles. (5) Razor blades (safety type). (6) Boots, shoes, and slippers. (7) Chinaware and porcelainware (not including sanitary or toilet ware) decorated

Listed goods which do not conform to the requirements when imported must be marked before being released from customs possession; this provision is interpreted to allow importers to mark examined goods in a customs warehouse or by arrangement under customs supervision on their own premises. Formally the importer is permitted to remedy marking defects after importation at his own expense under customs supervision. However, it is not practicable to remedy marking defects on some articles; chinaware and porcelain ware, for example, must be marked before being fired in the kiln. Regulations also prescribe the method and manner of marking of certain other items in considerable detail.

In addition, at one time, a marking duty of 10 per cent was imposed on goods not properly marked. This duty was collected until June 1950, when it was abolished by amendment of the Customs Tariff Act. Since then imported goods that do not comply with the marking requirements must remain in the possession of customs until properly marked but no extra duty is collected. The scope of the Canadian marking provisions has always been much narrower than that of the United States, but within its scope, from 1938 to 1950, the Canadian law imposed heavier penalties than the American.

Since the Canadian provisions require only a few items to be marked and since, because Canada is bilingual, they permit either the English or the French name of the country of origin to be used, they have occasioned much less delay and expense (at least in recent years) than those of the United States. Nevertheless, in the fields to which they do apply they serve to deter foreign producers who are concerned primarily with their own domestic markets from making

---

or undecorated as follows: (a) articles commonly used in connection with the serving of food or drink, or intended or designed for household use for ornamental or decorative purposes; (b) kitchenware and utensils; (c) Heraldic and souvenir ware. (8) Ladies' purses in the form of handbags, not including bags made of beads, metal mesh, or of a similar nature. (9) Thermometers of all kinds. (10) Pen knives, jacknives, and pocket knives of all kinds; scissors and shears. (11) Articles wholly of porcelain for electrical use. (12) Clocks and clock movements. (13) Packages containing fresh fruit, vegetables, or honey. (14) Glazed wall and hearth tile; and glazed or unglazed floor tiles over six square inches, and all sizes of ceramic mosaic tiles mounted on paper. (15) Vacuum bottles, carafes, flasks, jugs, jars, and other thermostatic containers and refills or inserts for use therewith.

In addition, entry is prohibited of goods manufactured in a foreign country which bear a trade mark registered in any British country unless the trade mark "is accompanied by a definite indication of the foreign state or country in which the goods were made or produced": Customs Tariff, item 1209.

sporadic and unplanned shipments to Canada. This is particularly true with respect to merchandise such as chinaware and porcelain-ware which must be marked during the manufacturing process; but, even more broadly, the additional cost of specially marking a small part of output (or the whole of the output when only a small amount is exported now and then) may be sufficient to discourage small and sporadic shipments even of commodities which can easily be marked after the ordinary processes of production are completed. Shipments which infringe the marking regulations are now seldom received in Canada except from firms experimenting with the Canadian market.

At times in the past, too, especially when public feeling was strong, the marking provisions have been applied to imports in which an un-popular country had a considerable cost advantage; under these circumstances the mark of origin provides information on which an informal boycott of the foreign goods may be based.[28]

On some matters Canadian practice has vacillated; sometimes the regulations have been more restrictive, sometimes less. Sometimes, for example, Canada has accepted the name of a state or well-known city in place of the country of origin, and sometimes not. Indeed, Cana-dian importers have complained that practice in this respect was not at all times uniform as between different ports of entry.[29] Even when protectionist sentiment is not widespread the very existence of the marking requirements may occasion considerable delay and expense. It even seems possible that at times the zeal and care of local officials may have been embarrassing to their superiors, as well as irritating to importers.

An account of a few annoying experiences of Canadian importers follows. In 1949 certain unmarked shipments of shoes from the United States involved the importers in the additional expense of marking

[28]Concerning "Produced in Canada" campaigns see S.D. Clark, *The Canadian Manufacturers' Association*, p. 93.

[29]At one time, for example, Montreal importers complained that imports of English cutlery marked "Sheffield" were accepted, when entered in Toronto, as fulfilling the marking requirements, while, when imported through Montreal, they were held until die-stamped and were charged the extra duty of 10 per cent. It is difficult, to maintain at all times strict uniformity between different publica-tions. In May 1952 two memoranda of the Department both supposedly in effect (Series D, no. 43, rev. dated Aug. 23, 1948, with its supplements, p. 8, and Series D, no. 1, rev. 1949 and dated Sept. 27, 1949) did not agree on this point. The Department of National Revenue in May 1952 stated that the name of a well-known city was acceptable, and explained that D, no. 43, was then being revised. D, no. 43, 2nd rev., dated June 25, 1952, corresponds with D, no. 1, rev. 1949.

and paying the duty of 10 per cent. The requirement that imported articles bearing a brand or trade name registered in Canada be marked to show country of origin has occasioned some unpleasant surprises. Disputes have occurred concerning the breadth of such items as "brushes" and "hand tools." An importer who received an unmarked shipment of small perforated price tickets in booklets containing 100 each was at first met with the demand that the country of origin be stamped on each individual ticket; but eventually they were released after each booklet had been stamped. A shipment of fountain pens from the United States was held because the mark "Made in U.S.A." was not stamped on the pen itself but only on the package containing it; on appeal to higher customs authorities the shipment was released. Such disputes and delays concerning marking are currently rare in Canada. These examples serve to show, however, that expense and annoyance must occur even when very few articles need to be marked and when there is no apparent tendency to be unduly restrictive in applying the regulations.

B. OTHER REGULATIONS

In each country, there are many acts, and regulations authorized by them, that control trade generally or trade across state or provincial borders, and therefore, incidentally, trade across international boundaries. In this section, the operation of such laws and regulations is illustrated in three important fields. One of these is the preservation of property by regulations concerning patents, trade-marks, copyright, and the prevention of unfair competition; a second, the safeguarding of health by regulating trade in drugs and food products; and a third, the prevention or control of plant and animal diseases.

If the fundamental purpose of these regulations is to be advanced, the regulations must be applied to importations as well as to domestic trade; but many countries have used them to discriminate against imports and to give widespread concealed protection to domestic producers. In this respect Canada and the United States have not been specially blatant offenders, for in most cases they have accompanied the inspection and regulation of imports with effective sanitary control over domestic, or at least interstate and interprovincial, trade.

(1) Property Regulations

The United States Federal Trade Commission is charged with the prevention of unfair practices in the import trade as well as in interstate commerce, and it has undertaken proceedings in a few cases concerning false claims for imported goods and misuse of foreign trade names. However, complaints of unfair competition in the import trade are usually laid under section 337 of the Tariff Act of 1930,[30] which empowers the President, on a finding of unfair practices by the Tariff Commission and subject to appeal by the importer on a question of law to the United States Court of Customs and Patent Appeals, to exclude the imports in question. There is some doubt whether this clause empowers the President to take action against unfair practices by non-residents, and in fact the Commission has interpreted its powers under this clause narrowly. Of the numerous complaints received between 1922 and 1938, sixteen only were deemed worthy of investigation. Of these, six were dismissed; eight of the others were found to involve violation of patent rights of United States producers; the remaining two involved simulation of an American product and misbranding.[31] One of the findings was reversed on appeal to the Court of Customs and Patent Appeals.[32]

The United States Tariff Act[33] prohibits the importation of foreign merchandise bearing a trade mark owned by a corporation or citizen of the United States and registered under its Trade Mark Act, if a copy of the certificate of registration has been filed with the Treasury Department, except with the written consent of the owner.[34] The Canadian Customs Tariff similarly protects trade marks by prohibiting the importation from any country of goods which would be forfeited under the provisions of Part VII of the Criminal Code, that is, goods from a foreign country which bear a name or trade mark of any product or dealer in Canada or the United Kingdom, unless accompanied by a definite indication of the foreign country of origin.[35] Under the first provision importation is currently prohibited of goods bearing some four trade marks.

Canada properly excludes unauthorized reprints of Canadian copyrighted works and reprints of unauthorized British copyrighted works which have been copyrighted in Canada.[36] The copyright laws of the United States have always afforded indirect protection to United States publishers. Originally no copyright protection was given to foreign

---

[30]Continuing s. 316 of the Tariff Act of 1916.

[31]Bidwell, *Invisible Tariff*, pp. 60–8, who cites U.S.T.C., *Sixth Annual Report*; and Viner, *Dumping*, p. 253.

[32]*In Re Amtorg Trading Corp.*, 22 C.C.P.A. 558, Feb. 25, 1935.

[33]U.S. Tariff Act, s. 526.

[34]S. 526. See also U.S.C.R., 11.14 to 11.17.

[35]Customs Tariff Act, s. 13 and item no. 1209.

[36]Customs Tariff, item no. 1202.

authors, and domestic publishers did a large business in pirated English works. The difficulties of American authors, subjected to competition of pirated foreign works, occasioned a change in the laws; the Copyright Act of 1891 permitted a foreign author to obtain copyright in the United States but only for a book which was printed there. This manufacturing requirement has given the domestic printing industry almost complete protection even against authorized reprints, and pirating has been largely abandoned. Until recently, if a work in the English language was copyrighted in the United States, importation was prohibited not only of pirated editions but of all copies printed abroad; exceptions were narrowly limited. Since 1949, however, if *ad interim* copyright in the United States has been obtained, 1,500 copies of the work may be imported within five years of first publication.[37] Any affected party is permitted to enter a complaint that a particular work is pirated but, to avoid delays occasioned by frivolous complaints, the regulations provide that, in disputed cases, the burden of proof is on the complainant to establish that the work is pirated. Moreover, if the importer claims that the delay of deciding the dispute will cause him loss or additional expense, the complainant is required to file with the collector a bond "conditioned to hold the importer harmless from any loss or damage resulting from it in case it is held by the Bureau of Customs not to be prohibited."[38]

(2) Health and Sanitation

As transportation facilities have improved, and specialization and commercial production have increased, most countries have found it necessary to regulate trade in food and drugs, and have taken precautions against the introduction and spread, through international or domestic trade, of the more serious plant and animal diseases. It is a necessary part of such programmes that importations be regulated at least as stringently as goods produced at home; but many countries from time to time have used sanitary regulations to prevent or discriminate against imports in order to give concealed protection to domestic agriculture and to counteract the liberalizing effects of international commercial agreements.

Canada and the United States, on balance, have been more important exporters than importers of foodstuffs. Perhaps as a consequence, they have not been the worst offenders in this respect. The primary purpose of most of their regulations has been, on the one

[37]Bidwell, *Invisible Tariff*, pp. 78–85; and 17 U.S.C. (Sup. III), 16.
[38]U.S.C.R., 11.20 (c).

hand, to provide their consumers consistently with wholesome foods clearly labelled to indicate their character and quality and, if packaged, the amount contained in the package; and, on the other, to improve or maintain the reputation of the country's products in export markets and to protect the crops and herds of domestic producers from pests and diseases that would reduce yield or quality.

However, the enforcement of high standards of sanitation by any country is almost certain to have more restrictive effects on imports, even from countries with equally stringent sanitary standards, than on domestic production and trade—even interstate or interprovincial trade. These effects are occasioned by a number of circumstances. In the first place, in international trade each shipment must come under the eye of a Customs examiner; accordingly, a large proportion of international shipments of certain foods subject to health inspection are more likely to be actually inspected than the shipments moving in domestic trade. More important, the goods are subject to inspection and often to analysis not by one, but by two, distinct national authorities; the standards, grades, and labels prescribed by these authorities are seldom identical; sometimes they are inconsistent. Finally, information concerning domestic regulations, and especially changes in them, is likely to be distributed more promptly and thoroughly to domestic than to foreign producers. Accordingly, even when sanitary regulations are framed without any intention of protecting domestic producers, they are almost certain to impose special costs, special delays, and special uncertainties on international, as compared with domestic, trade.

International co-ordination of grades, standards, and units of measurement, and the acceptance by one national authority of the licensing, inspection, and grading of another may diminish this protective effect; but, in fact, international differences in tastes and conditions, the intervention (or even the presence) of politically influential groups of domestic producers, and, at times, even the competitive pride of each inspectional and research organization in its own competence, make such co-ordination difficult and unusual.

More reprehensible, perhaps, but in Canada and the United States probably not more important than this general protective effect of the regulations, are the instances in which, under pressure from domestic producers, the authorities have introduced sanitary measures (or at least framed or applied them) with the primary objective of giving concealed protection to sensitive sectors of the economy. Agricultural interests in both countries have, to different degrees and with respect to different products, shown themselves to be not only sensitive to foreign competition but also aware of the advantages to be obtained by hindering the importation both of directly competing products and of substitutes for them. Generally speaking, Canadian interests have been more sensitive to the importation of fruit and vegetable products while those of the United States have been more active in obstructing the importation of animals, and of meat, dairy, and horticultural products.

Though seldom of crucial importance in the international trade of either Canada or the United States, the protective effects of sanitary regulations are worth considering here because it is very difficult indeed for domestic importers or foreign producers to obtain relief from this form of protection. To object publicly to the treatment accorded particular shipments, or to precipitate an investigation, is to publicize the fact that the products have been refused entry on sanitary grounds. Whatever the outcome of the investigation, the suspicion that the foreign article is unwholesome or inferior in quality is very difficult to remove completely. Accordingly, if the sanitary regulations of a country are not actually prohibitive, foreign producers usually try to conform; and their governments assist them by inspecting and restricting exports, and by research into productive methods. Whether protection by sanitary regulations is to be preferred to tariff protection is a complex question which cannot be discussed here. In any event it is concealed protection, whether it results from the largely unintentional, though pervasive, general effect of the regulations or from more specific and intentional protective episodes.

In what follows in this section, the general protective effects of the sanitary regulations as well as their more directly protective features are described and illustrated in the fields of miscellaneous foods and drugs, meat and meat products, fruit and vegetables and their products, and milk; a final section deals with plant and animal quarantine.

(a) *Food and drugs.* In each country a general act relating to foods and drugs is supplemented by other acts which provide for the commercial inspection, grading, labelling, or packaging of certain important kinds of foods and drugs. In the United States the Food and Drug Administration of the Federal Security Agency administers the regulations under the general Food, Drug and Cosmetic Act,[39] the Milk Import Act,[40] the Tea Importation Act, and the Caustics Pro-

[39]21 U.S.C. 801; U.S.C.R., Parts XII to XIV, relate to foods, drugs, and other special classes of merchandise.
[40]21 U.S.C. 141–9; U.S.C.R., 12.7.

ducts Act;[41] regulations under the Meat Inspection Act and section 306 of the Tariff Act are administered by the Bureau of Animal Industry of the Department of Agriculture.

In Canada the Food and Drugs Division of the Department of National Health and Welfare administers the general regulations under the Food and Drugs Act[42] and the Proprietary or Patent Medicines Act. Regulations concerning the commercial supervision, inspection, and grading of important foods are administered by other agencies. In the Department of Agriculture, the Fruit, Vegetables, Maple Products and Honey Division, as its name implies, inspects, supervises, and regulates the processing, grading, and packaging of important plant foodstuffs under authority of the Fruit, Vegetables and Honey Act,[43] The Maple Products Industry Act[44] and the Meat and Canned Foods Act;[45] the Livestock and Livestock Products Division and the Health of Animals Division perform similar functions in connection with animals and foodstuffs derived from them, under the Meat and Canned Foods Act as well as under the Animals Contagious Diseases Act; and dairy products are regulated by their appropriate division. The Department of Fisheries is similarly concerned with fish and their products under the Canned Food Act and the Fish Inspection Act.

In both countries, of course, still other acts affect the trade in foods or drugs; both, for example, regulate the sale and importation in insecticides or pesticides; in both, the federal regulations are supplemented by controls imposed by provincial (or state) and local authorities.

The regulation of the sale of food and drugs is not new. Canada passed the first Food and Drugs Act on the North American continent in 1874;[46] the United States Act was passed in 1906. In scope the Acts differ slightly. The United States Act applies to cosmetics (except soap) as well as food, drugs, and medical appliances; and, while the Canadian Statute relates to food for man only, the United States Act, more thoroughly biological, relates to "food for man and other animals." Both govern drugs for man and beast. Both acts define

[41]U.S., Federal Security Agency, Food and Drug Administration, *Annual Report*, 1951, p. 16.

[42]R.S.C., 1952, c. 123.

[43]S.C., 1935, c. 62; R.S.C., 1952, c. 126.

[44]S.C., 1945, c. 24; R.S.C., 1952, c. 172.

[45]R.S.C., 1952, c. 177.

[46]Can., Dept. of National Health and Welfare, *Annual Report for the Fiscal Year Ended March 31, 1951.*

adulteration and misbranding; prohibit trading in adulterated or mis-branded goods; and provide for the appointment of inspectors with adequate power to examine foodstuffs at all stages in the process of their preparation or distribution. Both Acts provide for the inspection of articles offered for importation in order to ensure that they conform with the standards of wholesomeness, purity, and labelling required of domestic products. The Canadian Act requires inspectors to pay, or offer to pay, for the samples taken for analysis from domestic sellers but it makes no such provision with respect to samples taken from articles offered for importation. The United States regulations require from the shipper a consular declaration that the merchandise offered for importation has not been manufactured, processed, or packed under unsanitary conditions, that it contains no added substance harm-ful to health, bears no false labels, and contains no added colouring or preservatives except as stated; and is not an untested drug not yet approved by the United States authorities. Domestic inspection im-poses these same conditions on domestic foods and drugs. In addition, the declaration must affirm that they are not "of a character to cause prohibition or restriction in sale in the country where made or from which exported."[47] It is clear that such a regulation adopted by all countries and rigorously interpreted and applied in detail with respect to contents, label, package, and advertising might easily be interpreted to require reconditioning, repackaging, or relabelling of all food im-ports except where, by accident, the details of the regulations were identical.

Under each system customs officials co-operate with food and drug officials. Each shipment of regulated goods must be held until the shipment (or a sample taken from it) is examined and passed by the appropriate inspecting authority. However, that authority may notify customs that merchandise of any specified kind of regulated goods need not be held for examination. In each country, when a sample is taken for analysis, the importer is notified; on completion of the analysis he is informed of the result. If he is dissatisfied he may present evidence in support of a request for re-examination which may or may not be granted. The result of a re-examination is conclusive as to the content and quality of the shipment at the time the sample was taken. However, after the goods have been released for sale in the domestic market they are, of course, subject to re-examination in the same way as goods produced within the country.

[47]U.S., Federal Security Agency, Food and Drug Administration, *Regulations under Food, Drug and Cosmetic Act*, 2.300, and 21 U.S.C. 381 (a).

When examination is required, the United States regulations provide that the merchandise must not be released except under a bond guaranteeing return of any, or all, of the merchandise at any time on the demand of the Collector of Customs;[48] the Canadian Act requires that a shipment be held, if a sample is taken, until the results of the analysis is reported.[49] In their practical results, however, the procedures are very similar; Canadian officials, in fact, typically release routine shipments to established importers who are known to be dependable, on the understanding that the merchandise will be returned to Customs if, on examination, it does not qualify for entry; while United States officials are unwilling to take advantage of their power to release the shipment even on bond, unless it appears from past experience with the importer that he will return the goods released promptly on request.

In the event that a shipment, on being examined, does not qualify for entry, it is held by Customs until the importer arranges for its disposal. Under both sets of regulations merchandise not admissible may be exported or destroyed; or, if it appears to the responsible officials that the defect can be corrected, the importer may be permitted to relabel the merchandise, or to sort or recondition it, in bond. The United States regulations require such permission to be given unless "the labeling constitutes a flagrant or intentional misbranding" or "the condition of the article is such as to indicate deliberate adulteration" or "the owner or consignee was informed with respect to any violation prior to the date of export" or "a public notice had been issued . . . that . . . such relabelling . . . would not be permitted";[50] the Canadian regulations provide that shipments may be released after compliance with the written conditions of the Dominion analyst who made the examination; but they also provide that the privilege of relabelling, cleaning, or similarly conditioning the merchandise may be refused if the importer, shipper, furnisher, or manufacturer has been informed of statutory violations in previous shipments.[51]

Canadian importers complain that in certain cases entry must be made and the duty advanced before the shipment is inspected by the Canadian Food and Drug authorities. This procedure is defended on

---

[48]U.S.C.R., 12.3.

[49]R.S.C., 1927, c. 70, s. 10; R.S.C., 1952, c. 123, s. 12(2).

[50]U.S., 21 C.F.R. (1949 ed.), 1.309 (c).

[51]Can., Dept. of National Health and Welfare, *General Regulations under the Food and Drugs Act*, s. viii.

the grounds that it helps to prevent the importer from shirking his own inspection; but at least one Canadian importer complains that importers are not permitted even to look at their shipments in bond prior to entry except after making a formal application, reciting the special circumstances which lead him to expect that the shipment is not in order. Others report that shipments marked by the exporter "Allow Inspection" may be inspected before entry is made and duty paid. United States publications warn foreign shippers of food and drugs to make entry promptly since, ordinarily, the Food and Drug officials cannot act upon a shipment until entry has been filed.[52] In any event, if the shipment is finally refused entry, and is exported or destroyed *under supervision of Customs and sanitary authorities*, a refund may be obtained of any duty paid with respect to that shipment.

The provisions for re-examination, reconditioning, or relabelling, and for refund of duty, afford an unfortunate importer some slight relief, but no matter how successful the attempt to administer the regulations justly, the special risks incurred by importers of drugs and foodstuffs (including the delays, expense, and difficulties involved in salvaging and the other losses on an unsatisfactory shipment) are very considerable. The regulations train importers to exercise unusually great care and restraint in importing foodstuffs subject to sanitary inspection; necessarily, therefore, they give some protection to domestically produced substitutes.

Though the provisions of the food and drug act of each country applies very broadly, each is supplemented by other Acts that control the production, import, and sale of special commercially important classes of food. Together, the general and the special Acts provide for comprehensive licensing, inspection, testing, and marking of domestically produced foods; and, as a matter of course, regulate the importation of foodstuffs as well. In Canada the Meat and Canned Foods Act, for example, applies primarily to establishments in which animals are slaughtered and in which meats, fish, shellfish, fruits, or vegetables are stored or processed if they are to be exported from the province (or, of course from the country). Generally speaking, such establishments must be licensed; all animals used in regulated establishments must be inspected before, and the carcasses after, slaughter; the fish, fruit, or other product used in preparing the foods must be sound, wholesome, and fit for food. The product is subject to inspection at

[52]U.S., Federal Security Agency, Food and Drug Administration, *Import Requirements of the United States Food, Drug and Cosmetic Act*, p. 45.

all stages in the process of preparation; and, finally, it must be marked or labelled in accordance with the Act or the regulations under it. Any canned or packaged food must bear the name and address of the packer or first dealer who obtained it from the packer and a true and correct description of the contents. However, any article prepared for export may be exempted from this regulation if it is established that such marking would hinder its sale in the markets of other countries.

The regulations with respect to domestic foods are applied, also, to imported foods. A shipment of meats and meat products is refused entry unless the standards of meat inspection in the country of origin are deemed satisfactory and the shipment is accompanied by an approved certificate of inspection. It is subject also to Canadian inspection at the port of entry and, like domestic products, at any time after it has entered the trade of Canada.

In the United States, similarly, the Food, Drug and Cosmetic Act is supplemented by the federal Imported Meat Act and the federal Meat Inspection Act, both administered by the Bureau of Animal Husbandry, and by the standards for processed fruits and vegetables prescribed by the Production and Marketing Administration of the Department of Agriculture.

In general outline the United States meat regulations resemble the Canadian. Except for farm slaughtering, the preparation and sale of meat and meat products is subject to thorough inspection and regulation and, as part of a general programme, importation of meat and meat products is prohibited unless they originate in a country which maintains a satisfactory meat inspection service and are accompanied by an acceptable certificate signed by an authorized official of that country to the effect that the products were derived from healthy animals, subjected to veterinary inspection before and after being slaughtered; that they have been handled, processed, and packed only in a sanitary manner; that they are sound, wholesome, and fit for human food; that they are not misbranded and contain no preservatives or dyes except as stated; and that their sale is not forbidden or restricted in the country of origin. On arrival the products are inspected by officials of the importing country and, if necessary, samples are taken for analysis.

If the shipment conforms with the regulations, it is marked "U.S. inspected and passed." If it does not conform, it is classified and may be marked "Refused entry"; and it is marked "U.S. condemned" when found unfit for human food or to contain substances in conflict with the laws of the country of export. Once the goods have been inspected and passed, they are subject to the same regulations as similar domestic goods.

Detailed regulations prescribe the labelling of outside containers of imported meats; and all labels and marks on immediate or true containers[53] as well as private brands on carcasses must be submitted to Washington for approval.[54] Shipments of meat products bearing labels that have not been approved must be held pending receipt of the report of the laboratory findings and the results of the examination of trade labels and the marks on shipping containers. Canned products bearing trade labels and other markings which have been approved and numbered must be inspected for soundness and checked for net weight. Samples of them may be collected for laboratory examination but the shipment may be released pending report of laboratory findings.[55]

Neither country, apparently, requires or imposes a higher standard on imported than on domestic meat and meat products; yet the imported product is subjected to inspection, sampling, and examination by two sets of officials, the domestic by only one. Canada and the United States each recognizes that the other maintains a satisfactory inspection service, and each treats the products of the other as favourably as the same products when imported from any other foreign country. Until the outbreak of foot-and-mouth disease in 1952, Canada was one of the few countries[56] from which meat and certain meat products could be imported into the United States. Formally then, the United States regulations did not discriminate against Canadian meats; and actually, in a sense, gave them a preferred position in the United States market.

In 1951, nearly 17,000 million pounds of meat products were prepared and processed under the supervision of the United States Bureau of Animal Industry, of which 7 million pounds were condemned and destroyed on reinspection. A total of 342 million pounds was passed for entry including 105 million pounds of fresh meat of which 95 million came from Canada and the rest from Cuba, the Dominican Republic, Ireland, and New Zealand; of the 237 million

---

[53]Except the marks of inspection of foreign governments embossed on metal containers or branded on carcasses.

[54]9 C.F.R. 27.17.   [55]9 C.F.R. 27. 14.

[56]At the time of the outbreak in Canada, the only important meat-producing countries free from the disease were Australia and New Zealand. See Can., Dept. of Agriculture, *Report of the Minister for the Year Ended March 31, 1951*, p. 72.

pounds of cured and canned meats, 133 million pounds came from Argentina and 28 million from Canada. Of the meats and meat products presented for entry, 1,452,000 pounds were refused entry and 149,000 condemned.[57] In terms of percentages about one-twentieth of one per cent of the domestic product was condemned on reinspection and about one-half of one per cent of meats and meat products presented for import were refused entry or condemned.

In each country standards are prescribed for other canned products and general regulations prescribe the form and content of the labels. Even more detailed conditions are prescribed for each type of product. In Canada, containers of fish products, for example, must be marked with the minimum weight in avoirdupois of the contents and, of shellfish, with the minimum weight of the dry meat in the can. Preserved fruit and vegetables, jams, and marmalade may be sold only in containers of prescribed shapes and sizes, which must carry on the label a circle of specified size within which appear the word "Canada" and the volume of the contents in fluid ounces. Regulations require, also, that certain information (concerning processing, degree of syrup, type of packing, and added ingredients, for example), be shown in letters equal in size and visibility to any other printing on the label; the minimum size of the letters is prescribed for each size of package. In addition, the marking must conform with prescribed grades and standards (as to quality and size, for example) defined in the regulations.[58]

Similar provisions govern imported canned fruit and vegetables. A shipment of preserved fruit or vegetables must be refused entry unless accompanied by an affidavit from the shipper that its manufacture was carried on under the sanitary conditions provided for in the regulations; that the product at time of shipment is sound, wholesome, and fit for human food; that the containers show the name and address of the manufacturer or fruit dealer; and that the description of the contents is true and conforms to the quality, container, and labelling requirements of the regulations. Shipments of any food product are refused entry, except for remanufacture, if of a quality below the minimum grade established for the product by the regulations. Even after entry, imported food products are subject to inspection and, upon condemnation by an inspector, are forfeit.

[57]U.S., Bureau of Animal Husbandry, *Report of the Chief of the Bureau*, 1951.
[58]See, for example, the Regulations governing the inspection of preserved fruits and vegetables under the Meat and Canned Foods Act, P.C. 3199, May 3, 1945; and S.O.R. 1949, Consolidated Food and Drugs Act, B.01.001 to B.01.01.

The standards applied by Canada and the United States, both to domestic and imported products, are kept as high as their advanced (and advancing) technologies permit. The primary motive for this procedure (as distinct from its effects) is not to protect domestic producers, it appears, but to hasten the adoption of the approved technologies at home and abroad.

The missionary zeal of the Food and Drug Administration of the United States is clearly expressed in its publications. The administration is required to reject as adulterated any food that "consists *in whole or in part* of a filthy decomposed substance. . . . this does not mean that food is necessarily condemned because of the presence of foreign matter in amounts below the irreducible minimum after all precautions humanly possible have been taken to prevent contamination." However, "As commercial practices improve, or insect infestation is brought under control, the basis of action may be lowered. This should not be a hardship on those who prepare the food in foreign countries, because, whatever may be the basis upon which actions are taken at the United States ports on filth and decomposition, it represents only what the careful producer or manufacturer can meet."[59]

The speed with which standards are stiffened by the Food and Drug Administration as technology improves contrasts with the obsolete phrasing and interpretation of the United States Tariff. This contrast may be attributable in part to the greater importance attached to assuring wholesome and pleasant foods; it may arise in part too from the fact that judicial appeal is not provided from the decisions of the Food and Drug Administration while it is from customs decisions; in addition, however, the changing of grades and standards to conform with changing domestic technology tends to protect domestic producers, whatever else it may be intended to do, while removing anachronisms from the Tariff Act is likely to weaken the protective effect and to allow trade more readily to be deflected from its former channels.

The detection and condemnation of foods, drugs, and devices which are dangerous to health is the most important function of the food and drug administrations. Performance of this function is universally regarded as being not only desirable but necessary, and its effect on trade will not be illustrated in this study. But though the most important, this function is not the one which requires the largest number

[59]U.S., Food and Drug Administration, *Import Requirements of the United States Food, Drug and Cosmetic Act*, p. 5.

of inspections or results in the largest number of warnings and seizures, or of delayed, refused, or conditional, entries. Much of the work of the officials charged with the control of drugs and foods in both countries consists in seeing that each import, as well as each domestic product, is actually the product that it purports to be; and therefore, of necessity, in defining in exact terms the margin at which it ceases to be that product and becomes something else. For example, while Italian olive oil was not available, many shipments to Canada marked "olive oil" were in fact wholly, or in part, cotton seed oil; they were relabelled or re-exported. This simple and clear-cut case of adulteration is an example of a large class of difficulties which, at the margins, when there is no intent to misrepresent, may require difficult decisions. These marginal cases are, on the whole, more likely to be discovered in international, than in domestic, trade.

Some seizures and rejections occur too because the standards of the importing and the exporting countries are not identical though neither may be wholly unreasonable. Differences may arise from allowing different, though substantial, safety margins with respect to contents which, if present in large quantities, might be harmful to the health of consumers. During one fairly recent period, for example, Canadian officials found, in certain imports of dehydrated fruits, a larger proportion of sulphur dioxide than was permitted by the Canadian standards, and occasionally, too, rather more spray residues.[60] Technological changes such as the development of new drying methods and the use of new sprays for controlling weeds, pests, and plant diseases, as well as the investigation of the effects of resulting residues on health, are likely to give rise to international differences in standards and consequent refusal of imports unless they have been specially processed for the export market.

Rejection of shipments of maple sugar and maple syrup at United States ports has occasioned considerable ill-will; the difficulties have arisen in part from differences in standards. In the 1936 reciprocal trade agreements with Canada, the United States conceded a reduction in the duties on maple sugar and maple syrup from 6 cents and 4 cents a pound, respectively, to 3 cents and 2 cents;[61] but the develop-

---

[60]The Canadian Regulations provide that "no person shall use sulphurous and/or sulphur dioxide in amounts greater than . . . (b) 2,000 parts per million in or upon dried fruits." S.O.R. 1949, Consolidated Food and Drugs Act, B.16.013, II, p. 1767.

[61]See also T.D. 44602 effective March 7, 1931, reducing duties from the 1930 rates.

ment of the trade was impeded by food and drug regulations. In 1938, for example, of 5,602,361 pounds of maple sugar entered, 5,000,000 pounds were inspected and 2,600,000 pounds rejected.[62] Some of the shipments of maple syrup were rejected on the grounds that they contained larger amounts of lead than the United States standards permitted. Canadian exporters claimed that the cans used in preparing the syrup were the same as those used in the United States for maple products, made by the same company using the same tinplate and the same solder. The rejection of numerous shipments of the product for this and other reasons led eventually to the passing of the Maple Products Industries Act,[63] which provides for the licensing of manufacturers and packers of maple products for interprovincial and export trade and the approval or rejection of labels by the Department of Agriculture. Shipments to the United States must be accompanied by analyses signed by a qualified chemist; and carlot shipments containing excess lead must be accompanied by a statement by the importer that the shipment is to be deleaded on his own premises. The Act further imposes on every manufacturer the requirements of observing certain sanitary regulations and provides for the seizure of adulterated products or products unfit for food.[64] The co-operation of the authorities in the two countries and the admission of syrup to be further processed has largely removed the former difficulties. In the latest report of the United States Food and Drug Administration no mention is made of maple products.[65]

The three following examples illustrate minor difficulties concerning packaging, labelling, and advertising encountered by Canadian exporters of foods. Scotch style oatcakes are brittle substances; in Canada they may be packed in a container large enough to prevent damage. The United States authorities, however, held that the containers were misleadingly large. They were permitted to enter but the Canadian exporter was warned that no more than three additional shipments would be permitted unless the packaging was changed. Objection was taken, too, to shipments of shortbread from Nova Scotia. The label contained the picture of a piper in kilts, and it was feared that this might lead consumers to believe that the shortbread was made in Scotland. Similarly a Canadian exporter of seafoods used the slogan

[62]Bidwell, *Invisible Tariff*, p. 189.

[63]S.C., 1945, c. 24; now R.S.C., 1952, c. 172. See also the Maple Sugar Industry Act, 1930.

[64]S.O.R. 1949, Consolidation III, p. 2436.

[65]However, co-operation has been required between federal and provincial officials to enforce the Canadian regulations. Can., Dept. of National Health and Welfare, *Annual Report*, 1951, p. 74.

"Health and Beauty from the Sea." This was held to be misleading since the product did not qualify as a drug or cosmetic. In these three cases it was possible to change the package, label, and display material.

Circumstances that would not affect the health of consumers, but might be distasteful if known, are more likely, it seems, to come to light in international than in domestic trade. A shipment of peanuts, for example, was held by Canadian authorities because rats had left their traces in the shipment. The nuts were to be used to produce oil by processes that involved sterilizing and purifying but they were finally admitted only on the condition that the oil from them be used for making soap and not for food. This action was taken as a matter of routine procedure even at a time when oils were in very short supply; protection was not intended.

Other defects not dangerous to health may in practice exclude commodities from international, but not from domestic, trade. Border inspection of Canadian freshwater fish has made for delay and higher costs. Shipments have been refused entry on the grounds that they are infested by a certain parasite; even though the infestation is conceded not to be dangerous to health, it is held to be repulsive. Complaints have been made that fish taken from the same border lake, and presumably equally infested, were allowed entry at least into local trade when captured by fishermen from the United States but not when imported from Canada. In order to reject the infested fish, it was considered necessary, at one time, to hold for examination all fresh Canadian whitefish; the costly and damaging delays which resulted threatened to destroy this important export industry. Eventually, after negotiation alone failed to remove the obstacle, regulations under the White-fish Export Inspection Act prohibited the export of whitefish from Canada unless they bore the stamp of an inspector certifying that the fish were in good merchantable condition at the time of inspection and that they complied with the other provisions under the Act; these included labelling regulations.[66] In this case a regulation of the United States effectively imposed similar standards on Canada; inspection and stamping were required on export shipments first, and only later extended to shipments in interprovincial trade. The United States Food and Drug Administration reports that "detentions of fish because of parasitic cysts have . . . decreased because of the new Canadian controls of exports."[67]

Shipments of solids such as dried figs and dates involve difficult

[66]The Regulations under the Act were revised in 1951. S.O.R. 151–89, 219, 523.
[67]U.S., Food and Drug Administration, *Annual Report*, 1951, p. 5.

problems, not only in setting appropriate standards but in devising methods of sampling and analysis suitable for examining large shipments quickly and efficiently. The most suitable methods are time-consuming and the delay is increased when there is no laboratory at the port of entry and the sample must be sent elsewhere for examination. A number of large shipments of figs have been denied entry into each of the two countries on the grounds that they contained an excessive number of dead larvae of the fig wasp which not only pollinates the fig blossoms but lays its eggs in the fruit. The larvae are not dangerous to health and almost all shipments contain some of them. When a large proportion of the shipments began to be excluded, some Canadian importers believed that the standards applied to figs had been raised without warning. Departmental officials, however, while admitting that the method of obtaining a representative sample had been improved, denied that the increase in rejections was attributable to any change in the standard or in the laboratory method used in examining the sample eventually chosen. They were inclined rather to attribute the increase in the proportion of imports rejected, in part at least, to a rise in the standards applied to figs by other countries, especially the United States, and the consequent selection of poorer fruit for shipment to Canada. The troubles of importers of foods, it appears, may be increased by changes in standards in third countries as well as by the regulations imposed by their own.

Whatever the cause, rejection of figs has occasioned heavy losses. As one importer phrased it, more succinctly and less profanely than some of his fellows, "Figs are dynamite. There is no way of telling before the shipment arrives whether it will be admitted or not; and even before shipment the importer has to put up an irrevocable letter of credit. Nuts are almost as dangerous." Sorting or reconditioning is not always allowed; sometimes it may be impracticable.

It should be pointed out, perhaps, that figs are not produced in Canada; and it seems improbable, therefore, that protection of domestic producers is directly intended. Nevertheless, and quite apart from the intentions of officials and legislators, the risks attaching to the importation of dried figs does discriminate in favour of the domestic producers of other dried or preserved fruits.

In spite of the fact that during 1950–1 several large shipments of dried fruits and nuts were refused entry, the Department of National Health and Welfare expressed the belief that "examinations and past refusals . . . were leading to a better quality of this kind of food being offered for import to Canada."[68] In 1951, however, the United

[68]Can., Dept. of National Health and Welfare, *Annual Report*, 1951, p. 75.

States Food and Drug Administration, reported that detentions of imported figs owing to infestations rose from 6.4 per cent of those offered for entry in 1950 to 29 per cent in 1951.[69] The experience with whitefish and maple products suggests that a rapid rise in the quality of an article offered for importation may be the result, in part at least, of transferring inferior goods to other international markets, or of compelling the exporting country to enforce the standards established by the importing country. In the long run, too, it may result in the adoption of productive methods which increase the proportion of the product which conforms with the regulations of large import markets; but the standards established by the importing country may well emphasize the quality produced by those processes in which historically it has had and has maintained a comparative advantage.

The laws and regulations of both countries control the labelling of canned or packaged foods and, accordingly, the size and type of the containers. Problems relating to the identity, purity, quality, and amount come to be centred on the control of label and container. A multitude of difficulties arise from international differences in these regulations.

With respect to canned fish, for example, the regulations promulgated under the Canadian Meat and Canned Goods Act require, in most cases, that the can contain only the variety named on the label; however, the Canadian standards for fish sold under certain names, for example Chicken Haddie and Flaked Fish,[70] require merely that the contents be made from wholesome edible fish of a specified colour. United States requirements are different. Shipments of canned "Chicken Haddie" were refused entry as not conforming with United States regulations because they contained hake as well as haddock. The United States authorities required that the label bear a statement, not only of the varieties contained, but the proportion in which they occurred in the package. Since it proved to be technically impracticable to ensure that a uniform proportion of each variety would be found in each can, this export was discontinued.

Partly for reasons of economy and partly to protect consumers who may not be sensitive to small differences in size or weight, the Canadian regulations prescribe the size and shape of containers for preserved fruit and vegetables, jam, and marmalade produced by inspected establishments or imported into Canada. For trade between Canada and the United States, this restriction is not of great consequence since the shapes and sizes prescribed in Canada are com-

[69]U.S., Food and Drug Administration, *Annual Report*, 1951, p. 3.
[70]The label of flaked fish must show the vernacular names of the kinds of fish.

monly used in the United States as well. It does tend, however, to exclude imports from other countries of certain specialty food products whose producers have developed a market for their specialties associated in the minds of consumers with containers of a different size or shape; or whose Canadian market is so small that it is not worth while to package specially for export to Canada. "Dundee Marmalade," for example, has been excluded from Canada by this regulation.

Standardization of the size of container is associated with another Canadian requirement: that the containers of canned fruits and vegetables and certain other foodstuffs bear on the label a distinctive marking stating the volume in fluid ounces rather than the weight of the contents. Since Canada uses Imperial measure and the United States wine measure, a statement of volume which is correct in one country is necessarily misleading in the other. As a consequence, the strict application by each country of a rule refusing entry to a product unless it could be sold without restriction in the country whence exported would preclude all trade between the two countries in preserved fruits, vegetables, jams, and marmalades.

Before a tin of grapefruit juice, legally saleable in the United States, could be sold in Canada, its label might require the following changes: "Contents 1 pt. 2 fl. oz." and "This is a No. 2 can. Contents 1 pt. 2 fl. oz. About 2¼ cups" cancelled and replaced by a circle "Canada 20 fluid oz. size"; "sweetened" replaced by "2% sugar added"; "enriched with dextrose" and "Rich in Vitamin 'C'" cancelled. Generally speaking, approved producers may submit proposed labels for approval; sporadic or initial shipments may be delayed, and corrective marking may be required. Such difficulties, when complicated by changes in other regulations, have sometimes had serious consequences.

One instance may serve to illustrate how such delay can cause inconvenience and loss. In the fall of 1947, a Canadian firm ordered a $30,000 shipment of canned vegetables from the United States, secured authorization from the Foreign Exchange Control Board to pay for it, and confirmed the order. However, shipment was delayed because the United States firm had to have special labels printed to conform with Canadian labelling regulations. Meanwhile, Canada imposed the emergency exchange conservation restrictions which prohibited imports of this kind. The special labels were not completed soon enough to have the shipment admitted. It is reported that neither the United States firm nor the Canadian was pleased by the outcome.

It has already been mentioned that the Canadian Food and Drugs

Act requires inspectors to pay, or to offer to pay, for samples obtained in domestic trade but typically importers are not paid for the sample in either country. Accordingly, one of the special costs of importing arises from the fact that some part of each shipment is (or may be) made unmerchantable by being submitted to laboratory analysis. Moreover, when one or more cases of a tempting or valuable delicacy are opened and left in the customs warehouse, the passerby is sorely tempted to do his own testing. The disappearance may form a substantial proportion of a small shipment. It is likely to form a relatively smaller proportion of a large shipment, but, as one importer remarked, "Ten per cent of a $40,000 shipment of candy isn't peanuts." Importers tend to suspect that inspectors take larger samples of the more valuable products than are strictly necessary on purely technical grounds; or that pilfering has taken place. This readiness to suspect helps to discourage the taking of large samples. It is probably not possible or desirable to prescribe upper limits to the size of samples inspectors are permitted to take, though minimum amounts are usually prescribed.[71] Nevertheless, it would help to reassure importers and to place responsibility for disappearances where it belongs if it were required of all inspectors, as it is now of United States inspectors of meat products, that they furnish importers with receipts for the amount of each shipment taken as a sample for analysis.

(b) *Fresh fruits and vegetables.* Most of the regulations concerning fresh fruits and vegetables apply equally to domestic and imported products. In Canada, commission agents, dealers, or brokers, who engage in interprovincial or international trade in fruit and vegetables, must be licensed. The principal fruits and vegetables grown in Canada may not be exported nor, typically, shipped in interprovincial trade unless accompanied by a certificate or other evidence that they have been inspected and graded; standard packages are prescribed. Shippers must apply for inspection and fees are charged, which, however, are not high relatively to the costs of the service. Each import shipment of these fruits and vegetables must be accompanied by a government inspection certificate of the country whence shipped, that the produce, as shipped, meets Canadian import requirements. It must be refused entry unless contained in packages marked "Inspected for Export." On these matters Canadian and United States authorities co-operate at least to the extent that the Canadian regulations set forth the

[71]See, for example, the minimum number of cans and cases to be withdrawn for laboratory inspection from shipment of canned salmon or herring. P.C. 1412 of March 11, 1952.

United States grades which meet the Canadian requirements.[72] Inspection certificates of each country are usually accepted by the other;[73] however, it is reported in Canada that when the price of vegetables drops suddenly importers frequently demand inspection of shipments that would otherwise be passed automatically.

The regulations respecting standard containers require that directly competitive imports conform with Canadian regulations; but produce which does not enter into competition with the same kind of Canadian produce may be imported in containers standardized for that kind of product in the country of origin though not in Canada. While this requirement may have some protective effects it can be defended on the grounds that the restriction imposed on domestic products must also be imposed on imports, while no Canadian regulation is necessary on kinds not grown in Canada.

One provision of the Act gives definite protection to those who trade in established channels, as well as to primary producers in Canada. At the height of the season in the United States fruits or vegetables are often shipped from the congested main markets without first being sold, and are allowed to "roll" until they reach a market in which prices are not yet unduly low. Formerly these "rollers" often ended up in Canada and were sold at prices lower than those that had to be paid by dealers buying regularly through ordinary channels. Now they are excluded from Canada by a provision which, subject to certain exceptions, denies entry to fresh fruits and vegetables unless the entry is "accompanied by conclusive evidence that the importer purchased such goods not later than 24 hours . . . after the time of shipment from the point of production."[74]

It appears that in 1938 Canadian officials enquired whether prohibition of "rollers" would be considered an infringement of her obligations under the trade agreement. At that time the United States Department of Agriculture favoured the proposal, but the State Department opposed it and it was dropped. It was adopted during the

[72]See Can., Dept. of Agriculture, *The Fruit, Vegetables and Honey Act and Regulations*, s. F, Exports and Imports, clause 3, pp. 107–8.

[73]There is a considerable degree of co-operation, generally between the two departments of agriculture. For an illustration of similar co-operation in fisheries, see the exchange of notes between Canada and the United States with respect to the certification of shellfish, Can., Dept. of External Affairs, *Treaty Series*, 1948, no. 10. There appears to have been less co-operation between the food and drug regulations of the two countries.

[74]Can., Dept. of Agriculture, *The Fruit, Vegetables and Honey Act and Regulations*, s. F, par. 9.

war after consultation with the United States as one of a number of measures designed to economize the use of refrigerator cars.

(c) *Milk and cream.* Imports of milk and cream into the United States are subject not only to state and municipal barriers but also to the provisions of the federal Milk Import Act of February 1927.[75] This Act imposes strict conditions on the importation of fluid milk or cream. It must be produced from animals shown to be healthy by physical examination and, if the milk is raw, by tuberculin test, not more than a year before importation, on a farm or in a dairy where sanitary conditions warrant a satisfactory rating; and the bacterial count and temperature when imported must not exceed prescribed maxima. No milk or cream may be imported unless the shipper holds a valid permit from the Secretary of Agriculture. Permits are issued to shippers, valid for one year only, after sanitary and veterinary inspection of herds and premises by officials of the United States, or, at the discretion of the Secretary of Agriculture, by foreign officials accredited by him. Under this latter provision, arrangements were made to issue permits to Canadian applicants on the basis of initial and subsequent inspection and of satisfactory reports by Canadian inspectors, supplemented by occasional visits from United States officials. In the three years prior to 1927, United States imports of milk from Canada averaged 6.7 million gallons; in the next three years, at 4.8 million gallons, they were smaller but still substantial. Increases in duty in 1929 and 1930,[76] as well as the effects of state and city regulations which became more protective in the early thirties,[77] almost completely eliminated Canadian milk exports by 1934. Exports of cream followed a similar pattern. In 1936 and 1939 the rates of duty were reduced (though not to the former level) subject to a substantial tariff quota, and co-operative arrangements for the issue of permits to Canadian producers were continued. However, Canadian exports of fluid milk and cream have remained very small.[78] Though increases

[75] 21 U.S.C. 141–9; U.S.C.R., 12.7; Bidwell, *Invisible Tariff*, pp. 177–83; also U.S., Bureau of Agricultural Economics, *Barriers to Internal Trade in Farm Products*, pp. 15–16.

[76] The duty on milk was raised from 2½ cents to 3¾ cents per gallon in 1929 and to 6½ cents per gallon in 1930; and on cream from 20 cents per gallon to 30 cents and then to 56.6 cents. In 1936 the duty on cream was reduced to 35 cents a gallon on a tariff quota of 1.5 million gallons and in 1939 to 28.3 cents. In 1939 the rate on milk was reduced to 3¼ cents on a quota of 3 million gallons.

[77] Some states and cities have made their inspection requirements all-inclusive and may require inspection at the source by their own inspectors of all dairy products (including condensed and evaporated milk).

[78] U.S., Food and Drug Administration, *Annual Report*, 1951, p. 16.

in relative costs and in the Canadian demand for milk may be partly responsible, it seems probable that state and local regulations in any case would effectively exclude foreign milk from the more important markets of the United States.[79]

Another protective regulation, important in the field of dairy products, relates to margarine. In the United States an internal revenue tax of 15 cents per pound has been levied on imported oleomargarine[80] and its importation into (and until recently its production in) Canada has been prohibited. It seems clear that these regulations were imposed to protect the dairy interests of each country. There seems little danger that margarine would be widely sold fraudulently as butter in countries whose food inspection services are as effective as those of the United States and Canada; and the fact that domestic production of margarine until recently was forbidden in Canada, and still is in certain areas, does not prove that the prohibition was not a protective measure. Prohibition of import, of course, was intended to protect domestic producers of butter (not of margarine) against the use of a product produced at least in part from foreign oils. The United States internal revenue tax of 8 cents per pound on filled cheese, apparently, has a similar protective intent.[81]

(d) *Animal quarantine.* The regulation of trade in animals and animal products warrants separate discussion. In this field both Canada and the United States have suffered, in the past, from sanitary regulations imposed by other countries, nominally for sanitary reasons but actually to protect their own domestic producers.[82] The current regu-

[79]For an account of the protective effects of state and local restriction on milk and cream in the United States, see U.S., Bureau of Agricultural Economics, *Barriers to Internal Trade,* pp. 5–11. At Geneva in 1947, the United States reduced the rates on cream to, and on milk below, the rates imposed before 1930. See testimony of H. R. Kemp and A. E. Richards, Can., Trade Relations, *G.A.T.T.,* 1947–8, pp. 98–104.

[80]For a brief history of federal and state treatment of margarine, see U.S., Bureau of Agricultural Economics, *Barriers to Internal Trade,* pp. 17–30. Entry of margarine into Canada has been prohibited since 1886; Simon J. McLean, *The Tariff History of Canada,* p. 30. For the relationship of this prohibition to the provision of the General Agreement, see testimony of L. Couillard, John Deutsch, H. R. Kemp, and H. McKinnon, Can., Trade Relations, *G.A.T.T.,* 1947–8, pp. 32–3, 136–8; and Can. Banking & Commerce, *G.A.T.T.,* 1948, pp. 205–7, 261–8.   [81]U.S., I.R.C., s. 2356.

[82]In 1879, for example, Italy and Austria-Hungary prohibited the import of pork products from the United States as did Germany, France, and other European countries a few years later; see Bidwell, *Invisible Tariff,* pp. 169–70. Great Britain gave Canada an early lesson in this field. In 1892 importation of Canadian cattle

lations of both countries owe much of their rigour to the requirements, past and present, imposed on their exports in foreign markets.

Normally, Canadians have little incentive to use the Canadian regulations to give protection in this field, since an important trade in competing imports from the countries most seriously affected would not develop even in the absence of the restrictions; United States producers have been more sorely tempted. However, the restrictions on imports of meats and animals have not been imposed solely or primarily to protect domestic producers against imports; in each country they are an essential part of an elaborate, costly, and, on the whole, effective system of safeguarding domestic livestock producers (or the consumers of their products) and of avoiding the imposition of sanitary embargoes against their products in export markets. The governments of each of the countries have sponsored large-scale measures against the more serious animal diseases. They have assisted, for example, in building up tuberculous-free areas and inspected and certified herds.[83] The regulations of the two countries are similar in many respects and the two departments of agriculture co-operate in many ways to prevent the spread of animal disease.[84]

Though Canada and the United States normally prescribe less rigorous precautions against imports of animals (and animal products) from each other, the general regulations laid down by each impose very serious handicaps on imports from most other countries. Under the general regulations of the United States relating to ruminants and swine, the importer must first obtain from the government a permit to

---

to Great Britain was prohibited except for immediate slaughter, because it was asserted that contagious pleuro-pneumonia had been detected in one animal in one shipment from Canada. The accuracy of the diagnosis was questioned at the time but all efforts to prevent the embargo were futile and it remained in force for more than thirty years. Meanwhile, no case of foot-and-mouth disease, cattle plague, or contagious pleuro-pneumonia was found in Canada. Can., Dept. of Agriculture, *Report of the Veterinary Director-General for the Year Ending March 31, 1927.*

[83]See Bidwell, *Invisible Tariff*, pp. 204–8; for a discussion of state, as well as federal, quarantine see U.S., Bureau of Agricultural Economics, *Barriers to Internal Trade*, pp. 85–97, especially pp. 92–93.

[84]". . . in matters pertaining to the administration of regulating measures necessary for the protection of the livestock industry from destructive animal diseases of foreign origin, and of the regulatory measures governing the movement of livestock products between Canada and the United States, the closest co-operation exists between the officials of the United States Bureau of Animal Industry and the officials of the Health of Animals Division." Can., Dept. of Agriculture, *Report of the Veterinary Director-General*, 1949, p. 6.

import the animals in question. The animals must be accompanied by a certificate signed by a veterinarian who is a salaried employee of the government of the country of origin that the animals have been in the country for 60 days and that during that time the country has been free from foot-and-mouth disease, rinderpest, contagious pleuro-pneumonia, and surra. Certificates for swine must show, as well, that the premises of origin and the adjoining premises have been free from hog cholera, swine plague, and erysipelas. In addition, cattle must be accompanied by a certificate showing that they have been tested with negative results for tuberculosis and brucellosis within 30 days of the date of shipment. Cattle must be quarantined for 30 days after arrival, at the expense of the importer, and are retested during the last ten days of quarantine. Other ruminants and swine are quarantined for 15 days. If disease develops during the period of quarantine, the animals are disposed of as directed by the Chief of the Bureau of Animal Husbandry.

Normally, however, animals from Canada and Mexico, accompanied by the appropriate certificates, are not quarantined or retested. If certificates are lacking, they are tested and held for three days. Cattle from tick-infested areas of Mexico, accompanied by a certificate that they have been dipped, are re-dipped and entered without quarantine. If satisfactory veterinary certificates are lacking, sheep and goats from Canada and Mexico are dipped, tested, and held in quarantine for ten days and swine are held for two weeks.[85] Animals imported from Canada for immediate slaughter need not be tested.[86] Normally, too, animal by-products from Canada are exempted from the strict regulations governing similar imports from most other countries.

One provision of the United States law concerning the importation of animals is definitely and avowedly protectionist. Section 306 of the Tariff Act of 1930, inserted between that which prohibits the importation of immoral articles and that which prohibits the importation of convict-made goods, prohibits the importation of ruminants or swine, or of the corresponding meats, when fresh chilled or frozen, from a country *in any part of which* the Secretary of Agriculture has determined that foot-and-mouth disease exists; cured meats from such a country are also prohibited unless they have been treated as specified

[85]New regulations (*Federal Register*, April 8, 1953) provide that sheep and goats from Canada if not certified or if found diseased on arrival or to have been exposed to disease shall be refused entry and destroyed, quarantined, or otherwise disposed of. *Foreign Trade*, May, 2, 1953, p. 27.

[86]Bidwell, *Invisible Tariff*, pp. 210–11; 9 C.F.R. 92.4 to 92.23.

in the regulations. This provision is more stringent than the restrictions that were imposed on domestic commerce in the United States during the nine outbreaks in the United States since 1870.[87] It was introduced to exclude shipments of beef and cattle from Argentina and was passed in spite of the opinion of the Secretary of Agriculture that his department already had adequate power to prevent importations which would tend to introduce contagious or infectious diseases among livestock in the United States.[88]

The administration of this regulation with respect to imports from the adjacent countries of Canada and Mexico has been as considerate as the statute permits but it has occasioned a greater disruption of trade than was necessary to prevent the disease from spreading to the United States.

In December 1946 an outbreak of foot-and-mouth disease occurred in central Mexico. Imports from the whole of Mexico were prohibited; a border patrol was instituted in 1947. The United States aided Mexico to combat the outbreak and by 1949 it had been controlled and confined to central Mexico. Meanwhile, when the cattle population of northern Mexico had increased dangerously, slaughter houses and meat-packing plants had been established there, and the United States contracted to purchase the canned products, though only for export to foreign countries; sales were made principally to the United States Army for use in occupied areas, and to Great Britain, Italy, and Austria.[89]

Prior to 1947, about 500,000 head of cattle normally entered the United States from Mexico. By 1951 only 368,000 animals entered the United States, almost all through ports on the Canadian border. None came from Mexico, a few from Ireland and one or two other countries.

On September 1, 1952, nearly six years after the outbreak occurred, the Secretary of Agriculture announced that the disease had been eradicated in Mexico and eventually the border was opened though under rather more restrictive conditions than before. It seems possible in this case that the stimulation given to the meat-packing industry

---

[87]See Bidwell, *Invisible Tariff*, pp. 211–20.

[88]During outbreaks of foot-and-mouth disease in the United States, for example, interstate shipments of dressed carcasses from healthy animals were permitted under regulation, while their importation from a foreign country under similar conditions is prohibited by statute. However, both in Canada and in the United States, domestic quarantines of particular areas are strictly enforced and movement of diseased animals from one district to another is prevented. State and provincial restrictions, moreover, are sometimes more rigorous than federal.

[89]U.S., Bureau of Animal Industry, *Report*, 1949.

in northern Mexico was more important than the protection given United States livestock producers beyond what was necessary to prevent the disease from spreading to the United States. During these years, too, Canada may have benefited slightly from the closing of the Mexican border.

The operation of the United States regulations is illustrated also by their application on the occasion of the first appearance of the disease in Canada. On February 21, 1952, the Canadian Department of Agriculture reported that a few cases had appeared in a small area in the neighbourhood of Regina, Saskatchewan. Immediately steps were taken to quarantine the area and slaughter all infected cattle. Initially, Canada established a complete quarantine to prevent outward movement of livestock from stockyards in Saskatchewan and Manitoba and prohibited shipment of meat from certain centres.

The United States Department of Agriculture was kept informed and, as was required by law, the United States immediately closed the border to imports of all ruminants and swine or their flesh or other products *from any part of Canada.*

Very shortly the United States modified its embargo to permit animal by-products and cured or cooked meats to pass through the United States under customs seal from one part of Canada to another and also to be moved similarly through Canada from one part of the United States to another. In addition, cured and cooked meats with bones removed were permitted to enter the United States if they had been treated and handled in a certain prescribed fashion. Hay and straw was permitted entry if it had been in a warehouse for at least 90 days, or otherwise purified; bone meal and certain other by-products were permitted to enter if disinfected at port of entry.[90]

Animals and meat, which ordinarily would have been exported to the United States, accumulated in Canada. As a partial remedy,[91] the Canadian Government prohibited the importation of livestock,[92] meat, and meat products except under permit. Arrangements were made, as well, to export meat from Canada to the United Kingdom in place of meat from New Zealand, which was sent to the United States. Meanwhile the Canadian Government undertook to support the prices of meat and meat products in Canada; this costly programme together with compensation for the animals destroyed served to prevent the disruption of the meat-producing industries of Canada.

[90]*Foreign Trade*, March 1 and 15, 1952.

[91]*Ibid.*, March 8, 1952, p. 271.

[92]P.C. 1234, March 4, 1952, under authority of the Export-Import Permits Act and the Emergency Powers Act.

Eventually, the United States Secretary of Agriculture declared Canada free from the disease and on March 2, 1953, the embargo on meat and animal imports from Canada was lifted. The Canadian import restrictions lapsed simultaneously.

It would be naïve, of course, to accept at face value the suggestions and insinuations of members of congressional committees or of the interested witnesses that appear before them. An amusing (and exasperating) interchange concerning imports of beef occurred in the hearings of the Senate Finance Committee in 1951:

Senator Butler: Mr. Lynn, this is a little off the subject you have just been discussing. . . . I would like to know the reason for the importation of a big cargo of Irish beef into New York when England, right alongside the Irish are importing it by the boatload from the Argentine, as the Senator says, with our money?

Mr. Lynn: I am not aware of that particular case.

Senator Butler: That would be a good subject for the Bureau [The American Farm Bureau Federation] to investigate.

The explanation, of course, was that inhabitants of the United States were not permitted to buy from the Argentine but they were from Ireland. Britain could buy from either. United States purchasers, accordingly, were compelled to pay enough for the beef imports from Ireland to make the price in that country higher than Britain had to pay to the Argentine, including transportation thence.[93]

The general Canadian regulations differ in some respects from those of the United States. They prohibit the importation of cattle unless the "district" (not the "country") from which they come has been free from the more serious diseases for six months (rather than 60 days); while swine, and ruminants other than cattle, must be held in quarantine for 30 days (instead of 15). No quarantine is normally imposed on certificated animals from the United States, except on swine; and a certificate of quarantine in the United Kingdom before shipment has been accepted, at times, in place of part of the period of quarantine in Canada.

That the operation of the Canadian regulations involves many changes and speedy action is shown by the history of the treatment of cattle imported from Scotland. The regulations have been changed to keep pace with the development and suppressions of outbreaks of foot-and-mouth disease in that country. When a new outbreak occurs, an embargo is imposed by cancelling all permits to import animals from the infected area, though an exception is made with respect to animals already embarked. The operation of the Canadian regula-

[93]U.S. Senate, On H.R. 1612, 1951, p. 414.

tions with respect to the United States can be seen from the records of the last outbreak of foot-and-mouth disease in the United States in 1929. The occurrence of a few cases of the disease in California was officially confirmed in January 1929. Immediately, Canadian authorities prohibited imports of animals, meat, and animal by-products from California, Oregon, Nevada, Arizona, and from the Mexican states of lower California and Sonora. The United States authorities took prompt action to suppress the outbreak, and the disease was declared eradicated by American officials on March 18, 1929. The Canadian embargo was withdrawn two months later, on May 18, 1929. Meanwhile, the original orders had been relaxed to permit bonded shipment through Canada under customs seal.[94]

Given a reasonable amount of good-will and ingenuity, it appears, then, that adjustments in the channels of trade and transfer of resources can do much to mitigate the incidence of livestock epidemics and sanitary regulations even under the existing statutes. Nevertheless, an outbreak of the disease might be made even less disruptive if the unnecessary provisions were removed from the United States Tariff Act which requires exclusion from *all parts* of a country in which the outbreak has occurred.

(e) *Plant and plant products.* Although, at a very early date, the Government of the United States prohibited interstate shipments of plants in violation of state quarantine laws, it was not given power with respect to the importation of plants until 1912 when the Plant Quarantine Act empowered the Secretary of Agriculture to restrict or prohibit the importation of plants and plant products in their movement in interstate commerce so far as he considered it necessary to prevent the entry of injurious pests or to control or eradicate pests which already had established a foothold in the United States.[95] In addition states are permitted to impose quarantines with reference to any dangerous plant disease or insect infestation not subject to a federal quarantine;[96] and, in fact, state quarantine regulations are numerous and varied.

Importations of nursery stock or other plants must be accompanied by a permit to import obtained from the Bureau of Entomology and Plant Quarantine, and the number of the permit must be shown on the consular certificate; a foreign certificate of inspection also is required if the shipment originates in a country which maintains an

[94]See Can., Dept. of Agriculture, *Report of the Veterinary Director-General,* 1929, 1930.

[95]Bidwell, *Invisible Tariff,* pp. 225–54; U.S., 37 Stat. 315.

[96]U.S., Bureau of Agricultural Economics, *Barriers to Internal Trade,* p. 86.

approved inspection service. The package containing the plants must show the kind and amount of plants, where grown, and the names and addresses of exporter and importer, and these must correspond with the permit to import. The importer must file a notice of arrival containing specified information with the port collector. On arrival, if the documents are in order, the shipment is inspected by the Department of Agriculture and, if not infested, may be released after payment of duty. Plants requiring fumigation or other processing as a condition of entry may be released upon a bond from the importer to be treated under the supervision, and to the satisfaction, of the Department of Agriculture. Release is refused to all plants concerning which notice of prohibition has been given by the Department of Agriculture.

Although the primary purpose of most of the plant quarantines has been to prevent the spread of pests or plant diseases, the regulations at times have been influenced by a desire to protect domestic (and local) producers against external competition. However, the agreements of the United States with Canada (as well as with several other countries) have contained a provision that sanitary restrictions on specified plants shall not exceed those necessary to combat the introduction of disease. It seems probable that the sanitary restrictions of the United States on plants and plant products have not greatly hindered imports from Canada. Canadian fruits and vegetables, for example, were exempted from the order of November 1, 1923, which required permits for, and inspection of, all fruit and vegetables originating elsewhere as part of the successful defence against invasion by the Mediterranean fruit fly. Indeed, at times, Canadian producers appear to have received unintended benefits from United States quarantine regulations undertaken partly to protect United States producers. From 1926 to 1935, for example, imports of narcissus bulbs into the United States were rigidly restricted; nominally as a quarantine measure only, actually, it seems, to protect United States bulb growers as well. As a result of the quarantine, there was a rapid increase in Canadian exports of cut flowers to the United States, in spite of a duty of 40 per cent, because the Canadian florists were still able to obtain bulbs from European growers, while those in the United States had to pay higher prices for home-grown bulbs, amounting, it was estimated, to 2.2 cents per flower.[97]

In Canada the export, import, and domestic shipment of nursery stock is subject to regulation under the Destructive Insects and Pests Acts. Generally speaking, a permit from the Department of Agriculture

[97]For this and other incidents see Bidwell, *Invisible Tariff*, especially pp. 235–47; and *Barriers to Internal Trade*, pp. 85–104.

at Ottawa must be presented before imports will be released; they must be accompanied by certificates of inspection in the country of origin; they may be entered only through one of the twelve customs ports where facilities for examination are provided, though if presented elsewhere they may be diverted to an authorized port on consent of the owner. On entering Canada they are subject to examination by officials of the Division of Plant Protection of the Dominion Department of Agriculture, and to treatment or destruction if necessary. Recently, in Canada, ten regulations have been in effect concerning domestic plant products and twenty concerning importations. Of the 10,133 import shipments of plant materials inspected in 1948–9, only 233 were turned back. There were 1,162 interceptions of insects and plant diseases.[98] The Division co-operates with the United States Bureau of Entomology and Plant Quarantine in order to enforce the regulations as efficiently and as conveniently as possible. No apparent use is made of these regulations to give protection intentionally by imposing on importers unnecessary costs or delays. On the other hand their existence makes possible occasional mistakes and consequent delay in releasing products exempt from inspection. It was reported, for example, that a shipment containing "damask roses," offered for entry at a port where there was no plant-protection examiner, was held and sent to a plant pathology laboratory for laboratory examination: it contained roses embroidered on damask. Similar care was shown with respect to another textile import invoiced as "Gladiolus-chenille."[99]

(3) Other Restrictions and the General Agreement

Many of the more recent commercial agreements have included a provision providing for consideration of complaints arising from sanitary and health regulations and for consultation by joint technical committees, and some provide for prior consultation before new sanitary regulations are introduced.[100] The General Agreement on Tariffs and Trade mentions many of the types of restriction discussed in this chapter.

[98]Can., Dept. of Agriculture, Report, 1948–9, pp. 103–4.

[99]Such errors, when they occur (and sometimes, perhaps, when they do not), supply newspapers with conveniently short and humorous news items. The story of a shipment of "whiffle-trees" sent to a plant pathology laboratory for examination seems to have played much the same part in the humour of the customs house as has the search for a "left-handed monkey-wrench" in the annals of rural humour.

[100]See Bidwell, Invisible Tariff, p. 132.

With respect to mark of origin, it requires the contracting parties to accord to each other Most-Favoured-Nation treatment; to permit marks of origin to be affixed at the time of importation whenever it is administratively practicable; and to co-operate with one another to prevent the misuse of trade names or harmful misrepresentation of origin; and it prohibits the imposition of a penalty duty unless the articles bear deceptive marking, or the marks of origin have been intentionally omitted, or corrective marking is unreasonably delayed.

These restrictions on marking requirements were reasonable though not revolutionary. The marking procedures of both countries now conform with them, at least for the most part. Neither now requires payment of additional duties on unmarked articles, if the marking requirements are met even after importation; the special marking requirements of the United States which excluded certain articles unless marked prior to importation have been repealed. In Canada only a small list of items must now be marked with the country of origin; it remains to be seen whether the increase in discretionary power granted the United States Treasury by the Customs Simplification Act will be used similarly to reduce the number of imported items that must be marked for entry into the United States.

With respect to protective and sanitary inspection and regulation, the General Agreement confirms the right of a contracting party to adopt or enforce measures necessary to protect public morals and human, animal, or plant life or health; to secure compliance with laws or regulations not contrary to the Agreement relating to the importation of gold and silver; to protect patents, trademarks, and copyrights; to conserve exhaustible natural resources, when accompanied by appropriate domestic restrictions. However, it subjects such measures to the requirement that they shall not be applied so as to discriminate arbitrarily or unjustifiably between countries where the same conditions prevail, nor so as to act as a disguised restriction on international trade.[101] Since it is extraordinarily difficult in these matters to secure unanimous agreement as to the kind and degree of discrimination or restriction that is essential for acknowledged and acceptable purposes, it may be doubted whether this proviso will be responsible for great and rapid reforms; but it may tend to discourage the introduction of blatantly protective regulations on the pretext that they safeguard property or health. Ultimately it may assist in developing a belief that such measures are beneath the dignity of self-respecting nations.

[101]G.A.T.T., art. xx.

IX

CONCLUSION

"Would you tell me, please, which way I ought to go from here?"
"That depends a good deal on where you want to get to," said the Cat.

Alice in Wonderland

CUSTOMS PROCEDURES in the United States and Canada supplement the rates of duty in varying degrees in discriminating against foreign, as compared with domestic products. In some respects the procedures in the two countries are very similar, in others different. It would be useful and interesting to know how these resemblances and differences are related in each country to their broader framework: to the geographic, economic, political, and sociological influences that have helped to make them what they are. In particular, it would be useful to know which of the characteristics of customs procedure are so closely knit with the more enduring characteristics of this framework that they are very resistant to change; which sorts of regulations may be more readily changed and in what ways; and which are likely to change with development. Methods have not been —and may never be—devised that would explain customs procedures completely in terms of these broader circumstances; and much of the application that might be, has not yet been made. This study cannot close these gaps or even recount all that has been done. In what follows, a few relationships are tentatively suggested as hypotheses.

The resemblances, past and present, between the customs procedures of the two countries are less puzzling than the differences. Both countries, in their early development, were subject to British colonial mercantile policy and customs procedures, as well as to British governmental and legal arrangements. To early food and raw material production, both have added substantial industrial output. In both, though in different degrees and at different times, labour and capital have been scarce relatively to natural resources. Both have been exposed to the influence of the frontier with its multi-dimensional

262

mobilities; both have experienced the exaggerated business cycles associated with the developmental fringes of western trade and technology; both have been separated by distances of decreasing significance from industrialized trading partners. In different degrees both have experienced the problems of preventing (or encouraging) smuggling across long and sparsely inhabited frontiers; both have experienced the financial problems of financing the construction and maintenance of long lines of internal communication, Canada more continuously and intensely; both have been exposed to the fluctuations in the commercial policies of Britain, of each other, and of other trading countries; both have experienced and reacted against Japan's invasion of world markets in textiles, pottery, toys, and other items. Both have been influenced, Canada much more substantially, by the possibility of gaining access to markets or other advantages by trade agreements; and the terms of the trade agreements in turn have influenced customs procedures.

In recent decades the United States and Canada have each come to produce an increasing proportion of the total output of non-communist countries; and the trade of each has become more important to the other. During war and rehabilitation, too, depletion of the more accessible supplies of raw materials has been accompanied by technological changes which favoured exploration and development of supplies on the geographic fringes[1] in Canada and elsewhere.

Similarities associated with geographical, economic, and political circumstances have been supplemented by the direct copying or borrowing of customs and other procedures; sometimes emulation has been stimulated by a competitive desire for excellence, sometimes enforced by smuggling, sometimes by the desire to retaliate.[2]

The differences in the timing, methods, and degrees of protection, including procedural protection, have been associated, similarly, with a completely interacting set of geographic, economic, and political circumstances. Canada's natural resources and climate were less varied than those of the United States; populated pockets of arable land were small and separated by larger non-arable tracts which, nevertheless, produced materials for export as their respective transportation problems were solved:[3] furs, lumber, wheat, non-ferrous minerals, hydro-

[1]See e.g. W. A. Mackintosh, "The People and Their History" in *Canada, Nation on the March.*

[2]Such direct effects of United States tariffs on Canadian tariffs are illustrated in McLean, *Tariff History,* pp. 45, 52–3.

[3]H. A. Innis, *Problems of Staple Production in Canada,* pp. 1–23 and elsewhere.

electric power, newsprint, aluminum, and iron. The inaccessibility of some of the natural resources, the smallness of the domestic markets and exclusion from the neighbouring one, delayed exploitation and industrialization until the competing and more readily accessible resources of the United States (and later of Australia) had been developed. Meanwhile the need to forestall American economic penetration on the frontier resulted in heavy expenditures on transportation. The consequent need for revenue, the sectional importance of exports, and the desire to foster or preserve national unity, affected the timing, the intensity, and the methods of Canadian protectionism. They prevented tariff policy from becoming more than mildly protectionist until 1879, and they precluded high protection except in the period from 1930 to 1932 or 1935: in the absence of varied and reasonably efficient domestic industries an exclusionist policy would have imposed substantial burdens on all, and insupportable hardships on some, sections of the economy.

In the United States, meanwhile, duties were used primarily for revenue until 1816. The protectionism following the Napoleonic wars culminated in the "tariff of abominations" of 1828 which almost occasioned civil war. Some reductions occurred, but by 1861 the varied output and a larger domestic market had permitted a return to high protection. The United States tariff remained high until 1945; it still contains many high protective rates.

Her more prolonged inclusion in Britain's colonial system, less varied resources, greater specialization of output, smaller population, more limited home markets, and consequent vulnerability to trade barriers, have predisposed Canada to offer and seek preferential treatment, if necessary, in order to gain access to markets. British Free Trade was associated with Reciprocity; abrogation of Reciprocity by the United States and continuous high protection with the National Policy and, later, with preferential duties; the Hawley-Smoot Tariff with the Ottawa Agreements.

On the whole also, in the past, consideration of national unity, geographic and climatic conditions, the need to obtain revenue from or for the railways, the dominance of the St. Lawrence waterway, and historical and sentimental ties with Britain have favoured the encouragement of east-west traffic and the maintenance of a three-column tariff. Discrimination against indirect shipments, introduced as a retaliatory measure against a similar United States provision,[4] has

[4]McLean, *Tariff History*, p. 52.

been transformed and is firmly fixed in the pattern of Canadian circumstances in the direct-shipment requirement, though it has been changed to remove some of its more objectionable features. The increase in population, wealth, and output, the development of the taxing system, the broadening of the band of inhabited pockets, the lowering of United States rates of duty, and the channelling of her direct investments to petroleum and to Canada, have diminished the incentives to maintain Imperial Preference and the need to discriminate in favour of east-west trade. But fear of United States protectionist tendencies, the historical attachment to Britain, and the desire to maintain an alternative market and source of capital seem likely to induce Canada to maintain a three-column tariff.

In their identification of imports and prescription of rates, the tariffs of both countries are burdensomely complex. The United States Tariff became gradually more complex as it became more protectionist; the Canadian Tariff was changed from a simple to a complex document with the adoption of the National Policy in 1879, and its continuance; both have become increasingly specialized by reason of trade agreements and the requirements of protectionism.

Introduced to minimize the divisive effects of protection, the peculiarly Canadian methods of defining items—by specific use, status of importer, and absence of domestic production—are likely to change in significance, in difficulty of administration, and perhaps in form. The increase in the size of market and in the variety of Canadian output has already diminished the significance of low-duty items relating to goods of a class or kind not made in Canada, and has increased the difficulties of distinguishing between goods which are and those which are not eligible for admission at the low rates. As more products are manufactured in Canada, and by more manufacturers, the unforeseen indirect effects of exceptions are likely to multiply, and the aggregate costs of administration to government and to importers to increase; as well as the difficulties of satisfying manufacturers that administrative reductions in duty are being reasonably apportioned.

Were it not for the continued sectional importance of export industries the increase in the variety of Canadian products, the growing importance of manufacturing, and the increasing importance of the home market to certain agricultural products might tend to favour or produce both an increase in Canadian protection and some offsetting simplification of the tariff schedule. Drastic simplification of the items, however, is unlikely to occur unless it is accompanied by reduction and similar simplification in the tariffs of Canada's principal trading partners, especially the United States. On the other hand, it should be possible for Canada to set an example by eliminating the few trick "wholly-or-in-part" items.

The principal manufacturing industries of the United States are now firmly established, and technologically advancing;[5] it should be easier, therefore, to simplify the United States Tariff and to arrange the products in broad rate groups, except for a relatively few, to which it may be considered desirable to give special consideration. It is not easy, however, to see how the simplification is to be brought about. The sensitiveness of congressmen to local interests in recent generations, in the absence of strong party and administrative discipline, has prevented substantial reduction of protection except by way of trade agreements; and though the United States has insisted that Canada and other countries give procedural concessions in trade negotiations, she has confined her own negotiations primarily to reductions in rate of duty. In spite of suggestions that the scope of trade agreements be broadened,[6] the President is prohibited from changing the classification of an item, for example, or transferring it from the dutiable to the free list. The reform of United States tariff classification by administrative action, in accordance with general policies adopted by Congress, will require substantial changes in Congressional behaviour.

That protectionist interests in the United States believe that Congress, as distinct from the administration, can still be influenced to favour procedural protection is suggested by the testimony which continues to be presented at the hearings of the Congressional Committees. "One fault I find, both in the previous and current analysis of the Customs Simplification Bill by the Treasury Department, is that they constantly state their explanations or justifications for changes in terms of efficiency in protecting the revenue. We feel that that is not the fundamental or basic purpose of our customs laws. Rather, the analysis of procedure, or a simplification of that procedure, should be

[5]Howard S. Piquet estimates that more than 40 per cent of the dutiable commodities that now enter the United States would not be noticeably affected by suspension of duties and that the "area of maximum import competition" in which imports will account for more than 10 and less than 90 per cent of domestic consumption "would include little more than a third of all dutiable imports." *Aid, Trade and the Tariff*, p. 349.

[6]See, e.g., H. D. Scully, "Canadian Problems of Industry, Production and Price Control," especially pp. 73–9.

looked at in terms of the protection and intended protection to be granted to American producers."[7]

The United States early established consular offices abroad and began to require consulation of invoices. Throughout the nineteenth century fees for certification of invoices more than supported the whole consular service of the United States.[8] Federal revenues are now collected from more varied sources, and the popularity of financing by fees is diminishing; with the lowering of rates of duties facilitated by the trade agreements it would appear that consular certification is no longer necessary and its abandonment has been strongly advocated in the United States and elsewhere.

The Canadian certificate of origin is associated with preferential treatment of imports produced in British and Trade-Agreement countries; it appears to be more closely tied to enduring elements of policy, but it is less burdensome than the United States consular certification. With the increase in the relative importance of trade with the United States, further exceptions might reasonably be made with respect to imports whose origin is self-evident.

In contrast with most other countries, Canada and the United States have adopted value in the foreign market as the primary basis for *ad valorem* rates of duty. In the United States this practice developed from the earlier procedure of accepting invoice value; it was then argued, too, that this basis of valuation was more equitable as between different ports than landed value. Canada borrowed the practice from the United States in 1856 partly, presumably, for the same reasons that had persuaded the United States authorities to adopt it; but partly, in addition, because it favoured imports from more distant countries and the use of Canadian transportation facilities; in reply to a charge that Canada was discriminating against the United States, Galt was able to reply that he was merely adopting the American method.

High rates of duty and fear that undervaluation might defeat efforts to exclude imports have favoured the adoption and continuation by the United States of time-consuming methods of enforcement, intricate definitions of value, and technical interpretations of them, which often raise dutiable value considerably above the invoice price and introduce wide margins of uncertainty as to the amount of duty payable. In addition, undervaluation duties imposed by the United

[7]Statement of John Breckenridge, on behalf of the Pin, Clip and Fastener Association, U.S. House, *On H.R. 5106*, 1953, p. 191.

[8]Smith, *Valuation*, p. 20.

States in 1818 were continued in one form or another until 1953.[9] In Canada the importance of the export industries, the desire to avoid national disintegration, a succession of strong governments, and parliamentary institutions, favoured more flexible and less technical, though perhaps less systematic, valuation procedures. In normal cases and normal times these procedures have resulted in values for duty that approximate export prices and invoice values; valuation provisions have been used from time to time to diminish the volume of certain imports but seldom to exclude them entirely, even during a serious depression. Again borrowing from the United States, Canada imposed, in her early years, a penalty duty for undervaluation but repealed it in 1904.

Willingness to grant necessary powers to a responsible ministry, coupled with the attitudes associated with a small domestic market neighbouring a large protected one, has favoured the use of official valuation and extension of dumping duties in preference to complicating the bases of valuation and using the resulting uncertainty to impose undervaluation duties. While its domestic market was small, faced with depression and large foreign productive capacity, the United States used official minimum values, after the Napoleonic Wars, to give very high protection to the textile industry; imposed on cotton in 1816, and extended to woollens in 1824, they played their part in fomenting sectional strife and provoking South Carolina to pass her nullification ordinance.[10] In Canada, official values, applied in the nineteen-thirties to textiles and to many other products as well, proved extremely effective in giving protection when combined with the dumping duties; in combination with other protective measures, however, they contributed to sectional antagonisms[11] as they had in the United States a century earlier.

Lagging seasons, less rapid industrialization, and the smallness of the Canadian market have predisposed Canada to apply dumping duties to cases of occasional and accidental dumping and to imports

---

[9]Smith attributes the persistence of penalty duties and other anomalies of United States valuation to legislative delays, to successful appeals of domestic producers, to the defencelessness of importers against chauvinist attacks, and to the anomalies and technicalities of court-made law. *Valuation*, pp. 335–6.

[10]*Ibid.*, pp. 53 *sqq.* They were abolished in substance in 1832. Minimum values were later reapplied, especially under the McKinley Tariff of 1890, to certain textiles and to cutlery and certain other manufactures of iron and steel. U.S. Tariff Commission, *The Tariff and its History*, p. 77.

[11]Can., Royal Commission on Dominion-Provincial Relations, *Report*, vol. 1, pp. 158–9. Also *Manitoba's Case*, part IV.

purchased at bargain prices when technically dumping does not exist. The sensitivity of certain industries may diminish with an increase in the size of the domestic market; and a strong government, in prosperous times, supported by exporters, consumers, and the provisions of the General Agreement, may be able to resist the demands of domestic producers to use official valuation and dumping duties to give hidden and unwarranted protection in a world where foreign trade restrictions are low or diminishing. The provision of flexible seasonal duties on fruits and vegetables and the provisions of the General Agreement may well prevent the application of dumping duties to the major fruits and vegetables; if so, it will no longer be possible for protected industries to use the lateness of the Canadian seasons to enlist the support of agriculture for broad application of dumping duties. The provisions of a commercial agreement are more likely than statutory amendment alone to limit the application of dumping duties. Even so, a weak government faced with less favourable conditions, at home or abroad, might be compelled to make some use, under the escape provisions of the Agreement, of its power to impose official values and dumping duties.[12]

The United States dumping procedures conform with the provisions of the General Agreement. They are consistent with United States tendencies to prescribe procedures by detailed statutes, and they seem unlikely to be changed, though a protectionist administration might reduce imports by undertaking a great many formal investigations. There seems to be rather more danger that United States may decrease the advantages of the Agreement by imposing quotas or raising rates of duty under the escape clause.

It is not yet clear how much the powers of the Canadian Government have been limited with respect to valuation, as a matter of actual practice. In any event, in the future as in the past, trade agreements, the importance of exports, dependence on imports, and party discipline associated with parliamentary government and flexible election dates, are likely to be more effective controls than mere statutory enactment on the use of customs procedures to give indirect protection. In the United States, on the other hand, the trade agreements which have lowered duties have had no effects on the valuation provisions of the statute and Congress has not amended them. Exasperation with delays,

[12]That even this guarded conclusion may be unduly optimistic is suggested by current proposals to re-revise the valuation sections in the Canadian Act. *Financial Post*, Nov. 14, 1953, p. 1. (This paragraph was written before Nov. 20, 1953. However, for changes in Dec. 1953 see chap. vii.)

inefficiency, and expense, coupled with growing willingness to concede (for strategic if not for economic reasons) that importing is not necessarily a nefarious and disloyal occupation, may eventually permit statutory revision; but the theory of separation of powers, the interests of customs attorneys and even (if finances are made available) of customs officials, may well require that the new statute be as detailed and intricate as the old. If so, it may be subjected to a long process of judicial testing and interpretation, especially if domestic producers retain the power to appeal from the decision of the collector or the appraiser.

The strictness of the regulations of the United States and Canada relating to health and sanitation is based in part on past conformity with the controls once imposed by other countries to protect their own food industries, in part on a level of income so high that cleanliness is no longer regarded as a luxury, on high and increasing technological competence in the preparation and distribution of foods, and on the political influence of the farm population. Of these, the first and last may diminish in importance; and international co-ordination of standards of identity and purity and labelling may occur as has co-ordination of grading, at least in some products; differences in weights and measures, however, may present more enduring difficulties.

Perhaps the most noticeable general difference between the customs procedures of the two countries is the greater importance or frequency of judicial appeal in the United States. This difference is based apparently on fundamental differences in political institutions and attitudes: separation of powers in contrast with parliamentary government; an administration closely and even jealously controlled[13] by statutes passed by the legislature and interpreted by the courts, in contrast with a government controlling, and dependent on, a majority in parliament, and capable of countering promptly an unwelcome administrative or judicial decision by issuing an order in council or securing such amendment of the statutes as it considers desirable and

[13]Distrust of the executive branch of government is expressed not only repeatedly but at times very forcibly by members of congressional committees, for example:
"Mr. Rosenthal: . . . Senator, I think in a democracy we must trust the executive branch of government to do certain things.
"Senator Millikin: Oh, No, No, No, No, No. Great Scott, Mr. Witness, do you not realize the trouble we are in today by doing that."
U.S. Senate, *On H.R. 1612*, 1951, p. 716.

politic;[14] a legislature extremely sensitive to sectional interests, in contrast with one where tight party discipline is associated with variable duration of parliament and date of election.

Both discretionary power and judicial interpretations can be used to liberalize customs procedure or to make it more protective. In Canada, consistently with the importance of the export trade and the impact of business cycles on the debtor fringes of the Western world, discretionary power has been used to increase procedural protection in depression and remove or decrease it in prosperous times; it has been regarded primarily as a political rather than a legal matter. In the United States the power of domestic producers to protest and appeal has varied from time to time; when granted it has been used to harass the importer. In United States, moreover, judicial interpretation has often proceeded in directions not closely related to changes in commercial practices and without consideration for the way the decisions affect marketing arrangements and tax structures at home or abroad. Both wooden and subtle judicial application have frequently had absurd results.

The importance of litigation, however, has probably tended to promote the development of a reasonably self-consistent set of Treasury decisions and regulations, more widely distributed and published in a more convenient form than Canada's, both for preservation and for current use; and litigation has been used, in place of responsible centralized authority, to control customs officials. The development of a group of specialized customs attorneys has helped to ensure that provision for appeal will not be unduly diminished.[15] But though the general importance of judicial appeal in this field is closely associated, apparently, with more enduring circumstances of the United States setting, it appears that its details may be changed. In particular, the right to bring action in the Customs Court was not granted to domestic producers until 1922;[16] the right to protest was partially withdrawn from 1934 to 1951, and was limited in 1938. It is not customary in the United States to allow one business man to bring action to have a competitor's taxes increased;[17] it seems possible, therefore, that this

[14]In Canada too, of course, the opposition at times has rightly complained of the breadth of the discretionary powers granted to the government.

[15]For example, on behalf of the Customs Bar of New York, H. S. King recommended that the term "estimates" should not be used in defining value lest it be interpreted "to vest irreviewable discretion in appraising officers.' U.S. House, *On H.R. 1535*, 1951, p. 437.

[16]Smith, *Valuation*, p. 142.   [17]*Ibid.*, p. 336.

power might be removed without great damage to the underlying framework of institutions and beliefs in the United States. If it were removed it would become easier to make declaratory rulings as to the classification of prospective imports and on certain other customs matters which would be binding at all ports for a reasonable time.

In Canada, appeals for judicial or quasi-judicial review of decisions as to value or rate of duty have never been frequent, though provision has been made and should be preserved to allow an importer to appeal to an independent tribunal. The right to be represented before the Tariff Board and to appeal from its decisions has been granted to domestic producers and even, contrary to practice in United States, to trade associations; though this practice is less likely to have important restrictive effects in Canada than it would have in the United States. The experience of the United States suggests, however, that extension of the privileges of domestic producers to appeal might tend to increase the uncertainties of importing into Canada. If procedural protection is not considered desirable, appeals by domestic producers should not be allowed to become an essential part of Canadian customs administration.

This chapter has been concerned primarily with the interpretation of past trends. Interpretation, however, is not justification, and past trends need not be projected forward. It has been assumed in this study that indirect methods of protection are inferior to direct methods: that if protective measures are to be adopted they should be pursued openly, so that their indirect effects can be taken into account as clearly as may be when their use is being considered for the promotion of whatever political or strategic objectives recommend themselves from time to time to the public or to the government. In addition, it should be remembered that protection, as well as other forms of governmental intervention and regulation, necessarily imposes procedural burdens.

BIBLIOGRAPHY

(The short form or abbreviation used in footnotes is shown in square brackets.)

American Import and Export Bulletin (New York, 1948).
Bell Report. See UNITED STATES, PUBLIC ADVISORY BOARD FOR MUTUAL SECURITY.
BIDWELL, PERCY W. *The Invisible Tariff* (New York, 1939).
BLAKE, GORDON. "Customs Administration in Canada" (unpublished Ph.D. thesis, University of Toronto, 1954). [Blake, "Customs Administration."]
BRADY, ALEXANDER. *Democracy in the Dominions* (Toronto, 1952).
CANADA
 Canada Gazette (weekly). [*Can. Gaz.*]
 Consolidated Statutory Orders and Regulations. [S.O.R.]
 Revised Statutes of Canada, 1927: 1952. [R.S.C.]
 Statutes of Canada (annual). [S.C.]
 DEPARTMENT OF AGRICULTURE. *The Fruit, Vegetables and Honey Act and Regulations, 1947.*
 ——— *Report of the Minister of Agriculture* (annual).
 ——— *Report of the Veterinary Director-General* (annual).
 DEPARTMENT OF EXTERNAL AFFAIRS. *Treaty Series* (annual).
 DEPARTMENT OF NATIONAL HEALTH AND WELFARE. *Annual Reports.*
 ——— *General Regulations under the Food and Drugs Act.*
 DEPARTMENT OF NATIONAL REVENUE [D.N.R.]. *Annual Reports.*
 ——— *Appraisers' Bulletins.*
 ——— *Customs Memoranda,* especially *Information for Exporters Concerning Shipments to Canada,* Series D, no. 43 (2nd rev., Ottawa, 1952); *Supplement,* no. 1 (Sept. 5, 1952).
 ——— *National Revenue Review.*
 DEPARTMENT OF TRADE AND COMMERCE, DOMINION BUREAU OF STATISTICS. *Canada Year Book* (annual).
 ——— *Canada's Balance of Payments* (Ottawa, 1939).
 ——— *Foreign Trade.*
 ——— *Trade of Canada* (annual).
 HOUSE OF COMMONS. *Debates.* [Can., Commons, *Debates.*]
 ——— *Sessional Papers.*
 HOUSE OF COMMONS, STANDING COMMITTEE ON BANKING AND COMMERCE. *Minutes of Proceedings and Evidence: Subject-Matter of the General Agreement on Tariffs and Trade . . . 1947–8.* [Can., Banking & Commerce, G.A.T.T.]
 ——— *Minutes of Proceedings and Evidence: Torquay Negotiations, 1951.* [Can., Banking & Commerce, *Torquay.*]

ROYAL COMMISSION ON CUSTOMS AND EXCISE. *Interim Report*, no. 10 (1926).
——— *Final Report* (1926).
ROYAL COMMISSION ON DOMINION-PROVINCIAL RELATIONS. *Report* (Ottawa, 1940).
ROYAL COMMISSION ON THE TEXTILE INDUSTRY. *Report* (Ottawa, 1938). [*Textile Report.*]
SENATE. *Debates.*
SENATE, STANDING COMMITTEE ON CANADIAN TRADE RELATIONS. *Proceedings of the Committee to Whom was Referred the Subject Matter of the General Agreement on Tariffs and Trade . . . 1947–8.* [Can., Trade Relations, G.A.T.T.]
——— *Proceedings in Respect to the Inquiry into . . . the North Atlantic Treaty, 1953.* [Can., Trade Relations, N.A.T.O.]
TARIFF BOARD OF CANADA. *Declarations on Appeals.* [T.B.C.]
——— *Reports.* [T.B.C., Ref.]
WARTIME PRICES AND TRADE BOARD. *Report, Jan. 1, 1946–Dec. 31, 1946.*

Canadian Importers and Traders Association Bulletin (Toronto, April 19, 1947).
CANADIAN MANUFACTURERS' ASSOCIATION. *Customs Aspects of Exporting to the United States.* Canadian Export Trade Series, no. 12 (Toronto, 1949).
——— *Industrial Canada.*
CHAMBER OF COMMERCE, JOINT CANADA–UNITED STATES COMMITTEE. *Customs Administration and Procedure between Canada and the United States: Report by the Canadian Sub-Committee on Invisible Tariffs, Approved by the Joint Canada–United States Committee Maintained by the Canadian Chamber of Commerce and the Chamber of Commerce of the United States* (n.p., n.d.).
CLARK, S. D. *The Canadian Manufacturers' Association.* University of Toronto Studies, History and Economics Series, vol. 7 (Toronto, 1939).
COLE, TAYLOR. *The Canadian Bureaucracy* (Durham, N. C., 1949).
COUNCIL ON FOREIGN RELATIONS. *Foreign Trade and United States Tariff Policy.* Ed. JOSEPH BARBER (New York, 1953).
CULBERTSON, W. S. *International Economic Policies* (New York, 1925).
DAWSON, R. MACGREGOR. *The Government of Canada* (2nd ed., Toronto, 1954).
DIEBOLD, WILLIAM. *New Directions in Our Trade Policy* (New York, 1941).
Dominion Law Reports (Toronto). [D.L.R.]
Financial Post (Toronto).
FLETCHER SCHOOL OF LAW AND DIPLOMACY. *International Trade Policy Issues.* Prepared for the Foreign Commerce Department of the Chamber of Commerce of the United States (Washington, 1953).
FUTRELL, WM. H. *The History of Customs Jurisprudence* (New York, 1941).
Globe and Mail (Toronto).
Gray Report. See UNITED STATES, *Report to the President.*
HAWKINS, HARRY. *Commercial Treaties and Agreements* (New York, 1951).
HAWTHORNE, N. *The Scarlet Letter.*
INNIS, H. A. *Problems of Staple Production in Canada* (Toronto, 1953).
INTERNATIONAL CHAMBER OF COMMERCE. *Resolutions Adopted by the 9th Congress.* Brochure no. 98 (1937).
——— *Invisible Trade Barriers.* Brochure no. 130.
INTERNATIONAL CHAMBER OF COMMERCE, UNITED STATES ASSOCIATES. *Simplifying United States Customs Procedure* (New York, 1949).

JAMES, R. W. *Wartime Economic Co-operation* (Toronto, 1949).

JEFFERS, WELLINGTON. "Finance at Large" (*Globe and Mail*, Jan. 1, 1952).

KNORR, KLAUS, and PATTERSON, GARDNER. *A Critique of the Randall Commission Report* (Princeton University, International Finance Section and Center of International Studies, 1954).

LARKIN, JOHN DAY. *The President's Control of the Tariff* (Cambridge, Mass., 1936).

——— *Trade Agreements: A Study in Democratic Methods* (New York, 1940).

LEAGUE OF NATIONS

    ECONOMIC COMMITTEE. *Report to the Council of the Work of the 35th Session* (Geneva, 1931).

    INTERNATIONAL CONFERENCE ON CUSTOMS AND OTHER SIMILAR FORMALITIES. *Proceedings* (Geneva, 1924).

    SUB-COMMITTEE OF EXPERTS. *Report to the 11th Assembly* (Geneva, 1930).

LEVETT, BENJAMIN A. *Customs Administrative Act of 1938* (New York, 1938, mimeo.).

——— *Reduction of Trade Barriers: What Have We to Offer?* (mimeo.).

——— *Through the Customs Maze* (New York, 1923).

MACKINTOSH, W. A. "The People and Their History" in *Canada, Nation on the March* (Toronto, 1953).

MANITOBA. *Manitoba's Case: A Submission to the Royal Commission on Dominion-Provincial Relations* (Winnipeg, 1937).

McDIARMID, O. J. *Commercial Policy in the Canadian Economy* (Cambridge, Mass., 1940).

McLEAN, SIMON J. *The Tariff History of Canada.* Toronto University Studies in Political Science, no. IV (Toronto, 1895).

NATIONAL COUNCIL OF AMERICAN IMPORTERS INC. *Customs Administration Law: Changes in Special Administrative Provisions of the Tariff Act of 1930 as Amended* (New York, 1945).

NUTTAL, J. A. *Functions of a Licensed Customs Broker* (Montreal, 1947, mimeo.).

PARKINSON, J. K. *Memorandum on the Basis of Canadian Commercial Policy 1926–38* (Paris, 1939, mimeo.).

PARKS, WALLACE. *United States Administration of Its International Economic Affairs* (Baltimore, 1951).

PATTERSON, GARDNER. *See* KNORR.

PIQUET, H. S. *Aid, Trade, and the Tariff* (New York, 1953).

RADCLIFFE, HARRY S. "The Tariff Act of 1930 as *not* Amended" (*American Import and Export Bulletin*, Dec. 1948).

Randall Report. See UNITED STATES, COMMISSION ON FOREIGN ECONOMIC POLICY.

SCULLY, H. D. "Canadian Problems of Industry, Production and Price Control" (*Proceedings of the Academy of Political Science*, vol. XX, no. 4, Jan. 1944).

SMITH, R. ELBERTON. *Customs Valuation in the United States* (Chicago, 1948).

TAYLOR, K. W. "Results of the Imperial Economic Conference in Relation to the Trade of Countries which are Members of the Institute of Pacific Relations" in CANADIAN INSTITUTE OF INTERNATIONAL AFFAIRS, *Canadian Papers 1933* (Toronto, 1933).

——— "Tariff Administration and Non-Tariff Methods of Trade Control" in *Con-*

ference of Canadian-American Affairs, 1935, ed. W. W. MCLAREN, A. B. COREY, and R. G. TROTTER (New York, 1936).

UNITED NATIONS. *Charter for an International Trade Organization* (London, 1948). [Havana Charter.]

——— *General Agreement on Tariffs and Trade* (New York, 1947). [G.A.T.T.]

UNITED STATES
    Code of Federal Regulations. [C.F.R.]
    Customs Regulations. [U.S.C.R.]
    Federal Register.
    Internal Revenue Code. [I.R.C.]
    Report to the President on Foreign Economic Policies (Washington, 1950). [*Gray Report.*]
    Statutes at Large.
    United States Code. [U.S.C.]

ADMINISTRATIVE OFFICE OF THE UNITED STATES COURTS. *Annual Reports of the Director.*

ATTORNEY GENERAL. *Annual Reports.*

BUREAU OF AGRICULTURAL ECONOMICS. *Barriers to Internal Trade in Farm Products.* By GEORGE R. TAYLOR, EDGAR L. BURTIS, and FREDERICK V. WAUGH (Washington, 1939).

BUREAU OF ANIMAL INDUSTRY. *Reports of the Chief of the Bureau.*

COMMISSION ON FOREIGN ECONOMIC POLICY. *Report to the President and Congress* (Washington, 1954). [*Randall Report.*]

——— *Staff Papers* (of the *Randall Report*) *Presented to the Commission* (Washington, 1954).

CONGRESS, HOUSE OF REPRESENTATIVES, COMMITTEE ON WAYS AND MEANS. *Customs Simplification, Hearings on H.R. 1612* (1951); *H.R. 1535* (1951); *H.R. 5505* (1952); *H.R. 5106* (1953). [U.S. House, *On H.R.* —.]

——— *Trade Agreements Extension, Hearings on H.R. 1211* (1949); *H.R. 1612* (1951); *H.R. 4294* (1953).

CONGRESS, SENATE, COMMITTEE ON ADMINISTRATIVE PROCEDURE (appointed by the Attorney General at the request of the President). *Administration of Customs Laws.* Monograph 27 (Justice Department, Washington, 1948, mimeo.). [A.G. Com., Mon. 27.]

——— *Final Report* (1948).

CONGRESS, SENATE, COMMITTEE ON FINANCE. *Customs Simplification, Hearings on H.R. 5505* (1952). [U.S. Senate, *On H.R.* —.]

——— *Trade Agreements Extension, Hearings on H.R. 1612* (1951).

COURT OF CUSTOMS AND PATENT APPEALS. *Decisions: Customs.* [C.C.P.A.]

CUSTOMS COURT. *Reports.* [U.S.C.C.]

DEPARTMENT OF COMMERCE. *Foreign Marks-of-Origin Regulations.*

——— *Preparing Shipments to Canada* (Washington, revised from time to time).

DEPARTMENT OF COMMERCE, OFFICE OF INTERNATIONAL TRADE, IMPORT ADVISORY COMMITTEE. *First Interim Report on Customs Administrative Laws* (Dec. 14, 1949, mimeo.).

DEPARTMENT OF COMMERCE, UNITED STATES ECONOMIC CO-OPERATION JOINT MISSION. *Report of the . . . Joint Mission to Investigate Possibilities of Increasing Western European Dollar Earnings* (Washington, 1949).

FEDERAL SECURITY AGENCY, FOOD AND DRUG ADMINISTRATION. *Import Require-*

ments of the United States Food, Drug and Cosmetic Act: A Guide for Foreign Manufacturers and Shippers. Miscellaneous Publications, no. 2 (Washington, 1947, with addenda and changes 1947–50 inclusive).

—— Regulations under the Food, Drug and Cosmetic Act.

PUBLIC ADVISORY BOARD FOR MUTUAL SECURITY. A Trade and Tariff Policy in the National Interest (Washington, Feb. 1953). [Bell Report.]

TARIFF COMMISSION (reports are listed in order of publication). Report upon the Revision of the Customs Administrative Laws (1918).

—— Dumping and Unfair Competition in United States and Canada's Antidumping Law (1919).

—— Basis of Assessment of Ad Valorem Duties in Foreign Countries (1932).

—— Methods of Valuation. Report no. 70, 2nd series (1933).

—— Regulation of Foreign Tariffs by Administrative Action. Miscellaneous series (1934).

—— The Tariff and Its History. Miscellaneous series (1934).

—— The [First] Trade Agreement with Canada. Report no. 111, 2nd series (1936). [U.S.T.C., Report 111.]

—— Extent of Equal Tariff Treatment in Foreign Countries. Report no. 119, 2nd series (1937).

—— Operation of the Trade Agreements Program: Third Report, April 1949– June 1950. Report 172, 2nd series (1950).

TREASURY DEPARTMENT. Annual Reports on the State of Finances.

—— Customs Regulations of the United States (1943).

—— Treasury Decisions [T.D.]

TREASURY DEPARTMENT, BUREAU OF CUSTOMS. Customs Information for Exporters to the United States (U.S. Government Printing Office, 1950).

VINER, J. Dumping (Chicago, 1923).

—— The Customs Union Issue (New York and London, 1950).

—— "Memoranda on Commercial Policy" in JOINT COMMITTEE CARNEGIE ENDOWMENT, INTERNATIONAL CHAMBER OF COMMERCE, The Improvement of Commercial Relations between Nations (Paris, 1936). Reprinted in J. VINER, International Economics (Glencoe, Ill., 1951).

WINSLOW, E. M. "Administrative Protectionism" in Explorations in Economics: Essays in Honor of F. W. Taussig (Cambridge, Mass., 1936).

INDEX

Lightning Source UK Ltd.
Milton Keynes UK
UKHW010005210722
406167UK00001B/120